RV CAM
BIBLE

Escape the Ordinary and Unleash Your Wanderlust: The Ultimate 7-in-1 Road Trip Guide! 3000+ Campgrounds & Attractions Across the US + Expert Tips for an Easy,

Safe & Fun Journey

Thiago and Elisa Davidson

TABLE OF CONTENTS

Introduction

For RV camping enthusiasts, this guide helps as an invaluable resource to meticulously plan and execute your next adventure. It is brimming with essential skills and expert tips that guarantee a successful trip, ranging from selecting the ideal RV camper to efficiently packing and setting up at a campground. One of the most valuable aspects of this guide is its handpicked collection of premier RV campgrounds and captivating attractions throughout the United States. These carefully curated recommendations eliminate the guesswork involved in trip planning and guarantee a comfortable and delightful stay for you.

This comprehensive guide goes above and beyond by featuring the finest campgrounds in each state, saving you precious time and effort that would otherwise be spent on researching and comparing various options. Rest assured that each recommendation has been carefully vetted for its quality and amenities, ensuring that you can fully concentrate on the joy of exploration and leisure. Whether you seek a serene and tranquil retreat or a lively and family-friendly atmosphere, you can rely on this guide to help you discover the perfect campground that aligns perfectly with your preferences and requirements.

There are different ways to explore the world, but RV camping has always been considered one of the most fascinating. It combines the classic road trip with the charm of the wide-open spaces, offering the convenience of a home away from home thanks to the camper.

RV camping is considered the best way to explore for several reasons:

- Mobility: With an RV, you have the freedom to move wherever you want. You can explore cities, visit national parks, stop along the coast or immerse yourself in the wilderness. You are not tied to a single destination, and you have the option of following personalized itineraries based on your interests.
- RV camping offers an experience of unparalleled comfort and convenience. Inside the motorhome, you have all the comforts of home at your disposal, such as comfortable beds, a fully equipped kitchen, a private bathroom and ample space to relax. There is no need to look for accommodation or worry about finding a restaurant every day, as you have everything you need at your fingertips. This convenience makes RV camping a convenient and enjoyable way to explore, providing the feeling of being 'at home' wherever you go.
- RV camping is an economic cost-effective option compared to other forms of travel. It allows you to save on accommodation and catering costs, as you have the option of cooking your own meals inside the motorhome and staying in campsites with more affordable rates. In addition, RV camping allows you to have finer control over your budget, as you can plan and manage your expenses more flexibly and adaptable to your financial needs.
- Camping in a motorhome offers you the opportunity to experience authentic contact with nature, immersing yourself in splendid landscapes and enjoying all its nuances. You can start your day by waking up to breathtaking views, explore pristine trails, picnic surrounded by natural beauty and admire the starry sky at night. This experience allows you to live in close contact with the surrounding natural environment, offering you total immersion in the beauty and tranquility of nature.
- RV camping gives you unprecedented flexibility. You have the freedom to decide how much time you spend in a specific location. If you particularly like a place, you have the option to extend your stay. You have total control of your itinerary and the freedom to tailor it

according to your needs and wishes. This flexibility allows you to explore places at your own pace, without time constraints or external pressures, fully enjoying every experience along the way.

In conclusion, camping in a motorhome gives you an unparalleled feeling of freedom, comfort comparable to that of home, unparalleled convenience and authentic experiences in the midst of nature. It's the perfect way to explore new places, create memories that will last forever, and fully enjoy the beauty of the world around you.

BOOK 1

GETTING STARTED WITH RV CAMPING

CHAPTER 1

Understanding the Different Types of RVs

Are you looking for an ideal recreational vehicle for your road trips? Whether you're looking for the perfect campervan for full-time living or you're just looking for the most affordable option for your weekend getaways, there's a wide range of campervans and travel trailers to choose from, all capable of meeting your needs.

Let's see what types of campers are available.

Camper

As the name suggests, RVs are motorized vehicles that provide mobile accommodations for full-time living. They offer more space, ease of driving, little or no installation time, and the ability to be used while travelling, things that towable RVs cannot provide.

However, campers are usually more expensive and require more maintenance. Also, due to their size, they can be more difficult to store. This is why they are often chosen by avid camper travelers or those who consider the camper as a way of life.

Class A

Class A RVs are the largest type of recreational vehicles available. Their length ranges from 22 to 49 feet, and they offer all the essentials for living on the road.

A-Class campers boast a spacious interior, ample storage space, comfortable seating and a smooth ride, making them the ideal option if you plan to spend a considerable amount of time on the road each year.

Class A campers are similar in size to an apartment and come with full-sized kitchens, bathrooms, and plenty of sleeping and lounging areas. Inexpensive Class A campers can be priced as low as $60,000, while more luxurious models, such as those with diesel engines, can fetch prices as high as $500,000.

Class B

Class B campers, often referred to as van campers, are a smaller and cheaper option than class A and C campers.

Resembling large vans, Class B campers are ideal for those traveling with small families and don't plan to spend all their time on the road. These RVs are well equipped and often have bite-sized kitchens, creatively configured sleeping spaces, and can fit into virtually any parking space. They usually range in length from 17 to 19 feet, and the price can range from $60,000 to $140,000.

Class C

Class C campers are somewhere in between class A and B campers. These vehicles have a much larger interior than class B campers, providing space for many of the same features found in class A campers.

Unlike class A campers, which resemble a bus, class C campers are much more like a truck. These vehicles offer the choice of gas or diesel engine options.

This type of camper has a distinctive cabin that extends above the passenger compartment and can be used as a sleeping area, storage space or entertainment center.

If you don't have the need to tow a trailer, this option offers fuel efficiency ranging from 8 to 15 miles per gallon (MPG). The average size of a Class C RV is 21 to 41 feet, and the price can range from $50,000 to $100,000. Class C campers are able to comfortably accommodate four to eight people.

The more compact size of Class C RVs allows them to access places where larger RVs may not be suitable, such as some campgrounds located in state parks. Thanks to their smaller size, C-Class campers offer greater maneuverability and flexibility, allowing travelers to explore a wider range of destinations and access more limited spaces. This makes them an ideal choice for those looking to explore state parks and other natural areas where access may be limited for larger campers.

C-Class RVs offer a huge selection of different floor plans, making them ideal for people who enjoy remote exploration and camping. This flexibility makes them particularly suitable for families and couples traveling together with friends, as they can choose the configuration that best suits their needs and preferences while travelling.

RUV (Recreational Utility Vehicle)

A RUV, or Recreational Utility Vehicle, is a combination of a camper and an SUV. RUV campers represent a new trend in the world of recreational vehicles and are considered an amalgamation of class A, B and C campers. This is due to their unique ability to offer a comfortable driving and living area, a spacious interior and an extraordinary mobility and maneuverability for a vehicle of this size. This makes them an attractive, medium-sized option for those looking to make short to medium-length trips. On average, RUVs are between 23 and 28 feet long and are easier to drive due to their compact size.

Travel Trailers

Travel trailers are a more affordable option for those interested in owning a trailer able RV.

Most travel trailers don't require a storage area with a height of 14 feet, which can result in savings in storage costs. Additionally, travel trailers offer more interior space than RVs because they lack driver and engine compartments, allowing for more room for activities. You can find more information about the different types of travel trailers below.

Fifth Wheel Trailers

Recreational vehicle enthusiasts who want to spend most of their lives camping should consider this option. This is a towed camper that looks a lot like traditional travel trailers, but with one key difference at the front.

Fifth Wheelers are known for being among the roomiest campers available on the market. This is due to their main feature: a section overlapping the cargo area of a truck, extending over the bed of the truck.

These campers offer an extended length which allows for more interior space for different areas, such as the kitchen, lounge area, bathroom and bed. Additionally, many fifth wheels feature slide-outs, which are retractable sections that extend when the RV is parked, providing additional living space. The slide-outs allow for greater width without compromising the maneuverability of the camper during transport.

They are especially popular with families or groups of friends traveling together and need ample space for all members to stay. In addition, fifth wheels provide more separate areas and privacy inside, allowing different people to have their own personal space.

Prices usually range from $36,000 to $135,000.

Conventional Travel Trailers

This type of trailer is what comes to mind whenever you picture a trailer being towed.

While sizes vary, most travel trailers can be towed by a standard SUV, van, car, or truck with a bumper and hitch.

Travel trailers offer a wide variety of floor plans and styles, making them suitable for different traveler preferences and needs.

Travel trailer floor plans can include different configurations of beds, kitchens, bathrooms, and seating areas. There are models that offer single beds, double beds, bunk beds and even separate rooms for more privacy. Kitchens can be equipped with stoves, refrigerators, sinks and storage spaces, allowing you to prepare meals while camping. Bathrooms can be equipped with showers, toilets and sinks for comfort during travel.

Additionally, travel trailers come in a variety of styles and designs. There are more traditional models that offer a classic and comfortable look, while others can have a more modern and contemporary look. Their weight is also quite variable. In fact, you can find trailers ranging from 4,000 to over 10,000 pounds.

The large selection of travel trailer floor plans and styles allows travelers to find the model that best fits their travel needs, whether a couple looking for an intimate RV or a family looking for space additional.

Travel trailers are easier to unhitch and install than fifth wheels. This allows travelers to enjoy the freedom of having a separate vehicle to explore their destination, while still being able to enjoy the comforts of a proper home unit wherever they go. This versatility makes them the preferred type of RV for many people.

These RVs usually range in price from $8,000 to $65,000.

Pop-Up Campers/Fold-Down Campers

Foldable camping trailers, also known as tent trailers or pop-up campers, are a great option for travelers who like to enjoy the outdoor breeze while they sleep. These trailers are designed with an expandable roof, which can be raised to create a larger living space when parked. This feature provides more sleeping and living space while camping.

Folding camping trailers are popular with those who want a more comfortable camping experience than just a tent, but who don't want to invest in an RV for the long term or spend large sums of money. They offer the possibility to enjoy nature and life outdoors, but with greater comfort than a traditional tent.

The prices of folding camping trailers can vary according to the dimensions, materials and specific characteristics of the vehicle. However, as you mentioned, they usually sit in the $10,000 to $20,000 range. It is important to note that prices may vary depending on the manufacturer, model and additional options you wish to include.

Before buying a folding camping trailer, make sure you do thorough research on the different options available on the market. Consider your travel needs, the number of people you will be accompanying, and any specific features you want, such as a kitchen, bathroom or storage space. This way, you will be able to find the folding camping trailer that best suits your needs and budget.

Hybrid Travel Trailers

Expandable travel trailers, also known as hybrid RVs, offer an attractive combination of space, light weight and affordability. These vehicles are designed to offer more living space than traditional pop-up campers yet are still lighter and more compact than rigid travel trailers.

Hybrid campers feature rigid sidewalls and an expandable roof, which can be raised to increase height and provide additional interior space. This configuration allows for more comfort and living space while camping, but at the same time keeps the vehicle light and easy to handle while driving.

A significant advantage of hybrid campers is the presence of an on-board toilet. This can be an important element for those who prefer to have a private bathroom during their travels, eliminating the need to make use of toilets in campsites or rest areas. Plus, thanks to the hybrid setup, RV setup is generally quicker than rigid travel trailers, which require more time and effort to get up and running.

The prices of hybrid campers can vary according to the size, characteristics and materials used in the construction of the vehicle. As you mentioned, they usually sit in the $15,000 to $35,000 range.

Teardrop Campers

Teardrop trailers are a fantastic option for those looking for a small travel trailer that can be towed by almost any vehicle. These compact RVs offer an affordable mix of tent camping and RV camping.

Teardrop trailers feature a streamlined teardrop shape, which is where they get their name from. This compact, profiled shape makes them lightweight and easy to tow, allowing for a variety of vehicles to tow them, including a smaller car. They are ideal for people on a budget who want a more comfortable camping option than the traditional tent, but without having to invest in a large camper.

Teardrop trailer prices can vary based on the size, materials, features, and options included with the vehicle. Prices can start at around $5,000 for base models and can go up to around $20,000 for models with add-on amenities.

Teardrop trailers are perfect for couples who only need sleeping space for two and want to take shorter trips.

The simplest teardrop campers feature a basic configuration that essentially consists of a bedroom on wheels.

However, the larger floor plans of teardrop RVs offer a fuller experience. These designs can include a sleeping area with a bed, a kitchen/dining area for preparing and eating meals, and a wet bathroom that includes a toilet and sink. The larger floor plans of Teardrop RVs are ideal for those who want a little more space and convenience while camping. They allow you to prepare meals, wash and rest without having to rely completely on external structures. This makes teardrop campers a popular choice for those looking for a self-contained yet compact camping option.

Truck Campers/Slide-In Campers

Truck campers are a great option for those looking for a portable and versatile travel option. If you already own a pickup truck, truck campers can offer a cheaper and lighter solution.

Truck campers are designed to fit in the back of a pickup truck and are easily installed and removed. This flexibility allows the truck to be used both as an everyday vehicle and as a means of exploring nature. These campers are particularly suitable for those looking to venture off the beaten track, as they offer more freedom of movement than traditional campers.

As far as pickup towing capabilities go, half-ton trucks are usually capable of supporting most truck campers available on the market. However, some larger slide-out models require a one-ton truck to ensure proper stability and towing capacity.

Truck camper prices can vary widely based on size, features, and options included. Prices can start at around $5,000 for the simplest models and can go up to around $60,000 for the larger, more luxurious models.

Before purchasing a truck camper, be sure to carefully evaluate its size, features, and travel needs. Consider the weight of the camper and the load capacity of your pickup, making sure you choose a model that is compatible with your vehicle. Also, do thorough research on the different options available and also consider your budget to find the truck camper that best fits your travel needs.

Toy Haulers

Toy haulers, also known as sport utility RVs, are vehicles specifically designed to haul ATVs, motorcycles, jet skis, and other similar recreational vehicles. These vehicles combine the living space of an RV with the storage capacity of a sport utility trailer, providing a versatile option for the motorsport enthusiast.

Toy haulers are ideal for those involved in the racing or equestrian communities, as they offer a convenient way to transport the recreational vehicles needed for these activities. They can be fitted with gooseneck hitches, allowing you to attach and carry additional trailers, such as horses or other loads.

These vehicles also offer ample storage space for motorsports. You can find specialized storage areas inside your RV or trailer, where you can store the ATVs, motorcycles, or other vehicles you want to transport.

It's important to note that toy haulers can be available as both full campers and travel trailers, so you can choose the option that best fits your needs and preferences.

CHAPTER 2

Choosing the Right RV for Your Needs

Are you looking for the perfect camper for you and your family, but can't decide which one to buy among the many models available on the market? In this chapter you will find all the useful advice to be able to choose the camper that best meets your expectations and needs.

The very first thing to do is understand why you want to buy a camper. Understanding why you want to own an RV is key to making the right choice. There are a number of reasons why people choose to have a campervan, such as the freedom to travel, explore new places, the comfort of a home on the go, or simply a desire for adventure. Choosing the right camper depends on your needs, preferences and travel goals. Take the time to carefully evaluate what you want out of your camper and consider the different options available to find the one that best suits your needs.

Having established why, now you need to establish your budget for the purchase of the camper. As with any major purchase, it's crucial to establish a budget before starting your search for an RV. RV price can vary widely, from a few thousand dollars up to over a million, depending on size, options, and technology.

Setting a budget limit will help you keep a realistic view and avoid falling in love with an RV beyond your financial means. This will allow you to focus on finding campers that are within your price range, saving you time and avoiding disappointment.

It is important to keep in mind that the larger the camper and the more advanced its features and technology incorporated, the higher the associated costs will be. So, it's essential to consider your budget in relation to the size and options you want in your camper.

Once you have determined your budget, you can initiate your search for RVs within your preferred price range. You'll find a wide array of options that perfectly align with your requirements and preferences, ensuring they remain within your financial constraints.

After establishing the budget, you need to think about what kind of camping you want to do. Choosing the type of camper depends on your lifestyle and travel preferences. It's important to consider where you plan to take your RV and how you want to spend your time on your travels.

If you plan to spend more time at RV resorts, you may want to opt for a larger, more comfortable RV that comes with all the necessary amenities and facilities. This will allow you to enjoy the comfort of a home unit while enjoying the resort facilities and activities on offer.

On the other hand, if you prefer off-grid or off-road camping, you may want to consider a more compact and rugged RV that can tackle tough terrain and is free from reliance on outside infrastructure. Off-road campers or 4x4 vehicles could be an option to consider in this case, as they offer greater maneuverability and better terrain adaptability.

If, on the other hand, you are a fan of camping in national parks or in various places, you may want to choose an RV that is suitable for different types of camping. It might be worth opting for a more versatile camper with features like mobility, a streamlined design, and good energy management to suit different camping situations.

The main goal is to align your travel style with the most suitable type of camper. Consider your personal preferences, the places you want to explore and the type of camping experience you want to have. This way you can make an informed choice and find the camper that best fits your lifestyle and travel needs.

Remember that you don't have to choose between just one type of camping, you can adapt your travel style to different situations. The key is to find an RV that fits your style and preferences to maximize your travel enjoyment.

Another important element that should never be underestimated is the seasonality factor. Different weather conditions and seasons can affect your comfort and travel needs throughout the year.

If you intend to camper all year round, you should look for an RV with adequate thermal insulation, an efficient heating system and possibly a cooling system for hot days. This will allow you to enjoy comfort regardless of the outside temperatures.

If you plan to travel mainly during the warmer months or to places with mild climates, you may not need such an advanced heating system. In this case, you might focus on features like good airflow, windows that open, and good ventilation to keep the camper cool during hot days.

On the other hand, if you intend to camp mainly during the cold months or in places with a harsh climate, you should pay attention to the heating system, insulation and protection against extreme temperatures. You might consider a camper with double glazing, good insulation, a gas heating system or a wood burning fireplace, depending on your preference.

Also, if you plan to travel to areas with different seasons, you may want to consider an RV with an air conditioning and heating system that will allow you to adapt to changes in the weather during your trip.

Also consider that some destinations may have seasonal restrictions or adverse weather conditions at certain times of the year. Make sure you are aware of local conditions and plan your trips accordingly.

You also need to consider how much space you need or how much space you want to have inside your camper. It's important to carefully consider the length of the RV, its floor plan, and available storage space to meet the needs of your family or lifestyle.

If you have a family with children and pets, you may need a larger camper with enough room to accommodate all family members comfortably. You can consider RVs with floor plans that include bunk beds or rollaway beds for children, as well as dedicated spaces for pets.

If you're a couple who prefer a minimalist lifestyle, you might want to opt for a more compact camper with a basic but functional living area. This will allow you to have the space you need for your basic needs without having to manage an RV that is too large.

If you have a crafting hobby or need extra space for specific activities, you may be looking for an RV that offers additional storage spaces or has a flexible layout that allows you to tailor the space to suit your needs.

Touring as many RVs as possible is a good idea, as it will allow you to see the different floor plans for yourself and evaluate the space usage based on your personal preferences. You may also want to make a note of your specific needs and discuss them with RV sellers or dealers for advice and suggestions.

After taking into consideration the space you need, you should now also keep in mind how long the camper you want should be and according to what needs it must meet.

Some campgrounds, state parks, and national parks may have length restrictions on permitted RVs. These limits are often enforced to ensure that campsites are suitable for the size and needs of the vehicles using them. Therefore, if your primary goal is to primarily access and use smaller campsites, it's important to give serious consideration to the length of RV you're considering.

Before buying a camper, it is advisable to check the requirements and restrictions of the campsites you intend to visit. This way, you will be able to determine what maximum length your camper can have to be able to access those specific campsites.

Keep in mind that not all campsites have length restrictions and that there are still plenty of camping options available for even larger RVs. However, if you prefer smaller campsites or if you would like the flexibility to be able to move to different camping areas, then the length of the camper becomes an important factor in your choice.

Now create a list to understand which functions you want to have in your camper, both inside and out. One of the first decisions you need to make is whether you want an RV that can be towed by a vehicle or if you prefer a vehicle-mounted RV, such as a Class C RV or Teardrop RV. If you already have a truck or vehicle suitable for towing, you may want to opt for a travel trailer or fifth wheeler that you can tow behind your vehicle.

Also, it is important to consider the motor type of the camper. You can choose between a petrol or diesel camper, each with its own specific features and benefits.

If you plan to go camping off the grid or in locations without access to external energy sources, you may want to consider installing an on-board generator or using solar panels to ensure adequate power supply during your travels. These options can offer the energy independence needed for off-grid camping.

After the outside we have to consider the inside. It's really important to consider your must-haves inside the RV and assess your needs room by room.

Once you've identified the features and options you want in your RV, it's important to factor them into your research and vehicle selection. Make sure you set a realistic budget and use your preferences as a starting point to find campers that match your needs and financial possibilities.

Once you've made a list of what you need, it's still a good idea to try to remain open to compromises. Buying a camper often involves a compromise between mobility and comfort, as well as personal needs and wishes. It's important to be aware of these trade-offs and make decisions based on your current priorities, but it's also important to understand that your needs can change over time.

As you begin to travel full-time, you may find that there are new needs and desires emerging. Your lifestyle adapts to travel, and you may want more space, more conveniences or different features in your camper. It's a process of adaptation and discovery, and it can take some time to figure out exactly what you need as you immerse yourself in this new experience.

If you plan to travel full-time in the future, it may be wise to choose an RV that offers some flexibility and ability to adjust to your evolving needs. Additionally, you may want to consider purchasing a used RV to get started, so you can experience your travel lifestyle and better understand what works best for you.

CHAPTER 3

New vs Used: Is it better to buy a new or used RV camper?

After reviewing the different RV options available in the market, you may also have come to a decision as to what type of equipment best suits your needs. However, there is still one important question to consider during your research: is it better to buy a new or used camper?

The consequences of this choice can be significant and can affect your satisfaction with your new home on wheels and the life experiences you will have with it.

Purchasing a new model, equipped with the latest features, technologies and interior styling can offer a few benefits over using an older model.

Furthermore, when it comes to choosing the desired floor plan and layout for an RV, buying a new vehicle offers the widest range of options and customization possibilities. Local dealers or RV shows are great places to explore a huge selection of RV models and variations available. An advantage of buying a new camper is that you can choose between different floor plans, color combinations and customization options offered by the manufacturer. You can find the model that best fits your needs and preferences, and even order a custom-made unit that meets your exact specifications.

In addition, newly manufactured implants generally come with a warranty which usually covers a period of one year. This warranty offers protection for many contingencies that could arise, but it is always advisable to research carefully and understand exactly what items are covered by the warranty.

However, it is important to consider that buying a new camper will result in a significant financial loss. As soon as you sign the paperwork and leave the parking lot, the value of your camper will drop rapidly and dramatically. Although it has not undergone any physical changes, it is classified as a used vehicle. The initial depreciation can even reach 20% of the purchase value.

Also, determining the true market value of an RV can be a confusing process. While it is known that you don't have to pay the full list price for a new vehicle, it can be difficult to determine the actual sale price at which the dealership is willing to pass it on. Negotiations can become awkward, especially when there is a lack of trust or pressure from the salesperson. It is important to conduct thorough research into the market value of the specific RV model, consider competitor offerings, and establish an adequate budget before engaging in negotiations with the dealer. Also, being prepared to negotiate and stand your ground can help you get a fair price and reduce any embarrassment or pressure during the buying process.

It must also be considered that it is very common for new campers to have some problems or defects that may have been overlooked during the manufacturing process or the dealer's inspection. The first year of ownership might feel like an experience filled with repeat visits to the dealership to fix these issues. Often, the first trip with your new purchase is referred to as a "shakedown trip," as it is during this trip that you spot many of the problems that may have been overlooked by the manufacturer or dealer.

It is important to note that this does not apply to all new campers, but is a common situation reported by many owners. However, some manufacturers and retailers offer an extended warranty period or dedicated customer service to address such issues promptly and ensure a better customer experience during the first few uses of the camper.

However, as they become more familiar with RVs and their travel needs, many people may prefer to buy a used RV rather than a new one.

One of the main benefits of buying a used RV is the potential money savings. If you are patient and put the time and energy into searching, it is possible to find a used camper that meets your needs and is only a few years old, but with similar features and specifications to a new model.

This means you can get a camper that still offers many of the latest features and technologies, but at a lower price than buying a new model. Often, camper owners may decide to sell them after only using them for a few years, perhaps because they want a different model or for other personal reasons.

The used RV market has experienced a notable surge in transparency and efficiency, largely attributed to the emergence of dedicated online platforms like RV Trader and RVUSA. These websites have revolutionized the process by providing comprehensive information and facilitating smooth transactions, making it easier than ever to navigate the used RV market. These sites offer a wide variety of used RV listings from dealerships and private sellers across the country. This allows buyers to have a wide choice and to compare the prices and features of the campers they are interested in.

Additionally, there are resources such as the National Automobile Dealers Association (NADA) guides that provide fair market valuations for used RVs. These guides can be used as a guideline in determining a fair and reasonable price for your desired camper, considering various factors such as age, features, condition and market demand.

Consulting these online resources and using appraisal guides can help buyers gain a better understanding of the true market value of their desired RV and avoid paying a much higher price than it is worth.

In addition to the cost-saving benefit, buying a used camper offers the opportunity to benefit from a vehicle that has already dealt with initial wear. Common problems that can arise in the first few years of using a new RV have generally been addressed and resolved by the previous owners. Also, previous owners may have made improvements and upgrades to the RV, such as installing newer technology, satellite TV systems, or solar panels. This means you can get a camper that offers more functionality and convenience than the original model, without having to carry out such upgrades yourself.

There are therefore many advantages in buying a used camper, but as there are pros, you must also weigh the cons.

When buying a used RV, it's important to take precautions to avoid running into hidden problems, such as structural damage or water intrusion. It is advisable to inspect the vehicle carefully or have it inspected by a specialized professional before finalizing the purchase.

A thorough inspection can reveal any hidden problems or defects that may not be apparent at first glance. If the seller is honest and serious, they may be willing to share the cost of the inspection or, in some cases, even cover it entirely. This shows their willingness to be transparent and to ensure a fair transaction.

Remember that a professional inspection may require an additional expense, but it's a major investment to avoid costly breakdowns or repairs in the future. Be sure to request full documentation of the camper, including maintenance records and any past repairs.

It is also to be considered that depending on your geographical location you may have to travel to find the desired replacement used equipment. This applies to both the purchase of used and new equipment. The availability and variety of offerings may vary from location to location, and you may need to broaden your search and consider options in different locations.

When buying used equipment, it's important to do your own research to determine a fair market price and to make sure you don't overpay. This is especially important when dealing with customized or modified equipment, where the owner may be looking to derive additional value from the work performed. To avoid overpaying, it's wise to look closely at similar market prices for similar used equipment and compare the features, condition, and upgrades offered.

During negotiations, you can evaluate the importance of custom jobs or upgrades and establish a fair market price by considering those factors. The key is to be well informed, ask the seller questions, and negotiate based on a thorough understanding of the equipment's value and market conditions.

Another possible downside to buying a used RV is that it may not automatically be covered by a warranty. Unlike buying a new camper, where a standard warranty is usually provided, with a used vehicle the situation can vary depending on where it is purchased.

In some cases, it may be possible to obtain an extended warranty or additional warranty coverage for the used camper.

It is important to carefully check the conditions of sale and discuss the warranty options available before buying a used camper. In some cases, you may need to consider purchasing a separate warranty or look for a vendor that offers some form of warranty coverage.

In any case, be sure to read the terms and conditions of the proposed warranty carefully, including specific coverages and limitations, so that you have a clear understanding of what is included in the coverage and how long it is valid.

Having said that, it should be emphasized that very often, individual preference becomes the determining factor in choosing between buying a new or used item. There are individuals who opt for a new camper, as they wish to be the sole owner of the unit and appreciate the exclusivity that comes with it. Conversely, there are other people who would never consider paying an extra cost for a completely new item and always prefer to shop on the used market.

CHAPTER 4

Renting an RV Camper: Useful Tips and Mistakes to Avoid for Renting the Best RV Camper

In this chapter, we'll look at the common mistakes people make when renting an RV, so you can avoid repeating them and ensure you have an amazing experience on your RV adventure.

If you are used to staying in hotels and are considering renting an RV for your holiday, it is understandable that the whole rental process can seem a bit daunting or new. However, with the right knowledge and attention to mistakes to avoid, you can face the experience with confidence and serenity and above all you will avoid mistakes and rip-offs.

Rent your Camper from an honest and reputable agency

A common mistake to avoid when renting an RV is to rely on an unreliable source. It is essential to choose a serious and reliable camper rental company or private individual with a good reputation.

When it comes to renting an RV, it's important to take into consideration where you're renting it from. While some people choose to rent directly from private individuals, there are risks associated with this option. If a problem occurs during your rental, there may not be immediate support or someone to help resolve it.

When choosing an RV rental company, be sure to read reviews, check rental policies, and make sure there is a proper support system in place. In this way, you can rent a camper with greater safety and peace of mind during your adventure.

Don't judge the Camper to rent based only on photos

When looking at camper rental options, pictures can provide a visual idea, but the description is just as important to gaining a complete understanding. That is why it is vital that you carefully read the description of the listing you are considering. That's why skipping the description is a common mistake to avoid.

By reading the description, you can obtain detailed information on the camper, including the services and equipment provided, the dimensions, the number of beds, any restrictions and other relevant information

Read the technical specifications carefully, such as the dimensions, the type of vehicle, the capacity of the water tank, the available electric energy, the heating and cooling system, as well as the accessories included.

Pay attention to rental policies, such as age requirements, mileage limits, restrictions on driving off-road or rough terrain, and RV return policies. Make sure you understand the rules and responsibilities associated with the rental.

You acknowledge any particular restrictions or conditions associated with the rental, such as no smoking or pets, or special requests for pick-up or return of the camper.

Reading the description carefully will help you make an informed decision and avoid unpleasant surprises during your rental. Make sure you complete your search by reading both the description and looking at the images to get a complete view of the campervan rental offer.

Check integrated services and amenities

It is another common mistake to assume that an RV will have certain services or amenities without checking them carefully. It's important to refer to the lists of amenities provided in your camper advertisement to make sure it includes everything you need to feel comfortable during your rental.

Make sure you carefully read the list of services provided in the camper advertisement. See if amenities such as a full kitchen, bathroom with shower, air conditioning, heating, Wi-Fi connection, dishes, bedding, outdoor tables and chairs, barbecue and other comforts you wish to have during your trip are listed. If you have specific needs, such as accessibility for people with disabilities or a child seat, check if these services are available.

If you have any doubts about the presence of a particular service or equipment, contact the owner or the rental company to request clarifications. It's best to ask in advance to avoid disappointment or inconvenience during your rental.

Having too high expectations for your Camper

When renting an RV, it's important to have realistic expectations about the level of comfort and amenities available. While it's reasonable to expect an RV that's clean and has working appliances, you can't expect the same level of service you'd find in a luxury hotel.

A camper offers the opportunity for a more adventurous and independent experience, but it also requires some adaptation. You will not get daily maid service or immediate support from service personnel. You will have to take care of your space and your needs during the rental, such as cleaning the camper, filling water and emptying the tanks, and managing any unforeseen events that may arise during the trip.

Have good communication with the host

When you rent a camper from a private individual, a relationship of mutual trust is effectively created. You need to be able to trust the owner with your holiday, and at the same time, the owner needs to be able to trust you with their caravan or camper.

It is important to answer questions promptly both before and during the camper rental from a private individual. Quick and effective communication helps maintain a good relationship and resolve any concerns or issues that may arise along the way.

Try to answer questions or messages from the camper owner as soon as possible. This demonstrates your commitment and interest in the rental and allows the landlord to feel supported and considered.

If you have any concerns or encounter problems while using the camper, it is essential that you let the owner know without delay. Clearly describe the situation and provide details for the landlord to understand and address the issue appropriately.

Read the cancellation policies carefully

The cancellation policy is an important aspect that owners must carefully consider when offering their camper for rent. Likewise, renters should take the time to read and understand these policies before confirming the rental. Unfortunately, many renters neglect to do this and may later regret it.

Before confirming the rental, take the time to carefully read the cancellation policy provided by the owner. This policy specifies the rules and conditions for canceling or modifying the reservation. Make sure you understand the terms and any penalties or restrictions associated with the cancellation.

If there are any parts of the cancellation policy that you do not understand or would like to clarify, please do not hesitate to ask the owner any questions. It is best to get all the necessary information before confirming the rental.

If you need to make changes to your reservation or cancel it, notify the owner as soon as possible so that he can adequately handle the situation. In this way, it may be possible to find an agreement that is satisfactory for both parties.

When renting an RV through a reputable peer-to-peer rental company, the cancellation policy should be easily accessible on each listing. It is important to find, read and keep in mind the cancellation policy when booking.

Remember that you will have to respect the cancellation rules established by the owner; therefore, carefully evaluate your decisions and consider the possible consequences before confirming the reservation. Maintaining a clear understanding of the cancellation policies will help avoid any misunderstandings or inconveniences during the camper rental process.

Go through the check-out procedures

When renting an RV, it is common for renters to have certain responsibilities to perform before returning the vehicle. These activities are important in getting the RV ready for the next renter and ensuring a smooth transition.

It's important to understand that some landlords may charge additional fees if renters don't properly complete checkout tasks, such as taking down beds, washing dishes, or draining tanks. These fees may apply to cover the additional costs incurred by the landlord in returning the RV to a clean, ready state for the next renter.

To avoid such extra expenses and end your trip on a positive note, I strongly recommend that you perform these simple tasks before returning your camper. Make sure you carefully read the instructions provided by the owner regarding check-out and follow the specific procedures indicated. By doing this, you will help maintain a good relationship with the owner and keep the experience positive for both parties.

CHAPTER 5

Preparing Your RV for the Road

Going on a road trip in your camper, whether new or used, can encompass a wide range of experiences, ranging from a long weekend getaway to an extended road trip. The pre-trip checklist for your camper depends on your destination and the length of trip you have planned. However, there are some essential mechanical checks and camper basics that you should always check before setting off.

Start with a technical inspection of your Camper

It is highly recommended to conduct a comprehensive technical inspection of the camper, ideally within the timeframe of 3 to 6 months before your planned trip. Before you hit the road, it's vital you check the condition of your camper and make sure it's safe and ready to travel.

In this regard, it is certainly advisable to have the camper inspected by a certified technician at least once a year. This will allow you to identify any problems or wear before they turn into costly or dangerous breakdowns during the journey. Preventive and condition-based maintenance are equally important. This means that you should take regular care of your camper, for example by carrying out oil changes, checking and replacing filters, lubricating moving parts, checking the integrity of hoses and cables, and looking out for any signs of deterioration or damage. Following the manufacturer's recommendations for maintenance and consulting a qualified technician for any necessary repairs or replacements is always good practice to ensure your RV is in top condition for the journey.

Check the roof of the camper

Another aspect to take into consideration is checking the roof of your camper. Over time, UV rays from the sun and exposure to water can cause damage to your RV's roof sealing coating.

Replacing an RV roof can be an expensive process, costing approximately $300 or more per linear foot, which includes both the labor and materials needed to complete the job. This price can vary considerably depending on the specification of the camper and the rates charged at the location where the work is being carried out.

Conversely, resealing your camper roof is generally a cheaper option than replacing it completely. However, costs can still vary, and resealing is estimated to cost between $250 and $500 total. This price will depend on the size of the roof, the type of sealant used, and the amount of work required to complete the job.

If the roof of your RV is walkable, you can walk on it carefully to inspect it closely for damage. If the roof is not walkable or if you do not feel confident walking on it, it is advisable to use a stable ladder to inspect the roof from a safe vantage point. Make sure you place the ladder on a solid surface and have an assistant or someone hold the ladder to ensure your safety during the inspection.

If you are not comfortable doing the inspection yourself or if you prefer to rely on an expert, you can contact a specialized service station. At these service stations, you can request a professional inspection of your camper's roof by experienced technicians, who will be able to identify any damage or problems and provide you with the necessary repair or maintenance recommendations.

Also, checking for cracks or broken seals around any element of the RV is an important step in pre-trip preparation. If there are any cracks or broken seals, you should take steps to repair or replace them before you leave on your trip. You can use sealant products recommended by the RV manufacturer or consult a professional for help repairing damaged seals.

Rubbing your hand on the surface of the RV roof is an effective method of checking the condition of the sealant. If the sealer is well maintained, it should have a chalk-like feel and there should be no white residue on your hand.

However, if you notice white residue on your skin while hand scrubbing the roof, it is a sign that the roof coating is deteriorating. These white residues may indicate that the sealant is losing its integrity and that the campervan roof now needs to be re-sealed.

Thoroughly washing the roof of the camper before inspection is good practice. Thorough cleaning of the roof makes it easier to identify any visible problems or damage. This will help you take the necessary preventive measures or plan any repairs before setting off on your journey.

Carry out a thorough check of the tyres

Be sure to carefully inspect the tyres on your camper and tow vehicle, if any. Don't forget to check the spare wheels as well. Tire failures are one of the leading causes of accidents when traveling in an RV. If your camper is parked and has not been used for an extended period, it is advisable to lift the tires off the ground to reduce the stress and deformation caused by the weight of the vehicle.

Carefully inspect the tread and sidewalls of your tyres for wear. Check the tread for signs of deterioration or obvious damage. Also, check the sidewalls of your tyres for any signs of damage or cracks.

Even if the tread appears to be in good condition, it is advisable to replace tyres after the manufacturer's recommended lifespan. You can verify the age of your tires by looking at the manufacturing date code stamped on the sidewall of your tyres. The last four digits after "DOT" indicate the week and year of manufacture. Typically, the recommended tyres life for campers is around 6 years.

Check for proper tyres pressure, as tires tend to lose pressure over time. Be sure to check the tire pressure using a reliable pressure gauge and ensure it falls within the recommended range set by the manufacturer. During storage, tyres can lose approximately 2-3 PSI per month. Also, check for any air leaks.

Inspect the lug nuts on your tires for tightness and wear. Make sure the nuts are securely fastened and show no signs of damage or corrosion.

Carry out a complete and correct mechanical inspection of the camper

It is advisable to have a complete camper overhaul carried out, whether you choose to have it done by a qualified professional or decide to do it yourself. It's also important not to neglect the maintenance of your towing vehicle, as towing puts additional stress on it, requiring more frequent maintenance than a non-towing vehicle.

If this is your first road trip of the RV season, you can combine the pre-trip inspection with an annual overhaul performed by a qualified RV maintenance technician. If your RV owner's manual recommends having a specific service performed by a certified technician, you should follow that recommendation. It is important not to ignore any warnings or suggestions given in the manual and check the specific warranty requirements.

Also make sure that both the tow hitch and the towing equipment are in perfect condition. remember that the towing configuration and towing must be compatible with the load capacity of your camper. Before leaving, check if there is wear, corrosion or loose parts and arrange to fix or replace all the parts that are not working.

Try to book campsites well in advance of your intended departure date

It's a good idea to contact campsites near your destination and make a reservation in advance. In many locations, especially during peak seasons or during special events, campsites can fill up quickly and it may not be possible to get a spot without a reservation.

Some campsites that are very popular or located in busy tourist spots may have limited capacity. In some localities, campsites have specific regulations that prohibit arrivals without a reservation. A limited number of guests or reservations may be required to ensure an enjoyable experience for all campers.

Also, making a reservation in advance allows you to better plan your route. By knowing where and when you'll have a placc to camp, you can organize your itinerary more efficiently and plan for necessary stops along the way.

Before leaving, it is good practice to plan a route that is suitable for campers

When thinking about an RV trip, route planning may require some additional considerations than a traditional road trip.

Route planning will require a different approach when embarking on an RV trip. It is important to consider several things, such as:

RVs are larger and heavier than a regular car; therefore, it is important to consider the size of your RV when planning your route. Check that the roads you intend to travel on are wide enough for your camper and that there are no height, width or weight restrictions that could cause problems along the way.

When planning, look for gas stations that offer large, accessible parking spaces for RVs. Avoid petrol stops that may have parking spaces that are too narrow or difficult for your camper to maneuver.

Beware of roads that have steep inclines or tight switchbacks. These stretches could be challenging to travel with a camper; therefore, look for alternative routes that avoid such difficulties or approach them with caution.

Check to see if there are any bridges or tunnels along the way that have restrictions on carrying propane tanks. Make sure you avoid such restrictions by planning an alternate route or refueling before facing them.

Also look in advance for a place that is suitable for parking your Camper

When traveling by RV, unplanned layovers can be more complicated to manage than a traditional road trip. However, calling points of interest along the route ahead of time and asking about RV parking is a great strategy for meeting this challenge.

Booking in advance at campsites or attractions along the route will ensure you have adequate spaces to park your camper and avoid any frustration or inconvenience. Asking for specific details about RV parking, such as the maximum size allowed or availability of amenities, will help you plan accordingly.

However, there will always be situations where you might come across interesting stops along the way that weren't planned. In these cases, you can follow some tips to evaluate if you will be able to access the place with your camper:

- Check the satellite map view on your smartphone to assess the accessibility of the area. Look at the size of the parking lot, the layout of the roads, and potential obstacles that could make navigating an RV difficult.
- Look for online reviews or information about other people who have visited the destination with an RV. You may find useful travel tips or experiences that can give you an idea of the feasibility of accessing the place with your own vehicle.
- If you come across an interesting stop along the way, you can also ask the locals if it's possible to park an RV in that area.
- Either way, it's important to exercise caution and evaluate the situation carefully before committing to an area that could present accessibility challenges for your RV. Planning remains the best strategy, but when you encounter an unexpected stop, use the resources at your disposal to evaluate the feasibility of accessing the place with your camper.

Before leaving, check that you have all the essentials

When traveling with a small house on wheels, it is important to ensure that you have the essential items with you to ensure comfort and safety during the trip. Here are some key elements to keep in mind:

- Make sure you have your ID card or passport, credit and debit cards with you. These documents are essential for personal identification and for financial transactions along the way.
- Bring all necessary medical documents with you, such as prescriptions, medical records and health insurance information. These documents can be important in case of medical emergencies or health care needs while travelling. Remember to also include any pet health related documents, such as veterinary certificates.
- If you are taking any prescribed medications, be sure to bring enough with you for the duration of your trip. It's a good idea to have a copy of your prescription as well, in case you need to refill while traveling.

- Make sure you have valid insurance cards with you, which cover both medical emergencies and road accidents. These cards can be requested if you need medical treatment or roadside assistance during your journey.
- If you are traveling with children, don't forget to bring along their favorite comfort items, such as stuffed animals, blankets or toys. These elements can help create a familiar and comfortable environment for the little ones while travelling.
- Making a checklist of all the essentials before you leave can help you avoid forgetting anything important. Make sure you have a safe place to store these items in your tiny house on wheels, so you can easily access them when you need them.
- Make sure you bring enough clothing to cover a variety of weather conditions. Include seasonal clothing, such as jackets, sweaters, pants, t-shirts, and waterproof clothing. Remember to also bring comfortable clothing for relaxation, such as tracksuits or pajamas.
- Bring along food supplies that suit your preferences and dietary needs. This can include non-perishable foods, snacks, beverages and drinking water. Make sure you also have essential cooking utensils, such as cutlery, plates, glassware, and pans.
- Bring enough sheets, blankets, pillows, and towels for you and other members of your party.
- Bring along personal cleaning supplies, such as soap, shampoo, conditioner, toothbrush, toothpaste, and paper towels. Also make sure you have RV cleaning supplies, such as dish soap, dish soap, sponges, and cleaning cloths.
- Include basic tools, such as a first aid kit, flashlights, spare batteries, screwdrivers, and pliers. It may also be helpful to have camping equipment, such as folding chairs, a portable table, a camping grill, or outdoor activity equipment, such as bicycles or fishing gear.

CHAPTER 6

RV Upgrades: DIY Projects and Upgrades for Your RV

You can greatly improve your motorhome experience by making a few modifications and new upgrades to your vehicle. Even simple upgrades can have a significant impact on your comfort level and overall travel satisfaction.

The beauty of many of these modifications is that they don't require an engineering certification or an advanced scientific background.

Whether you're looking to optimize storage space or increase comfort in your RV, upgrades can definitely be worth it. These improvements can make your journey more enjoyable and functional, giving you a more organized and comfortable environment during your time in your motorhome. Whether it's installing additional shelving, upgrading your heating and cooling system, or upgrading your mattress, investing in RV upgrades can make a real difference to your travel experience.

Change or update the mattress

It is possible that some motorhome manufacturers have not done extensive tests on the mattresses that are installed in their platforms. It's important to keep in mind that standard-supplied mattresses may not offer the same level of comfort and quality as the high-quality mattresses found in hotels or private homes.

Many mattresses that come standard with RVs are designed to accommodate the space restrictions and weight requirements of the unit, rather than prioritizing optimal sleeping comfort. However, that doesn't mean that all RV mattresses are low quality.

If you'd like to improve the quality of the mattress in your RV, there are several options available. You may consider purchasing a custom RV mattress that fits the dimensions and specifications of your vehicle. There are specialist companies that offer mattresses specifically designed for RVs, which can offer better comfort and support while sleeping.

Alternatively, you could also consider adding a mattress topper, which can be placed on top of your existing mattress to add an extra level of cushioning and comfort.

Camper door lock replacement

Interestingly, there are only a few different keys for the standard RV door lock. This means that it may be possible for another person to possess a key that matches your lock if you spend a lot of time in campsites and RV parks.

To increase the security of your RV, a recommended option is to upgrade to a lock specifically designed for RVs. These locks offer additional security features over standard locks, such as using a PIN code to unlock the door instead of a physical key.

PIN code RV locks can offer several benefits. Firstly, they eliminate the risk of losing keys and the need to duplicate them. They also allow you to easily share your PIN code with family or friends without having to physically manage your keys.

It's important to choose a high-quality RV lock that is durable and reliable. You can find a variety of options available on the market, with additional features such as built-in alarms or wireless connectivity features.

Modify your kitchen with a stick-and-peel backsplash

It's true that most RV manufacturers avoid installing ceramic tile due to its weight and complexity of installation. However, there are lightweight alternatives like stick-and-peel tiles that can provide a similar look without adding an excessive weight load to your RV.

Stick-and-peel tiles are self-adhesive tiles that can be easily applied to smooth surfaces, such as walls or countertops, without the need for glue or special tools.

With a little patience and attention to detail, you can transform the look of your kitchen using stick-and-peel tiles. Make sure you clean the surface thoroughly before applying to ensure proper grip. Start by applying the tiles from the center and work your way out, pressing them firmly to make sure they adhere properly.

However, it's important to note that these tiles may not be as strong or long-lasting as traditional ceramic tile. Therefore, it is advisable to avoid excessive exposure to water or intense heat to ensure the best durability.

Add a digital type thermostat

Upgrading your RV thermostat from an analog to a digital one can bring benefits in terms of accuracy and temperature control. Digital thermostats offer the ability to view the current temperature and precisely set the desired temperature, eliminating the guesswork of knob adjustment.

With a digital thermostat, you can easily control and adjust the temperature inside your RV to suit your personal preferences. This allows you to create a more comfortable environment during your travels.

Plus, if you choose a programmable digital thermostat, also known as a programmable thermostat, you can program your desired temperature based on the time of day. This allows you to set different temperatures during the day, for example, raising the temperature slightly in the morning to make waking up more pleasant or lowering the temperature during the night to promote a comfortable sleep.

Installing a digital thermostat or programmable thermostat may require some basic electrical skills and an adequate understanding of your RV's heating and cooling system.

Add trash cans hidden under the kitchen cabinet

Solving the garbage storage space in your RV can be a challenge, but there are creative solutions like using a hidden trash can. There are types of bins on the market that are specifically designed to fit under a kitchen cabinet or in a hidden corner, allowing you to easily store your rubbish out of sight and out of the way.

Concealed RV trash cans come in many different sizes and styles to fit different furniture and space configurations. You can find models that fit perfectly into a specific space or bins that can be pulled out or folded when not in use to maximize the available space.

When choosing this type of trash can, be sure to consider capacity and practicality. Opt for a size that fits your garbage disposal needs and look for features like a lid that seals tightly to prevent odors or an easy-to-use open/lock mechanism.

Change the camper's batteries to lithium batteries

The batteries that come standard with many RVs can be of inferior quality and can limit life and energy efficiency when camping off the grid. If you want to significantly improve the performance and energy range of your motorhome, one option to consider is upgrading lithium batteries.

Lithium are lighter, more compact and have a higher energy density, which means they can store more energy in a smaller space. Furthermore, lithium batteries have a higher charge and discharge efficiency, allowing you to make better use of the available energy.

Upgrading your campervan batteries to lithium can provide several benefits. You'll enjoy more reliable and longer-lasting power when camping off the grid, allowing you to use electrical devices for a longer period without having to frequently recharge your batteries.

High-quality lithium batteries can cost more than traditional batteries, and you may also need to make changes to your RV's power system to accommodate the new batteries.

Before deciding to upgrade, carefully consider your camping style, level of energy usage, and available budget. Also consider the life of lithium batteries, which typically outlast lead-acid batteries, but may require proper charge management and precautions to maintain performance over time.

Install solar panels on the roof of your Camper

Installing solar panels on the roof of your RV can be a great complement to upgrading your lithium batteries. Solar panels can provide a sustainable, renewable source of energy to recharge your RV batteries while camping off the grid.

Solar panels transform solar energy into usable electricity, which can be stored in RV batteries. This allows you to make the most of the solar energy available during the day and use it to power electrical devices and keep batteries charged even when you are not connected to an external power source.

Installing solar panels on the roof of your camper offers several advantages. You can reduce your reliance on traditional energy sources, such as generators or camping power outlets, allowing you to camp in more remote locations and without having to make frequent stops to recharge your batteries. Additionally, solar panels are low maintenance and can last a long time with proper care.

Before installing solar panels on your RV, consider a few important factors. Evaluate the size and capacity of your lithium battery system to determine how much solar power you need. Make sure you have adequate space on the roof of the camper to accommodate the solar panels and choose an installation that blends well with the aesthetics and shape of the vehicle.

Position the panels to obtain the optimum exposure to the sun during the day and consider the use of adjustable stands to be able to adjust the angle of the panels according to the angle of the sun.

Add a wireless RV backup camera

Installing a wireless RV backup camera can increase your safety and ease the reversing process.

The size and shape of RVs can make rearward visibility difficult when backing up. A backup camera strategically installed at the rear of your motorhome allows you to have a clear view of the area behind you, helping you to avoid obstacles, vehicles or other potentially dangerous situations when reversing.

Wireless RV backup cameras are designed to be easy to install and use. They usually come with a portable monitor that you can place inside the vehicle, allowing you to view what the camera is filming in real time. This gives you an additional view and improves your awareness when reversing.

They can help you position yourself more precisely and avoid accidental collisions with walls, obstacles or other vehicles.

Before buying an RV backup camera, make sure you consider a few important factors. Check the compatibility of the system with your camper and the ease of installation. Look for a camera with good video resolution and a wide viewing angle to get the best possible view. Also, consider battery life or power options and weather resistance to ensure reliable performance over time.

While installing an RV backup camera can take some time and effort, the benefits in terms of safety and ease of operation can be substantial. You will have the peace of mind of having better visibility when reversing and you will be able to protect your motorhome from possible damage caused by accidental collisions.

BOOK 2

RV CAMPING: USEFUL THINGS TO KNOW ABOUT FINANCING, INSURANCE, AND REGULATIONS

CHAPTER1

Getting Your RV Insurance

Why to have a RV insurance

RV insurance, also known as recreational vehicle insurance, is a kind of insurance indemnity specifically designed for RV. It provides protection for motorhomes, travel trailers, camper vans, and other kind of RVs.

RV insurance typically includes the following kinds of coverage:

- Collision coverage: This coverage helps repair or replace your RV if it's damaged in a collision with another vehicle or object, regardless of who is at fault.
- Liability coverage: This coverage protects you if you are found legally accountable for leading an accident that results in property damage or bodily injury to others. It covers medical expenses, legal fees, and damages you may be forced to pay.
- Comprehensive coverage: this kind of coverage gives protection against non-collision incidents like theft, vandalism, fire, falling objects, or other disasters depending by nature. It helps cover the cost of repairing or replacing your RV in these situations.
- Uninsured/underinsured motorist coverage: This kind could provide protection for you once you're included in an accident with a driver who either has no insurance or insufficient insurance to cover the damages.
- Personal belongings coverage: This coverage reimburses you for the loss or damage of personal belongings kept inside the RV, such as clothing, electronics, appliances, and other items.
- Roadside assistance: Many RV insurance policies offer roadside assistance services, which can be helpful if your RV breaks down or you encounter other issues while on the road. Roadside assistance may include services like towing, battery jump-starts, fuel delivery, and locksmith services.

It's important to note that RV insurance requirements and coverage options may vary depending on the type and size of your RV, how it is used (recreational use or full-time living), and the insurance provider. Be sure to consult with an insurance agent or company to discuss your specific needs and find a policy that suits you.

RV Insurance Benefits

Having RV insurance is important for several reasons. Here are some benefits when you get an RV insurance:

- Protection for your investment: An RV is a significant financial investment, and RV insurance helps protect that investment. It provides coverage for physical damage to your RV in case of accidents, theft, vandalism, or natural disasters. This coverage can be useful whenever you wish to repair or replace your RV, ensuring you don't face a significant financial burden.

- Liability coverage: It covers medical expenses, legal fees, and damages you may be legally forced to pay.
- Personal belongings coverage: RV insurance often includes coverage for personal belongings stored inside the RV. In this kind of coverage could embrace clothing, electronics, furniture, and other personal items. If your belongings are stolen or damaged while traveling, the insurance can help cover the cost of replacement.
- Roadside assistance: Many RV insurance policies offer roadside assistance services, which can be invaluable when you're on the road. If your RV breaks down or you encounter a mechanical issue, roadside assistance can provide services like towing, fuel delivery, battery jump-starts, and locksmith services.
- Full-time coverage: If you live in your RV full-time, standard auto insurance may not provide adequate coverage. RV insurance policies can be specifically tailored to meet the unique needs of full-time RVers, including coverage for personal property, liability, and additional living expenses if your RV becomes uninhabitable.
- Campsite liability coverage: Some RV insurance policies offer campsite liability coverage, which protects you in case someone is injured while on your campsite.
- Financial protection during storage: If you store your RV during certain periods, RV insurance can still provide coverage. It can protect your RV from theft, vandalism, fire, and other risks that can occur even when it's not being used.

All coverage options and benefits can change because of the different insurance provider and policy you choose.

How to get a RV insurance

To get RV insurance, there are few simple passages, and we will show you them below:

- Research insurance providers: Start by researching insurance providers that offer RV insurance. Look for reputable agencies that have experience in providing coverage for recreational vehicles. You can check online, seeking for recommendations from other RV owners, or ask to an insurance agent who specializes in RV insurance.
- Determine your coverage needs: Consider the type of RV you have, its value, how you plan to use it (recreational or full-time living), and any specific coverage requirements you may have.
- Gather necessary information: Before contacting insurance providers, gather the necessary information about your RV. This may include details such as the make, model, year, VIN (Vehicle Identification Number), mileage, and any modifications or additional features installed in the RV.
- Get multiple quotes: seek for different insurance providers to get quotes for RV insurance. Provide them with the information about your RV and the coverage options you desire. Compare the quotes you receive, considering not only the cost but also the coverage limits, deductibles, and additional benefits offered.
- Review policy terms: review with so many attentions the terms and conditions of each insurance policy you're considering. Make sure the policy aligns with your coverage needs and budget.
- Ask questions: If you have any doubts or questions about the policy, contact the insurance provider and ask for clarification. It's important to have a clear understanding of what the policy covers and any limitations or restrictions.
- Purchase the policy: Once you've chosen the insurance provider and policy that best meets your needs, complete the necessary paperwork and provide the required information to

purchase the policy. Review the policy documents carefully and ensure that all details are accurate.

- Pay premiums: RV insurance typically requires you to reward premiums to keep coverage. Determine the payment schedule and method of payment accepted by the insurance provider.

Once you have got your RV insurance, it's quite vital to review your insurance policy periodically to make you quite sure it keeps on meeting your needs. As your RV or circumstances change, you may need to adjust your coverage or seek different options.

CHAPTER 2

RV Financing: Tips for Getting the Best Deals

RV financing: what we are talking about

RV financing refers to the process of obtaining a loan or financing arrangement to purchase a recreational vehicle (RV). An RV is a motor vehicle or trailer equipped with living quarters, amenities, and features designed for temporary accommodation, travel, or recreational purposes.

When it comes to RV financing, there are a few options available:

- RV Dealership Financing: Many RV dealerships offer financing options to their customers. They work with financial institutions or have in-house financing departments to help buyers secure loans. Dealerships may have special promotions or offers, but it's still important to compare rates and terms with other lenders.
- Banks and Credit Unions: these classical financial institutions, in which are included not only the banks but also credit unions offer RV loans as well. You can apply for a loan directly with them, and if approved, they will provide the funds to purchase the RV.
- Online Lenders: these can be specialized in giving RV loans. These lenders often have a streamlined application process and may offer competitive rates. It's essential to research the lender, read reviews, and ensure they are reputable before proceeding with an online loan.

When seeking RV financing, several factors may affect your eligibility and loan terms:

- Credit Score: A good credit score enhances your possibilities of securing favorable loan terms. Lenders normally review your credit history to assess your creditworthiness.
- Down Payment: Making a significant down payment can reduce the loan amount and potentially lead to better terms.
- Loan Term: The length of the loan term can vary, but RV loans normally range from 10 to 20 years.
- Interest Rates: Interest rates can change depending on your creditworthiness, the loan amount, loan term, and the lender's policies. It's crucial to make a comparison between rates from different lenders to ensure the most favorable rate.
- Monthly Payments: Consider your budget and ensure the monthly payments fit comfortably within your financial means.

Anyway, when you are at the point of finalizing any financing agreement, you should review with more attention the terms and conditions, including interest rates, fees, repayment options, and any potential penalties for early repayment. It's advisable to calculate the total cost of the loan, including interest, to determine its affordability over the loan term.

How to finance an RV: a step-by-step guide

To properly finance an RV, you can follow these steps:

- Determine your budget: Before you start looking for RV financing, it's important to assess your financial situation and determine how much you can afford to spend on an RV. Consider factors like your income, expenses, and savings to establish a realistic budget.
- Research RV financing options: Explore different financing options available to you. This includes RV dealership financing, banks, credit unions, and online lenders. Look for their interest rates, loan terms, eligibility criteria, and customer reviews to reach out the best fit for your needs.
- Check your credit score: Request a copy of your credit report and review your credit score. A massive credit score can be aids for you about qualify for better loan terms. If your score is lower, consider taking steps to enhance it before asking for financing.
- Save for a down payment: Saving for a down payment is beneficial when financing an RV. It reduces the loan amount and can make you surer about better terms. Aim to save at least 10% to 20% of the RV's purchase price as a down payment.
- Get pre-approved: consider to be pre-approved for RV financing. Pre-approval gives you with a transparent budget and can be useful on streamlining the purchasing step.
- Gather necessary documentation: Lenders typically require specific documents for loan applications. These may include proof of income, employment verification, identification, and sometimes proof of insurance.
- Submit loan applications: Once you have chosen the lender(s) you want to work with, submit your loan application(s). Fill out the necessary paperwork accurately and provide all requested documentation. Be prepared for the lender to conduct a thorough review of your financial information.
- Review loan offers: After submitting your applications, carefully review the loan offers you receive. Consider the total cost of the loan over its duration and choose the offer that best suits your needs and budget.
- Complete the loan process: If you accept a loan offer, work with the lender to complete the loan process. This involves signing the loan agreement and any other required paperwork. Be sure to understand the terms and conditions. In these terms and conditions, you may find repayment schedules and any penalties for early repayment.
- Finalize your RV purchase: Once your loan is approved and finalized, you can complete the RV purchase. Follow the necessary steps, including negotiating the purchase price, arranging for insurance, and ensuring the title and registration process is completed correctly.

It's important to consider all the processes involved: from reading all documents carefully, to asking any questions you may have, and seeking professional advice if needed. By taking these steps, you can navigate the RV financing process and secure the funds to purchase the RV of your dreams.

Tips for getting the best deals

When seeking the best deals on RV financing, here are some tips to help you secure favorable terms and save money:

- Check your credit score: Before applying for RV financing, review your credit score and credit report. A higher credit score generally leads to better loan terms. If your score is littler, think about taking steps to make it bigger before applying.
- Save for a down payment: Saving for a substantial down payment can help lower the loan amount and potentially qualify you for better interest rates. Aim for a down payment of 10% to 20% of the RV's purchase price, if possible.
- Shop around and compare rates: Don't settle for the first financing option you come across. Research and obtain quotes from multiple lenders, including RV dealerships, banks, credit unions, and online lenders.
- Consider pre-approval: Getting pre-approved for RV financing can provide you with a clear budget and negotiating power when shopping for an RV. It allows you to know the maximum loan amount you qualify for, helping you make more informed decisions.
- Negotiate the purchase price: Just like buying a car, negotiating the purchase price of an RV can have a significant impact on your financing. Try to negotiate a fair price with the seller or dealership, as it can reduce the loan amount and save you money in the long run.
- Understand the loan terms: Ensure you are comfortable with the monthly payments and have a clear understanding of the total cost of the loan over its duration.
- Consider financing alternatives: Explore alternative financing options such as personal loans or home equity loans. Depending on your financial situation and assets, these options may offer more favorable terms or interest rates compared to traditional RV loans.
- Be mindful of the total cost of ownership: Remember that the cost of owning an RV includes more than just the monthly loan payments. Consider additional expenses such as insurance, maintenance, fuel, storage, and campground fees. Factor in these costs to ensure the overall affordability of the RV.
- Read reviews and check reputability: Before finalizing any financing agreement, research the lender or dealership. Read customer reviews, check their reputation, and ensure they are trustworthy and reliable.

By implementing these tips, you can increase your chances of securing the best deals on RV financing and make an informed decision that aligns with your financial goals.

CHAPTER 3

Understanding RV Laws and Regulations

Understanding RV laws and regulation: the main concepts

RV laws and regulations can vary by country, state, and even local jurisdictions. It's important to you to have a complete knowledge about precise laws and regulations that apply to recreational vehicles (RVs) in your area. However, I can provide you with some general information and common considerations regarding RV laws and regulations. Keep in mind that this aspect is based on the knowledge available up until September 2021. We had more updates or changes so far. It's always best to consult the relevant authorities and legal resources for the most accurate and up-to-date information. Here you are the main concepts:

- Licensing and Registration: In most jurisdictions, RVs require proper licensing and registration. The requirements for obtaining a license and registering an RV can vary, but typically involve providing documentation such as proof of ownership, proof of insurance, and payment of applicable fees. Some places may require a special license or endorsement to operate larger RVs, such as Class A motorhomes.
- Size and Weight Restrictions: Many jurisdictions have restrictions on the size and weight of RVs that can be driven on public roads. It's important to be aware of the maximum allowable dimensions and weight limits for RVs to avoid legal issues.
- Driver's License Requirements: Driving an RV may need of a specific type of driver's license or endorsement. The requirements can change based on the size and weight of the RV. For example, in the United States, different classes of motorhomes may require a regular driver's license (Class C), a commercial driver's license (CDL), or a special endorsement. Check with your local department of motor vehicles or licensing authority to determine the specific requirements in your area.
- Parking and Overnight Stays: Regulations regarding parking and overnight stays in RVs can differ from place to place. Some jurisdictions have designated RV parks, campgrounds, or specific areas where overnight parking is allowed, while others may have restrictions or prohibitions on overnight stays in RVs outside of designated areas. It's important to research and comply with the local rules and regulations regarding where you can park or camp with your RV.
- Road Safety Regulations: RVs are subject to general road safety regulations, including speed limits, traffic rules, and regulations for towing trailers or other vehicles. It's crucial to adhere to these regulations for the safety of yourself and others on the road.
- Prohibited Activities: Some jurisdictions may have specific rules and regulations regarding activities within an RV. For example, it may be illegal to consume alcohol while driving or occupy certain areas of the RV while it's in motion. Familiarize yourself with any restrictions on activities within an RV to ensure compliance with the law.

Remember, the information provided here is a general overview, and it's essential to research the specific laws and regulations that apply to your location. Always consult the official sources, such as government websites or legal resources, to obtain the most accurate and up-to-date information regarding RV laws and regulations in your area.

What are main RV laws ?

The main RV laws can vary depending on the jurisdiction, but here are some common areas of regulation that are typically covered by RV laws:

- Licensing and Registration: as we said just above, RVs are often required to be properly licensed and registered. This includes obtaining the appropriate license plates, stickers, and documentation from the relevant motor vehicle department or authority.
- Size and Weight Restrictions: There are usually regulations regarding the size and weight of RVs that can be operated on public roads. This includes limitations on the height, width, and length of the RV, as well as weight restrictions to prevent overloading.
- Driver's License Requirements: Depending on the size and weight of the RV, a specific type of driver's license or endorsement may be required. This ensures that drivers have the necessary skills and knowledge to safely operate larger vehicles. Different classes of RVs may have different licensing requirements.
- Traffic Laws: RVs must adhere to general traffic laws, including obeying speed limits, traffic signals, and signs. Additionally, RV drivers must be aware of any specific laws or regulations related to passing, merging, and turning with a larger vehicle.
- Towing Regulations: If you are towing a trailer or another vehicle behind your RV, there are typically specific rules and regulations that govern towing. This can include requirements for hitching, braking systems, safety chains, and weight restrictions for towed vehicles.
- Parking and Overnight Stays: Many jurisdictions have regulations regarding where you can park or camp with your RV. This may include restrictions on overnight stays in certain areas, requirements to use designated RV parks or campgrounds, and limitations on parking in residential or urban areas.
- Prohibited Activities: Certain activities may be prohibited within an RV, such as drinking alcohol while driving, occupying certain areas of the RV while it's in motion, or engaging in other distracting behaviors. These regulations are in place to ensure the safety of both the occupants of the RV and other road users.

It's essential to see that RV laws can vary significantly from one jurisdiction to another, so it's crucial to research and make you sure about the knowledge of specific laws and regulations that are present in your location. Consulting the official sources, such as government websites or legal resources, is the best way to obtain accurate and up-to-date information about RV laws in your area.

What are main RV regulations?

RV regulations typically encompass a range of areas to ensure safety, compliance, and environmental responsibility. Here are some main RV regulations that are commonly encountered:

- Construction and Safety Standards: RVs are subject to construction and safety standards to ensure they are built to specific specifications. These standards can cover various aspects, including electrical systems, plumbing, structural integrity, fire safety, and more. Compliance with these standards may be verified through inspections and certifications.

- Vehicle Equipment and Safety: RVs must adhere to regulations regarding vehicle equipment and safety features. This can include requirements for headlights, taillights, turn signals, mirrors, brakes, tires, seat belts, and other safety-related components. Regular maintenance and inspections are often required to ensure ongoing compliance.
- Propane and Fuel Systems: Regulations govern the use and installation of propane and fuel systems in RVs. This includes safety standards for propane tanks, storage, and usage, as well as regulations for fuel tanks, lines, and ventilation systems.
- Waste Disposal and Water Systems: RVs typically have onboard waste disposal and water systems. Regulations may exist regarding the proper installation, maintenance, and operation of these systems. This includes guidelines for handling and disposing of gray water, black water (sewage), and fresh water.
- Environmental Regulations: RVs are subject to environmental regulations to minimize their impact on the environment. This can include regulations regarding emissions from RV engines, requirements for proper disposal of hazardous materials, and guidelines for responsible waste management.
- Campground and Park Regulations: When using RVs in campgrounds or parks, specific regulations may apply. These can cover topics such as campground rules, quiet hours, pet policies, waste disposal, and adherence to park-specific regulations and guidelines.
- Accessibility Standards: Some jurisdictions have regulations to ensure RVs are accessible to individuals with disabilities. These regulations may include requirements for accessible entryways, interior features, and bathroom facilities.

It's important to note that RV regulations can vary significantly depending on the jurisdiction and the type of RV. Additionally, regulations are subject to change over time, so it's essential to consult the relevant authorities, such as government agencies or RV industry organizations, to obtain the most accurate and up-to-date information regarding RV regulations in your area.

RV ownership costs

The costs associated with RV ownership can vary depending on various factors such as the type of RV, its age, usage, location, and personal preferences. Here are some common ownership costs to consider:

- Purchase Price: The initial cost of buying an RV can vary significantly depending on factors like the type (motorhome, travel trailer, etc.), brand, size, features, and condition. RVs can range from a few thousand dollars for older or smaller models to hundreds of thousands of dollars for larger, newer, or more luxurious models.
- Financing: If you require financing to purchase an RV, you'll need to consider the cost of interest payments. The interest rate and loan term will impact the total amount you pay overtime.
- Insurance: it is necessary to cover your investment and give protection from potential liabilities. The cost of insurance can be linked to some aspects such as the kind of RV, its value, your location, driving record, usage, and coverage options. Comprehensive coverage, liability insurance, and specialized coverage for specific needs (such as full-time RVing) may add to the cost.
- Registration and Licensing: RVs typically require registration and licensing fees, which can vary by state or jurisdiction. These fees are typically renewable annually or biennially.

- Maintenance and Repairs: Regular maintenance is crucial to have your RV in good working condition. Costs can include oil changes, tire rotations, filter replacements, and general inspections. Additionally, repairs and unexpected maintenance issues can arise, especially as the RV ages. Budgeting for these costs is important, as repairs for mechanical issues, appliances, or body damage can be significant.
- Fuel and Propane: Motorized RVs require fuel, while propane may be needed for cooking, heating, and powering appliances. Fuel costs will depend on factors such as the size of the RV, driving distance, fuel efficiency, and fuel prices. Propane costs will depend on the frequency of usage and the price of propane in your area.
- Campground and Park Fees: If you plan to stay in campgrounds or RV parks, there will be associated fees. Costs can vary depending on the location, amenities offered, and duration of stay. Some locations may offer discounts for longer-term stays.
- Storage: If you don't have space to store your RV on your property, you may need to rent a storage facility. Storage costs can vary depending on the size of the RV, location, and availability of amenities like security and covered storage.
- Depreciation: Like any vehicle, an RV depreciates over time. The rate of depreciation will depend on factors such as the RV's age, condition, brand, and market demand. Understanding the potential depreciation can help you plan for long-term ownership costs.

It's crucial to understand that these costs are general estimates, and individual circumstances may vary. Creating a detailed budget and considering all potential expenses will help you have a clearer understanding of the specific costs associated with owning an RV.

BOOK3

PLANNING YOUR RV TRIP

CHAPTER 1

Choosing Your Destination and Finding the Best Campgrounds

There are apps (see book number 6.) that are very useful in helping you choose your travel destination. In the book n. 7 you'll find a careful selection of the best Campgrounds found in the 50 U.S. states that meet all kinds of budgets (divided into free or paid campgrounds). Here we will show you all you should know about RV trip and how to choose your destination.

What is an RV Trip?

Traveling by camper is one of the most adventurous and at the same time unique experiences that a traveler can have. You have maximum freedom when moving, you can change itinerary even during the trip without worrying about having to book accommodation, and you have all the comfort you want at your disposal. The camper is a small house on wheels equipped with all the necessary comforts to make a pleasant and relaxing holiday.

For being more specific an RV trip, also known as a recreational vehicle trip, is a journey or vacation taken using a recreational vehicle (RV) as a mode of transportation and accommodation. An RV is a motorized or towable vehicle that combines transportation and living quarters, providing amenities like those found in a home. It typically includes sleeping areas, a kitchen, a bathroom, and sometimes entertainment systems.

During an RV trip, individuals or families travel to various destinations, staying overnight in RV parks, campgrounds, or other designated areas that accommodate RVs. The trip can involve exploring natural landscapes, visiting national parks, touring cities, or simply enjoying the freedom of the open road. RV trips offer the convenience of bringing your own living space with you, allowing for flexibility and the ability to travel at your own pace.

RV trips provide an opportunity to experience the outdoors, enjoy camping activities, and create lasting memories. They are popular among adventure seekers, nature lovers, and families looking for a unique and immersive travel experience. The freedom to choose different destinations and the comfort of having essential amenities on board make RV trips a popular choice for those who enjoy road travel and the convenience of a mobile home.

How to choose your destination?

The best advice we can give to you, especially for your first motorhome holiday it is to plan a travel itinerary.

That's because once you are sure about where you wish to be is essential to choose in advance the campsites in which to stop, the equipped rest areas in which to stock up on water and the unmissable destinations that you will find along your route. This organizational step is not secondary to the choice of vehicle: on the contrary, it is essential to understand what type of camper we need, for how long, with what services and much more. So, don't forget to prepare a travel plan, perhaps even a generic one, but where the stops and the type of travel are clear elements right from the start.

Indeed, choosing a destination for your RV trip can be an exciting part of the planning process. So, let us show you some principal steps to help you choose the right destination:

- Determine your interests: Consider what activities and attractions interest you and your travel companions. Do you prefer outdoor adventures, historical sites, scenic landscapes, or vibrant cities? Identifying your interests will help narrow down potential destinations.
- Consider all the costs: If you think you already have a global idea of how much your motorhome holiday will cost just because you have quantified the amount of fuel you will use, you could be a mistake.
- Research RV-friendly locations: Look for destinations that have RV parks or campgrounds that can accommodate your RV. Check for amenities like hookups, dump stations, and access to necessary facilities. Websites and apps like Campendium, RV Park Reviews, and AllStays can be helpful resources for finding suitable RV-friendly locations.
- Consider the season and weather: Consider the time of year you plan to travel and the weather conditions of potential destinations. Some areas may be more enjoyable during certain seasons, while others may have extreme weather conditions that you prefer to avoid.
- Plan your route: Determine the route you want to take and consider the distance and travel time between destinations. Factor in your preferred pace of travel, stops along the way, and the overall duration of your trip. Ensure that the destinations you choose are within a reasonable distance of each other.
- Seek recommendations and reviews: Read reviews and seek recommendations from fellow RV travelers or online communities. They can give you valuable insights and firsthand experiences about different destinations. Websites like TripAdvisor and RV forums are excellent sources for gathering information and tips.
- Create a bucket list: Make a list of destinations that have piqued your interest and prioritize them based on your preferences and available time. Consider factors like scenic beauty, attractions, activities, and the overall experience you seek.
- Plan for diversity: If you have an extended trip, aim for a mix of destinations that offer diverse experiences. This could include a combination of natural wonders, cultural sites, and urban areas to add variety and cater to different interests.
- Be flexible: even if you have set a general complete plan, be open to flexibility. Discovering unexpected places along the way or adjusting your itinerary based on recommendations from locals or fellow travelers can lead to amazing experiences.
- Decide where to sleep before leaving once you have planned your itinerary, it is right to identify which campsites and equipped areas you will find along the way. In this way you will have the possibility to choose in advance where to stop, informing yourself in time about the services offered and the costs to be incurred. Plus, you'll know for sure when you'll have a chance to refill your tanks and avoid having to wash by drawing on your supply of drinking water.

- To find a place to stop, in the past it was necessary to resort to word of mouth or articles from specialized magazines. Today, the camper 2.0 fears no surprises: download the specialized apps on your device and you will have all the campsites and rest areas available along your itinerary in one fell swoop. We will keep this discussion in the sixth book.

These are only some simple and general guideline for planning an RV trip destination, but you always must remember to consider your budget, travel restrictions, and any specific requirements or preferences you have when choosing a destination. With careful consideration and research, you can find the perfect destination for your RV trip and embark on a memorable adventure.

How to find the best campgrounds?

As for the national parks, which are assumed to be the main stages of a nice on the road tour of the USA in a camper, always check the availability of equipped parking areas! Don't worry: these areas are never lacking in the main parks, and the opportunity is truly tempting... sleeping in your camper, in the extraordinary nature of the park you have chosen to visit, is a priceless privilege; or rather, it would have (and salty!) if you slept in the lodges and hotels of the parks!

So, first, log on to the Recreation.gov site. looking for information on recreational vehicle (RV) areas in individual national parks (excluding Navajo-managed parks, such as Monument Valley, so you'll have to plan differently).

Attention, in most cases it is advisable to book the pitch well in advance since they are snapped up. In this regard, we recommend that you do not camp where it is not permitted.

Looking for the best RV campgrounds needs of research and consideration of your general needs and preferences. So, let's see some principal steps to give you an aid for finding the ideal RV campgrounds for your trip:

- Utilize online resources: Websites and apps dedicated to RV camping are valuable tools for finding campgrounds. Some popular platforms include Campendium, RV Park Reviews, ReserveAmerica, and AllStays. These websites offer reviews, ratings, and detailed information about campgrounds, including amenities, pricing, and nearby attractions.
- Look for reviews and ratings: so, seek for reviews and ratings from fellow RVers. Pay attention to comments about the cleanliness, facilities, customer service, and overall experience. Look for campgrounds with consistently positive reviews and high ratings.
- Take into consideration the amenities and facilities: Identify the amenities and facilities that hold significance for you. This could include full hookups (water, electric, and sewer), Wi-Fi, laundry facilities, showers, swimming pools, playgrounds, pet-friendly areas, and recreational activities. Make a list of the amenities you prioritize and look for campgrounds that offer them.
- Check campground policies: Read and understand the campground policies, such as check-in and check-out times, reservation requirements, cancellation policies, and any specific rules or restrictions that may impact your stay. Ensure the campground's policies align with your preferences and needs.
- Always check the campsite check-in times: If you've never been camping, know that to enter you need to go through the check-in procedures, like in a normal hotel. The difference lies in the fact that most campsites do not allow this operation at night, nor during lunchtime.

- Always check the times when you can access the campsite: alternatively, you can always park your camper in the immediate vicinity and start enjoying your holiday in the camper before the staff go back to work.
- Location and proximity: Consider the location of the campground in relation to your planned activities and attractions. Determine whether you prefer a campground in a serene natural setting, near a specific city or national park, or closer to amenities like grocery stores and restaurants. Check the proximity of the campground to your desired destinations and assess accessibility.
- Campground size and layout: Consider the size and layout of the campground. Some campgrounds are large and offer plenty of space, while others may be more compact. If you prefer privacy and space, look for campgrounds with larger sites and ample distance between them.
- Research campground fees and availability: Take note of the campground fees and availability for your travel dates. Some popular campgrounds may require reservations well in advance, especially during peak seasons. Determine whether the campground fits within your budget and if reservations are necessary.
- Seek recommendations: Ask for recommendations from fellow RVers, friends, or online communities. These firsthand recommendations can be valuable in finding hidden gems or lesser-known campgrounds that may not be as widely advertised.
- Respect the highway code and that of campers: In addition to the Highway Code, which imposes seat belts on all passengers during travel, it also respects the unwritten code that all respectable motorhome owners abide by. If you have to stop in urban centers, make sure that parking is permitted and avoid parking near shops and monuments, while if you decide to stop outside the cities, check that the land is not private property and, if necessary, ask for the permit. It will hardly be denied to you. In all cases, be respectful of your camper neighbors.

Remember to plan ahead, especially for popular destinations, holidays, or peak seasons when campgrounds can fill up quickly. By conducting thorough research, reading reviews, and considering your specific needs and preferences, you can find the best RV campgrounds that will enhance your overall RV trip experience.

CHAPTER 2

Planning Your Route and Stops and Creating a Travel Itinerary

Plan an RV-friendly route

Before start planning this kind of route, we want to give you a definition. So, an RV-friendly route refers to a road or highway that is suitable and accommodating for recreational vehicles (RVs) to travel on. These routes take into consideration the specific needs and challenges that RVs present, such as their size, height, weight, and other restrictions.

Let's see now what the principal characteristics of an RV-friendly route are:

- Adequate clearance: RVs, especially those with taller heights or extended features like air conditioners or satellite dishes, require sufficient clearance under bridges, overpasses, and other structures. An RV-friendly route will have ample vertical clearance to accommodate these vehicles.
- Wide lanes: RVs are typically wider than regular cars, so an RV-friendly route will have wider lanes to provide enough space for safe navigation. This allows RV drivers to maneuver their vehicles without the risk of scraping against curbs or other obstacles.
- Avoidance of low bridges and tunnels: RVs have height restrictions due to their taller profiles. RV-friendly routes will avoid low bridges, tunnels, or other obstacles that may pose a risk of collision or damage to the vehicle.
- RV facilities and services: An RV-friendly route may have designated rest areas or campgrounds along the way that are specifically designed to cater to the needs of RV travelers. These facilities often provide amenities such as dump stations, freshwater fill-ups, electrical hookups, and waste disposal facilities.
- Scenic and enjoyable: RV-friendly routes often consider the scenic beauty and attractions along the way, offering travelers opportunities to enjoy picturesque landscapes, national parks, campgrounds, or tourist destinations that are accessible for RVs.

It's important for RV travelers to plan their routes carefully, considering factors such as road conditions, fuel stations, availability of RV services, and any specific restrictions or regulations in the area they plan to visit. Additionally, there are GPS navigation systems and online resources that can help identify RV-friendly routes to ensure a smooth and enjoyable journey.

Anyway, when you are planning an RV-friendly route, you should remind, as first thing, that this palling involves considering factors such as road conditions, fuel stations, campgrounds, and attractions along the way. Here's an example of planning an RV-friendly route from San Francisco, California, to Yellowstone National Park in Wyoming:

Day 1: San Francisco, CA to Sacramento, CA

- Start your journey in San Francisco and head east on Interstate 80 towards Sacramento.
- The route is RV-friendly with wide roads and several rest areas along the way.
- Stay overnight at a campground near Sacramento.

Day 2: Sacramento, CA to Reno, NV

- Continue on Interstate 80 eastbound towards Reno, Nevada.
- The route passes through the beautiful Sierra Nevada, Mountain range.
- Be cautious of the steep grades and winding roads, but most RVs can handle this route.
- Consider staying overnight at a campground near Reno.

Day 3: Reno, NV to Elko, NV

- Take Interstate 80 eastbound from Reno to Elko.
- The extend of road is not so flat and RV-friendly.
- Elko offers a few campgrounds where you can spend the night.

Day 4: Elko, NV to Twin Falls, ID

- From Elko, head north on US-93 towards Twin Falls, Idaho.
- The route is scenic, passing through the high desert and offering beautiful landscapes.
- Ensure you have enough fuel, as there are some stretches with limited services.
- Stay overnight at a campground in Twin Falls.

Day 5: Twin Falls, ID to Pocatello, ID

- Take Interstate 84 eastbound from Twin Falls to Pocatello.
- This route is RV-friendly, and there are rest areas and fuel stations along the way.
- Pocatello has several campgrounds where you can spend the night.

Day 6: Pocatello, ID to West Yellowstone, MT

- Continue on Interstate 15 northbound towards West Yellowstone, Montana.
- The road is generally well-maintained and suitable for RVs.
- Make sure to stop by the scenic Idaho Falls along the way.
- Once you arrive in West Yellowstone, there are several campgrounds available for RVs.

Day 7-10: Exploring Yellowstone National Park

- Spend a few days exploring the wonders of Yellowstone National Park.
- The park has several RV-friendly campgrounds, but it's advisable to make reservations in advance.
- Visit attractions like Old Faithful, Grand Prismatic Spring, Yellowstone Lake, and the wildlife-rich Lamar Valley.

You can change this route always taking into consideration what you like more and the duration of your trip. A truly good idea can be to check for road closures, weather conditions, and any other relevant information before starting your fantastic RV journey.

Research RV parking in advance

One of the fundamental aspects to keep in mind is always to plan your trip in advance to avoid surprises on the day of departure!

In addition to following the advice in the previous chapter, you need to find the ideal destinations and parking areas for your stays in a motorhome. Bear in mind that the rules to follow in campsites in Europe or overseas are not the same. For example, it is strictly forbidden to sleep in a parking lot (public or private) or on the side of the road. You can therefore choose whether to stay overnight in the campsites provided for RVs, in the motorway rest areas (often equipped with various services to guarantee the comfort of travellers) or in the car parks of supermarkets or hypermarkets.

However, researching RV parking in advance is an excellent idea to ensure a smooth and enjoyable trip. Here are some steps you can take to research RV parking options:

- Identify campgrounds: Look for campgrounds along your route and near your intended destinations. Websites like ReserveAmerica.com, Recreation.gov, and KOA.com provide comprehensive listings of campgrounds across the United States, including information on amenities, availability, and reservation options.
- Check RV park directories: Utilize RV park directories such as Good Sam RV Travel & Savings Guide (goodsam.com) or AllStays (allstays.com) to find RV parks and campgrounds in specific areas. These directories often include user reviews, pricing, and detailed information about amenities and services.
- National Park Service: If you plan to visit national parks, visit the official website of the National Park Service (nps.gov) to check for RV camping options within the parks. Many national parks have dedicated RV campgrounds, but they can fill up quickly, so it's essential to make reservations in advance.
- State park websites: Research the websites of state parks along your route. They often have RV-friendly campgrounds and provide information about availability and reservations. State parks can be an excellent alternative to commercial campgrounds, offering beautiful natural settings and often more affordable rates.
- Online forums and RVing communities: Explore online forums and RVing communities such as iRV2 (irv2.com) and RV.net to gather recommendations and insights from experienced RVers. These platforms are an excellent resource for finding hidden gems and getting firsthand information about RV parks and campgrounds.
- Review apps and websites: Utilize apps and websites specifically designed for RVers, such as RV Parky, Campendium, and RV Trip Wizard. These platforms provide user reviews, ratings, and detailed information about RV parks, including the availability of amenities like electric hookups, dump stations, and Wi-Fi.
- Make reservations: Once you have identified suitable RV parking options, make reservations as early as possible, especially during peak travel seasons. Many campgrounds and RV parks allow online reservations through their websites or popular reservation platforms like ReserveAmerica or Recreation.gov.

By conducting thorough research and making reservations in advance, you'll have a better chance of securing RV parking at desirable locations, ensuring a more enjoyable and stress-free trip.

Adjust your estimated time of arrival

To adjust the estimated time of arrival for an RV trip, you need to consider factors such as driving speed, rest stops, road conditions, and potential delays. Here are some helpful tips to help you adjust the estimated time of arrival:

- Calculate driving time: Determine the distance between your starting point and destination using online mapping tools like Google Maps or GPS navigation systems. Take note of the estimated driving time without factoring in breaks.
- Consider driving speed: Determine the average speed at which you plan to drive your RV. Keep in mind that RVs usually travel at a slower pace compared to regular vehicles due to their size and weight. Generally, an average speed of 55-60 mph is a good estimate, but adjust it based on your comfort level and road conditions.
- Account for rest stops: Plan for regular rest stops to stretch your legs, use the restroom, and grab meals. Factor in these breaks during your estimated time of arrival. It's a good idea to schedule breaks every 2-3 hours, depending on your needs and preferences.
- Check road conditions: Before setting off, check for any potential road closures, construction, or traffic delays along your route. Websites or apps like Waze or your state's Department of Transportation can provide real-time traffic updates and alerts.
- Be mindful of RV restrictions: Some areas, particularly mountainous regions, may have restrictions or advisories for RVs due to steep grades or narrow roads. Plan accordingly and consider adjusting your estimated time of arrival to account for potential slowdowns or alternative routes.
- Allow for extra time: It's always a good idea to add extra time to your estimated arrival to account for unforeseen circumstances like heavy traffic, unexpected road closures, or inclement weather. Adding a buffer of 1-2 hours to your estimated driving time can help alleviate stress and provide flexibility.
- Adjust for specific stops or attractions: If you plan to make specific stops or visit attractions along the way, remember to factor in the time you'll spend there. This includes sightseeing, exploring, or any activities you have planned.

Remember that these are general guidelines, and actual travel times may vary depending on various factors. It's crucial to be flexible during your trip and adjust your estimated time of arrival as needed. Prioritize safety, take breaks when necessary, and enjoy the journey at a comfortable pace.

CHAPTER 3

Budgeting for Your RV Trip

Budgeting your RV trip: what to take into account

RV trips are excellent plans, but to avoid surprises you need to plan your expenses, if the trip lasts only a weekend or a month, it doesn't matter, the important thing is to limit your expenses and not go over the budget you have available. However, this risk shouldn't cancel out the possibility of having a great motorhome trip. Here are our tips for planning a move to a mobile home for any itinerary and budget.

The program

Everyone's desire is to unplug from work for a set time and hit the road with their camper. It's not always possible, so when you decide to move around with four wheels, it's important to figure out how many days the camper will travel on the road and how many it will remain stationary.

When planning a travel plan, everything should be considered, and this includes:

- Fuel
- Rest stops
- Eat
- Sleep
- RV check
- Any maintenance that may occur
- Insurance.

If the budget is tight and you don't have many days to travel by camper, the program must contain the place you want to reach and what you want to see. From there it is decided how to achieve the set goals.

The best way is to find an action-packed destination where everything is in one area. The more travel with the camper is reduced, the greater the savings will be. Instead of traveling on four wheels, you can decide to park the camper in a safe area and then move around with the available public transport: for a few euros you can travel a whole day on the rails and visit many places at the same time and then in the evening return to the camper and plan the next stop.

To eat it is cheaper to go shopping and cook in the mobile home, if this is not possible, the main meal can be replaced with a sandwich or pizza by the slice, without going to the restaurant.

It is important to think where you will spend most of your time, campsites can be very expensive, you get advantageous discounts if you stay in one place for a long period of time, moreover there are various memberships, if you have a camping subscription you can save a lot of money.

Generally, this option is chosen by those who have decided to live in a camper or stop in one place even for a month, for those who move continuously it is advantageous to find a safe parking area and stop until the next day, when it turns on again the engine and off to a new adventure.

Things you can't do without

If you can avoid going to a restaurant or staying at the campsite, the same cannot be done when it comes to fuel, insurance and maintenance. These are three elements that cannot be missing from the budget, spending can be resurrected with a few tricks, but not canceled from the list.

Fuel

The price of fuel varies throughout the country, and if you cross the border, savings are guaranteed, in fact, in Italy the price of fuel is the highest ever. Sometimes it is enough to travel a few tens of kilometers more to refuel at a reduced cost, so before setting off it is reasonable to consider where it is cheaper to refuel.

Vehicle insurance

Another expense to add to your budget is vehicle insurance. You need to pay attention to the policy, you don't just need to choose the cheapest option, but understand what it's used to cover. If the intention is to live on the road full time, you will need a motorhome insurance policy which covers for 365 days, but if the motor vehicle is only used at certain times of the year, it is advantageous to take out a policy with coverage of the time considered. Some insurance policies also include coverage in the event of a breakdown, for a few tens of dollars more it is appropriate to integrate it into the policy.

Vehicle maintenance

Sooner or later, some maintenance will have to be done to the motorhome, whether it is a change of tyres, replacement of filters or mechanical interventions. Newer RVs will likely need less work than older ones, and the need to replace tires depends on mileage. This expense item varies from person to person. However, we must not forget the maintenance to be done before starting a journey.

Other expenses to be spread over the budget

When planning an RV budget trip, it's important to consider all the expenses involved and allocate your budget accordingly. Anyway, the camper is a home and daily expenses must be considered. Here are some additional expenses to consider and spread out over your RV trip budget:

Foodstuffs

Living in a campervan can lead to spending more because you prefer to eat out in restaurants, having dinner or lunch in a restaurant costs a lot, so it is advisable to establish a budget for eating out to keep costs down. If you spend the day out hiking, it is advisable to prepare a packed lunch to take with you to reduce costs. So, set aside a budget for groceries and meals during your trip. Consider the cost of groceries, snacks, and any dining expenses at restaurants or local eateries.

Fuel Costs

Fuel expenses will likely be one of the most significant factors in your budget. Calculate the estimated fuel consumption of your RV based on its mileage and plan for fuel costs accordingly. Consider the distance you'll be traveling and the current fuel prices in the areas you'll be visiting.

Campground Fees

Research campground fees in the locations you plan to visit. These kinds of fees can change based on the amenities offered, location, and time of year. Consider both public and private campgrounds and allocate funds for these fees.

Laundry

Washing the laundry can prove to be a big expense for those traveling by camper, but it all depends on the days you are away from home. If it is a question of a week, it is not necessary to look for a laundry, but if the travel time gets longer it is advisable to go to the laundromats or go to a camper park where it is usually equipped with cleaning equipment of the laundry. When buying a camper, it is advisable to take into consideration the presence of a washing machine and a dryer, what is spent more is then recovered over the years by saving on the cost of the laundry.

Fun

One of the advantages of traveling by camper is that you can always see new places. It is necessary to establish a budget that includes entrance tickets to museums, local parks, sports activities, excursions and anything else included in the program.

Some attractions may have entrance fees, such as national parks, museums, or amusement parks. Allocate funds for these activities based on their individual costs.

RV Maintenance and Repairs

It's essential to have a contingency fund for any unexpected RV repairs or maintenance that may arise during your trip. RVs, like any vehicle, can have mechanical issues, and having some funds set aside for such situations will provide peace of mind.

Miscellaneous Expenses

Don't forget to include a buffer for miscellaneous expenses that may arise, such as laundry, toiletries, tolls, parking fees, Wi-Fi access, or souvenirs.

One thing to remember is to research and estimate costs specific to your planned destinations and the duration of your trip. Having a comprehensive budget that considers these additional expenses will help you better plan and manage your finances during your RV adventure.

These are the main items to take into consideration, after making a calculation you will have a clear budget to help anyone who wants to embark on new adventures in a camper.

How to plan an Rv trip budget: a step-by-step guide

Summarizing and combining what we have just shown in the first two paragraphs, we can say that planning an RV trip budget includes considering various factors and estimating the costs associated with each aspect of your journey. Here's am ultimate step-by-step guide will be useful to you on setting your RV trip budget:

- Determine the Duration of Your Trip: Decide how long you plan to be on the road. The duration will affect many aspects of your budget, including fuel costs, campground fees, and food expenses.
- Create a Travel Itinerary: Outline your travel itinerary, including the places you want to visit and the routes you plan to take. This will help you estimate the distances you'll be traveling and identify potential attractions or activities that may have associated costs.
- Calculate Fuel Costs: Estimate the fuel consumption of your RV based on its mileage per gallon and the distance you'll be traveling. Consider current fuel prices and calculate the approximate fuel expenses for your entire trip. Keep in mind that fuel costs can fluctuate, so it's wise to have some flexibility in your budget.
- Research Campground Fees: Look for campgrounds along your route or in the areas you plan to visit. Research their fees and amenities to determine an average cost per night. Multiply this cost by the number of nights you expect to spend at campgrounds to estimate your overall campground fees.
- Estimate Food Expenses: Create a food budget by considering the number of people traveling with you, the duration of the trip, and your eating habits. Account for groceries, meals eaten out, snacks, and any special dietary requirements. Don't forget to factor in the cost of cooking supplies and utensils if you need to purchase them.
- Plan Activities and Attractions: always look for the activities and attractions you wish to experience during this RV travel. Check entrance fees, ticket prices, and any additional costs. Allocate funds for these activities based on their individual costs.
- Account for RV Maintenance and Repairs: Set aside a contingency fund for unexpected RV repairs or maintenance. It's advisable to have some emergency funds to cover any unforeseen issues that may arise during your trip.
- Consider Insurance Costs: Review your RV insurance coverage and contact your insurance provider to make you sure enough you have the required coverage for this adventure. Check if any additional costs are associated with extending your coverage or if you need to make adjustments.
- Allocate Funds for Miscellaneous Expenses: Include a buffer for miscellaneous expenses such as laundry, toiletries, tolls, parking fees, Wi-Fi access, and souvenirs.
- Track Your Expenses: As you progress through your trip, keep track of your actual expenses to ensure you stay within your budget. Adjust if necessary and be mindful of any unexpected costs that may arise.

It's important to consider a regular review and adjusting of your budget as required during your RV trip. By planning and allocating funds for each aspect of your journey, you can have a more accurate estimate of your expenses and better manage your finances while on the road.

11 tips on how to save on your RV trip

In the previous paragraphs we have explained to you how to set your budget for the RV trip. With the costs of everything on the rise, including travel, it can seem like a vacation is a much bigger expense than it should be. But you deserve a far journey to explore a new place and give your mind a break. And it's still possible to have an affordable RV trip, especially with these 11 travel tips! Then, to end this chapter, check out our top tips to make your trip cheaper and even more fun!

1. Choose a smaller motorhome

When renting an RV, people often think they need more than expected. For example, many choose a motorhome with toilets or showers, even if they already know they are staying in a campsite where they can use all the toilets. By doing so, you will not only choose a larger and more expensive vehicle to rent, but it will also consume more fuel and be more difficult to park.

Really consider what you need in your campervan hire and chances are you could opt for a smaller van. This will save you a lot in terms of rental fee and fuel consumption. Before choosing one with extra amenities like toilets, showers, or TVs, think about whether you'll actually use them.

Most people don't need a bathroom in their motorhome, as they will be able to use the on-site facilities and petrol stations along the way. Also, it's quite a chore to clean an RV's toilet, so it's not always worth it! If you can, opt for a smaller, simpler van to save on your RV trip.

2. Choose your campsite carefully

Just as people choose RVs that have more than enough, so do campsites. People flock to resort complexes with swimming pools, saunas and tennis courts. Consider what you are looking for in your trip and adjust your camping plans accordingly. If there's a beach nearby, you may not need or want a pool at your campsite. If you're not traveling with children, you don't need a family-friendly holiday village.
Another way to find cheaper campsites is to stay further away from cities. Campsites closer to a big city will be much more expensive. If your main goal is to immerse yourself in nature and only occasionally visit the city, opt for accommodations farther away and save up to $15 per night!

3. Book in advance

You can save a lot of money by simply booking well in advance! To ensure that you receive reservations well in advance, many establishments offer discounts if you organize your trip months in advance. It can be difficult to plan ahead, but it's a great way to save money. This also permits you to do proper research and compare multiple options.

4. Travel in the off season

We often travel in the summer just because that's what we've always done. But if you're not limited to summer vacations from the kids to school or work, traveling outside the peak season can save you a lot.

Not only is RV rental cheaper in the off season, so are campgrounds and attractions. The entire journey will cost essentially less by simply moving it forward to May or later to October.

You'll also avoid crowds and traffic jams, the latter of which will reduce fuel consumption and therefore costs too! It will be much calmer and allow you to do more things. Plus, you can enjoy the summer in your city!

5. Compare fuel prices

You'd be surprised how much fuel costs can vary between gas stations. Especially now with costs higher than ever, it's worth seeing where the best deal is. Use apps like Waze to compare fuel prices and then plan accordingly.

6. Slow travel

Another way to save on fuel is to use less. Seems obvious enough, but how? We have many tips on how to use less fuel while driving, but the main one is to travel light. Make sure you always drive your RV with an empty or nearly empty water tank. Just bring a few bottles of water for the road. Also empty the gray water tank before leaving. This can make such a difference to the weight of your RV.

Check your tires before setting off, as worn tires consume more fuel. Also try to drive steadily, as constant braking will use up more fuel. Drive in a higher gear and maintain the same speed.

Don't forget that you don't have to go that far from home for an RV trip. If you are looking for an affordable getaway, stay closer to home and appreciate the area. Slow travel is the cheap way to travel nowadays.

7. Make a checklist of what to bring

Preparation is key to keeping things affordable! Make a list of what you need before you travel or use our RV travel checklist. Preparation allows you to spend less in other areas. For example, buy food at your local supermarket to avoid higher prices in tourist areas. Make a meal plan so you don't buy more than you need and can reuse ingredients.

By bringing things to do in your RV, you're less likely to get bored and spend more money later. It's easy to spend an entire day of an RV trip on a budget, simply having things to do outdoors, card games for the evening, and food from a local market.

8. Eat!

Speaking of food, your RV comes with a kitchenette, so make use of it! Shop for plenty of groceries at the start of your trip and enjoy cooking in your RV. There are loads of delicious camping meals you can prepare and it's a big part of the experience.

Pack some snacks for the drive so you aren't tempted to buy those usual sandwiches from the service station for a few dollars. Aim for a local restaurant where you can enjoy fresh produce, rather than a chain restaurant in a city.

9. Go outside

The best way to avoid spending extra money is to just walk out! You can spend a day walking in a national park or area of outstanding natural beauty. You could bring your bike and follow the many trails available. If you pack a picnic, you won't even have to spend on lunch.

To keep things interesting, you might want to try geocaching to make your walk even more fun. You can download a birding app and see how many you can spot.

Alternatively, you can swim in a lake or visit a beach for a free activity.

10. Visit free museums

Museums can be more expensive than you think. And while we all want to savor a little culture while traveling, there is a way to do it on the cheap. There are countless free museums and art galleries all over Italy, so visit those. You can easily fill a rainy day with free cultural activities.

11. Avoid tourist centers

Places that can be interest of many tourists will always have higher cost, whether it's for admission to museums and attractions, food and drink in restaurants or campsites.

It's easier than ever to take an affordable RV trip this summer. With a little planning and flexibility, you can make your RV trip more affordable and still a lot of fun!

BOOK4

ESSENTIAL RV CAMPING SKILLS

CHAPTER 1

Setting Up Your RV Camper at a Campsite

How to set up your camper at a campsite: a mini guide

Setting up your RV camper at a campsite can be a truly funny part of the camping adventure. Here's a step-by-step guide will be useful to you once you get started:

- Choose a suitable campsite: Look for a campsite that accommodates RVs and offers the amenities you desire, such as water and electrical hookups, sewage disposal, and level parking spots.
- Arrive at the campsite: Drive your RV to the designated campsite and position it according to any guidelines provided by the campground or park. Ensure you're parked on a level surface to avoid any stability issues.
- Stabilize the RV: Engage the parking brake and use leveling blocks or stabilizing jacks to ensure your RV is stable and doesn't rock or sway when parked.
- Connect to utilities:

a. Electrical hookup: If the campsite offers electrical hookups, locate the power pedestal and ensure your RV's electrical system is switched off before connecting the power cord. Plug your RV's power cord into the appropriate outlet on the pedestal.
b. Water hookup: If there is a water hookup, connect your freshwater hose to the spigot and the other end to your RV's water inlet.
c. Sewage hookup: If your RV has a built-in sewage system or portable holding tanks, locate the campground's sewage hookup. Connect your RV's sewer hose to the sewer outlet at the campsite, ensuring a secure connection. Use appropriate attachments like elbow connectors or donut seals if needed.

- Level the RV: Use a bubble level to check if your RV is level from side to side and front to back. If adjustments are necessary, use leveling blocks or jacks to raise or lower specific areas of the RV until it is level.
- Deploy slide-outs and awnings: If your RV has slide-outs or awnings, ensure the surrounding area is clear before extending them. Follow the manufacturer's instructions to safely extend and secure these features.
- Set up outdoor amenities: Arrange your outdoor furniture, such as chairs, tables, and grills, to create a comfortable outdoor living space.
- Connect utilities inside the RV: Once the RV is leveled and stable, you can turn on the electrical power inside your RV. Switch on the circuit breakers and ensure all appliances are

functioning correctly. If your RV has a propane system, ensure the propane tanks are open and functioning.

- Set up the interior: Arrange the interior of your RV to make it comfortable and functional during your stay. Open windows and vents for fresh air, and make use of any available shades or curtains for privacy.
- Safety check: Before settling in, conduct a safety check to be quite sure about all is in proper working order. Test the smoke detectors, carbon monoxide detectors, and fire extinguishers. Familiarize yourself with emergency exits and procedures.

These are only general guidelines, but if there is something essential to keep in mind is to consult your RV owner's manual for specific instructions related to your RV model.

Connecting to Utilities: Hooking up Your RV Camper to Campground Electrical, Water, and Sewer Hookups

When it comes to RV camping, "connecting to utilities" typically refers to the process of hooking up your recreational vehicle (RV) to essential services such as electricity, water, and sewer.

So, we have e fundamental utilities:

- Electricity: Connecting to the electrical utilities involves plugging your RV into a power source at the campsite. Most campsites provide electrical hookups, commonly known as shore power or RV pedestals, which allow you to access electricity to run your appliances, charge devices, and power the various systems within your RV.
- Water: Many RV campsites have water hookups, which enable you to connect your RV's water system to a fresh water supply. This connection allows you to have a consistent water source for drinking, cooking, cleaning, and using the bathroom facilities in your RV. It's important to note that not all campsites offer water hookups, so you may need to fill your RV's water tank before arriving or use alternative methods such as bringing your own water or using campground facilities.
- Sewer: RVs have holding tanks for wastewater, including gray water (from sinks and showers) and black water (from toilets). When you connect to sewer utilities, it means linking your RV's waste system to a sewer hookup at the campsite. This allows you to drain and dispose of your RV's wastewater directly into the campground's sewer system, avoiding the need to empty your tanks manually.

While connecting to utilities enhances the comfort and convenience of RV camping, not all campsites offer these amenities at every site. Some may only provide electrical hookups, while others may have partial hookups (electricity and water) or full hookups (electricity, water, and sewer). It's essential to check with the campground or RV park beforehand to determine what utilities are available and whether you need to make any specific arrangements.

Now, let's see specifically how to connect to every single each utility.

Hooking up Your RV Camper to Campground Electrical

To hook up your RV camper to campground electrical hookups, follow these steps:

- Prepare your RV: Make sure the main power switch in your RV's electrical distribution panel is turned off. This will prevent any electrical surges or issues when connecting to the campground's power supply.
- Gather your equipment: You will need a suitable power cord and any necessary adapters or extensions based on the electrical hookup provided at the campground. Most campgrounds use 30-amp or 50-amp electrical services, so ensure you have the appropriate cord for your RV.
- Locate the campground's power pedestal: The power pedestal is usually a metal box with outlets and circuit breakers. It may be positioned at the rear or side of your campsite.
- Assess the power supply: Check the campground's power pedestal to determine if it provides 30-amp or 50-amp service. Look for the corresponding outlets labeled with the amperage.
- Connect the power cord: Take one end of your RV's power cord and plug it into the matching outlet on the power pedestal. Twist it to secure the connection and ensure a tight fit.
- Connect the other end of the power cord to your RV: Locate the external power inlet on your RV, usually located on the side or rear. Eliminate the protective cover and link the power cord to the inlet, twisting to secure the connection.
- Turn on the power: Once everything is securely connected, go back to the power pedestal and switch on the circuit breakers for your RV's electrical service. If you have a 30-amp service, you will typically have one circuit breaker to turn on. For a 50-amp service, you might have two circuit breakers that need to be switched on.
- Test the power supply: Inside your RV, turn on the main power switch on the electrical distribution panel. Check if the lights, appliances, and other electrical components are working correctly. If there are any issues, double-check the circuit breakers on the power pedestal to ensure they haven't tripped.
- Monitor your power usage: Depending on the capacity of the campground's electrical service and your RV's electrical demands, you may need to be mindful of your power consumption. Avoid running multiple high-wattage appliances simultaneously to prevent overloading the circuit.
- Safety precautions: you must prioritize safety when addressing with electrical connections. Ensure your hands are dry when handling cords and connectors, and never force a connection. If you notice any electrical issues or abnormalities, contact the campground management or a professional for assistance.

It's also important to note that electrical hookups may vary between campgrounds, so adapt to the specific setup accordingly.

Hooking up your RV camper to campground water

To hook up your RV camper to campground water, follow these steps:

- Prepare your RV: Ensure that your RV's fresh water system is turned off before connecting to the campground's water supply.
- Gather your equipment: You will need a potable water hose specifically designed for RV use. These hoses are typically white or blue and are made of non-toxic materials suitable for

drinking water. Make sure you have a hose of sufficient length to reach the campground's water hookup.

- Locate the campground's water hookup: The water hookup is usually a spigot or faucet located near your campsite. It may be positioned at the rear or side of the site or on a central water station.
- Assess the water supply: Take a moment to inspect the water hookup and determine if it is potable (safe for drinking) or non-potable (for general use only). Most campgrounds provide potable water, but it's always good to confirm.
- Connect the water hose: Attach one end of the water hose to the campground's water hookup. Twist it onto the spigot or faucet to create a tight seal, ensuring there are no leaks.
- Connect the other end of the water hose to your RV: Locate the freshwater intake valve or connection point on your RV's exterior. Remove the protective cover if present, and connect the other end of the water hose to the intake valve, twisting to secure the connection.
- Open the water supply: Once both ends of the hose are securely connected, slowly open the campground's water supply. This will allow water to flow into your RV's fresh water system.
- Check for leaks: Inspect the connections at both ends of the water hose, as well as the freshwater intake valve on your RV, for any signs of leakage.
- Fill and pressurize the water system: Inside your RV, open the faucets and run the water to remove any air from the lines. Start with the closest faucet to the freshwater intake valve and work your way to the furthest faucets, including the kitchen and bathroom sinks, shower, and toilet. Ensure that water is flowing smoothly and consistently from each faucet.
- Monitor water usage: Be mindful of your water consumption while connected to the campground's water supply. Avoid leaving faucets running unnecessarily and address any leaks promptly to conserve water.
- Use a water pressure regulator (optional): It's recommended to use a water pressure regulator between the campground's water supply and your RV to protect your plumbing system. This device helps regulate the water pressure, preventing high pressure from damaging your RV's pipes and fixtures.

Remember to use a potable water hose designated for RV use to ensure the safety and quality of the water supply. It's also advisable to sanitize your RV's freshwater system periodically, especially if you've been using non-potable water or if the RV has been in storage for an extended period.

Hooking up your RV camper to campground sewer hookups

To hook up your RV camper to campground sewer hookups for wastewater disposal, follow these steps:

- Prepare your RV: Ensure that your RV's waste tanks are closed and securely sealed before connecting to the campground's sewer hookup.
- Gather your equipment: You will need a sewer hose, which is a specialized hose designed for wastewater disposal, along with any necessary adapters or fittings. It's important to use a dedicated sewer hose for hygiene and safety reasons.
- Locate the campground's sewer hookup: The sewer hookup is typically a threaded pipe or PVC pipe with a screw-on cap, or a designated sewer drain located near your campsite. It may be positioned at the rear or side of the site or in a central location within the campground.

- Assess the sewer hookup: Take a moment to inspect the sewer hookup and determine if it requires any specific adapters or fittings to connect your sewer hose. Some campgrounds may provide different types of connections, such as threaded or bayonet-style fittings.
- Connect the sewer hose to your RV: Locate the RV's sewer outlet, usually found on the rear or side of the RV. Remove the protective cap or cover and connect one end of the sewer hose securely to the outlet. Twist it onto the fitting to ensure a tight seal.
- Connect the other end of the sewer hose to the campground's sewer hookup: Attach the opposite end of the sewer hose to the campground's sewer hookup. If required, use any necessary adapters or fittings to make a secure connection. Twist it onto the fitting at the sewer hookup to create a tight seal.
- Create a secure connection: Some sewer hookups may have a threaded connection, while others may have a bayonet-style fitting. Ensure that you secure the connection by twisting the hose onto the fitting in a clockwise direction. This will prevent any accidental disconnection or leaks.
- Set up a sewer hose support (optional): To assist with the flow of wastewater and prevent any kinks or blockages in the sewer hose, you can use a sewer hose support. These supports elevate the hose off the ground, making it easier for the wastewater to flow downhill into the sewer hookup.
- Open the RV's waste valves: Inside your RV, open the waste valve(s) for the specific tank(s) you want to empty. Start with the black water tank (toilet waste) first and then proceed to the gray water tank(s) (sink and shower water). Allow the wastewater to flow through the sewer hose and into the campground's sewer system.
- Monitor the wastewater flow: Keep an eye on the flow of wastewater to ensure it is moving smoothly and consistently through the sewer hose. If necessary, use a sewer hose clear adapter or attachment to check for any blockages or buildup. If you encounter any issues, adjust the hose or address the problem promptly.
- Rinse and clean the sewer hose: After emptying the tanks, you can use a designated hose or a separate hose specifically for rinsing to flush clean water through the sewer hose. This helps remove any residue or debris from the hose. Use designated sewer hose rinsing stations if available at the campground.
- Disconnect the sewer hose: Once you have finished emptying and rinsing the tanks, disconnect the sewer hose from both the RV's sewer outlet and the campground's sewer hookup. Rinse and store the sewer hose in a designated storage compartment, ensuring it is clean and dry before stowing it away.

Always follow proper sanitation and waste disposal practices when handling your RV's wastewater. Be considerate of campground regulations and guidelines regarding wastewater disposal.

CHAPTER 2

Dumping Your RV Tanks: Best Practices

How to manage the black water discharge of the camper

Unloading the sewage from the camper is a fundamental operation for the maintenance of your vehicle.

Draining sewage from a camper is part of those routine operations necessary for the proper management and cleaning of your vehicle.

It is also one of the most widespread and feared problems, especially by inexperienced motorhome owners, who have difficulty managing this operation, especially when they are travelling.

Let us try to clarify the matter, starting from a fundamental distinction, namely that between:

- Clear waters
- Gray water
- Black waters.

Clear water is nothing more than clean water, i.e., the unused water that will flow from the sink taps, into the toilet flush and into the shower.

Gray water, on the other hand, refers to wastewater from sinks and showers. While, consequently, the sewage is very simply the toilet discharges.

Water management inside the camper is not difficult, but it can be complex for beginners. In this paragraph we will try to go deeper into the topic, explaining how black water works and how to correctly manage its discharge.

How to manage the sewage discharge of the camper

Among the most important "routine" tasks to know for the correct use of your recreational vehicle, the management of sewage certainly plays a role of primary importance.

Especially in the hottest periods of the year, the wastewater tanks must be regularly checked and emptied, to avoid inconveniences and bad smells spreading throughout the living unit.

Undoubtedly, emptying the black water tank of a camper is never a pleasant operation to do, but it shouldn't be underestimated either.

How to discharge black water? The steps are roughly the following:

- Connect the flexible hose of the collector to the appropriate outlet and open the valve of the wastewater tank
- Drain all drains, close the lid and fill the tank with fresh water
- Reopen the valve to eliminate the contents of the tank, always using a transparent hose to check what is expelled
- Continue the operation until only clean water comes out of the tank
- Once the tank is clean, close the wastewater valve and open the gray water tank valve.

The emptying operation must be carried out daily, even several times a day if the crew on board the camper is numerous.

It should always be accompanied by a thorough cleaning of the tank - as we will see later - and the use of sewage disintegrating products, to prevent the formation of bad smells.

No less important is the place where to unload. Read on to find out where it is allowed to discharge black water according to the law.

Wastewater discharge area of a camper: where to do it?

Before delving into where to discharge the water, we must make an important distinction between the two different types of black water tank:

- Cassette toilet
- Nautical toilet.

The nautical toilet is present above all on older campers. It is a system that has a large built-in tank, unlike the cistern toilet which, as it is easy to guess from the name, consists of a removable cistern of limited size.

When dealing with limited freedom of movement, the cassette toilet offers the benefit of being removable and emptiable without the need to relocate the camper. In contrast, the marine toilet requires emptying the tank exclusively in a designated area equipped with a proper drainage system.

Consider usingHaving said that, for recreational vehicles equipped with cassettes and removable tanks, the management of the discharge is certainly easier, since the wastewater can easily be discharged even in a public toilet or in the bathroom at home.

The situation is different for those campers that have integrated and non-removable tanks. For these vehicles, unloading is permitted only in equipped areas, i.e., areas which bear the specific blue sign of an equipped unloading area.

How to empty the sewage from the camper on the motorway?

When you are travelling, the unloading and loading operations of the water must be carried out in special facilities which take the name of motorhome parking areas. These are equipped loading/unloading areas, usually free, present in some service areas of the motorway network.

The motorhome parking areas are equipped with a ground drainage grate or tank and a service column with clean water that allows you to wash the waste residues and fill the freshwater tank.

To carry out the unloading operations at a camper service you must:

- Position the camper so that the drainage outlet is located exactly on the ground drain grate/tray
- Manually open the drain taps or activate the appropriate command if you have a black water drain mechanism on your electric camper
- Immediately close the drain union when the operation is finished and clean the camper service with a jet of clean water.

Tips for cleaning the black water tank of the camper

The management of the wastewater discharge also includes the maintenance and regular cleaning of the tank.

This is because a tank that is not properly cleaned could produce bad smells and, even worse, become a source of bacteria or cause unpleasant blockages in the entire drainage system.

If you want to clean the black water tank, here's what you need to do:

- Put approximately one liter of water inside the tank to which a disintegrating liquid must be added, necessary to dissolve the organic material present
- Empty the tank completely of its contents, in a special camper service or area equipped for unloading
- Rinse the cassette abundantly with running water at least two or three times and replace it in the appropriate compartment.
- Periodically it is necessary to carry out a more thorough cleaning of the tank with specific detergent products or, if necessary, with bleach.
- However, in the latter case it is advisable to rinse the tank well to prevent the disinfectant from interfering with the sewage disintegrant.

Best practices for dumping your RV tanks

As we have just seen above, dumping the tanks of your RV is an essential part of its maintenance and proper operation. So, let's see together what the best practices to follow are when dumping your RV tanks:

- Safety First: Before starting the dumping process, put on disposable gloves and ensure you have eye protection. This will help protect you from any potential spills or splashes.
- Choose the Right Dumping Station: Locate an appropriate dumping station that can accommodate your RV's tanks. Many campgrounds, RV parks, and service stations have designated dumping areas.
- Prepare Your RV: Ensure that all faucets, showers, and toilets are turned off inside the RV. Double-check that the dump valve is securely closed to prevent any leaks.
- Position the RV Correctly: Position your RV in such a way that the dump valves are aligned with the dumping station. Use leveling blocks if needed to ensure a smooth and consistent flow.
- As first step, dump the Black Tank: you can begin with dumping the black water tank first. Open the black water tank valve, allowing its contents to flow into the dumping station. Allow

ample time for the tank to empty completely. You can also use a tank rinse or flush system to clean the tank thoroughly.

- Dump the Gray Tank Second: After emptying the black water tank, open the valve for the gray water tank. The gray water, which includes water from sinks and showers, helps flush out the sewer hose and ensures a more thorough cleaning.

- Rinse and Flush: Once both tanks are emptied, close the valves securely. Use the designated hose or a separate hose with a dedicated spray nozzle to rinse and flush out the sewer hose and connections. Properly clean and store the hose afterward.

- Use Tank Treatments: After dumping and cleaning the tanks, consider using tank treatments or chemicals designed to help break down waste and control odors.

- Practice Good Hygiene: After completing the dumping process, thoroughly wash your hands with soap and water, or use hand sanitizer if water is not readily available. Clean and disinfect any surfaces that may have encounter the RV tanks or waste.

- Maintain Regular Dumping Schedule: To prevent tank issues and unpleasant odors, establish a regular dumping schedule based on your RV usage. This helps ensure that the tanks don't become overfilled or allow waste to solidify.

Anyway, properly maintaining and cleaning your RV tanks will help keep your vehicle in good condition and ensure a more enjoyable travel experience.

CHAPTER 3

Maintaining Your RV on the Road

RV camper general maintenance

Regular maintenance is crucial for keeping your RV camper in good condition. Here are some general maintenance tasks to consider:

- Clean the exterior: start with cleaning the exterior of your RV in a regular manner to take away dirt, grime, and road debris. Use a mild soap specifically designed for RVs and avoid using abrasive materials that could damage the paint or finish.
- Inspect the roof: Check the roof for any signs of damage, such as cracks, leaks, or loose seals. Clean the roof regularly and ensure it is free from debris. Consider applying a roof sealant or coating as recommended by the manufacturer.
- Check and maintain the seals: Inspect all seals, including window seals, door seals, and roof seals.
- Lubricate moving parts: Regularly lubricate hinges, locks, slide-outs, and other moving parts to prevent friction and ensure smooth operation. Use an appropriate lubricant recommended for your RV.
- Check and maintain the tires: check for signs of wear, cracks, or bulges of the tires. You should be secure about the fact that tires must be regularly inflated depending on the manufacturer's recommendations. Make often a rotation of the tyres and substitute them when necessary due to age or wear.
- Service the batteries: Inspect and clean the battery terminals regularly. Check the battery water levels if applicable and top up with distilled water as needed. Test the batteries and replace them if they are no longer holding a charge.
- Check the electrical system: Test all lights, including interior, exterior, and signal lights. Inspect the wiring for any signs of damage. Check the functionality of electrical outlets and appliances and address any issues promptly.
- Maintain the plumbing system: Inspect the plumbing system for leaks, cracks, or damaged pipes. Ensure the water pump is functioning properly. Clean and maintain the water heater and the toilet system.
- Service the HVAC system: Clean or replace the air filters in the HVAC system regularly. Test the heating and cooling functions to ensure they are working efficiently. If necessary, have a professional service the HVAC system.
- Conduct regular safety checks: verify the smoke detectors, carbon monoxide detectors, and fire extinguishers to be certain of they are in working normally. Replace batteries as needed.

- Store and winterize properly: If you're storing your RV for an extended period or during the winter, take appropriate measures to prepare it for storage. This may include emptying water tanks, adding antifreeze, and protecting the RV from the elements.

By following these general maintenance tips and addressing any issues promptly, you can prolong the life of your RV camper and ensure a safe and enjoyable travel experience.

How much does it cost to maintain an RV?

The expenses necessary to maintain a camper are not the same for everyone: they depend on how much you actually want to do maintenance and invest in quality.

Maintenance, insurance and storage are certainly fundamental factors, but not the only ones.

Rest areas, for example, require payment both for the pitch itself and for services such as electricity and drainage.

This doesn't mean that you can't save money with a camper, especially if there are more than two people on board, comparing the prices of a hotel.

At the same time, however, everything relates to how many times the vehicle is used: the more you use it, the more you save.

Managing the costs of a camper in the best possible way is essential to enjoy your home on wheels to the fullest without any worries.

Like a car, the camper is subject to various expenses, many of which belong to purely bureaucratic aspects, such as insurance or road tax. These are necessary to travel by camper in complete serenity.

Maintaining your RV camper on the road

Maintaining your RV camper while on the road is vital to be certain about its longevity and no trouble operation. At this point, we want you to understand some essential maintenance tricks to consider:

- Regularly inspect the exterior: Check for any signs of damage, such as leaks, cracks, or loose seals. Inspect the roof, windows, doors, and awnings. Address any issues promptly to prevent further damage.
- Monitor tyres pressure: Keep a tire pressure gauge handy and regularly check the tyres pressure on all wheels, including the spare. Maintaining the proper tire pressure is crucial for safe and efficient travel.
- Perform routine engine checks: If your RV has an engine, conduct regular checks on oil levels, coolant levels, and other essential fluids.
- Check the electrical system: Inspect the batteries and ensure they are properly charged. Test the operation of lights, appliances, and other electrical components. Carry spare fuses and bulbs in case of emergencies.
- Clean the interior: Regularly clean the interior of your RV to keep it fresh and comfortable. Vacuum the floors, wipe down surfaces, and clean the kitchen and bathroom areas. Proper sanitation is especially important for maintaining a healthy living environment.
- Monitor propane levels: If your RV uses propane for cooking, heating, or other purposes, keep an eye on the propane levels. Refill or replace the propane tanks as needed.

- Maintain plumbing systems: Check for leaks in the plumbing system and fix them as soon as possible. Flush the holding tanks regularly and use appropriate RV-friendly toilet paper to prevent clogs.
- Keep an eye on the weather: Be aware of the weather conditions in the areas you're traveling through. Extreme temperatures, heavy rain, or snow can have an impact on your RV's systems. Take necessary precautions or seek shelter if needed.
- Follow regular service intervals: Adhere to the manufacturer's recommended service intervals for your RV.
- Carry essential tools and spare parts: bring a basic toolkit with essential tools with for addressing minor repairs. Additionally, carry spare fuses, light bulbs, and other commonly used parts that may need replacement during your journey.

These are some general tips but if you're not confident in performing certain maintenance tasks, it's always a good idea to consult a professional RV technician or visit a specialized RV service center for assistance.

3 useful tips for proper maintenance of your motorhome's service battery

A very important component of the camper is the battery, or rather, the batteries, one of which is used to start the engine (starter) and the other is used for the various services inside the camper, such as TV, heating, freezer, water pump, water etc.

Very often due to the misinformation of the user on the correct use of the batteries and on the various methods of recharging, the batteries do not last as long as expected but it is necessary to replace them much earlier than the estimated time.

Now we want to recommend to you 3 precautions to campers that will allow the batteries to last over time.

Tip N 1: Always charge the batteries

There are three types of service batteries in a camper:

- AGM
- Gel
- free acid

batteries should never be left discharged for a long period of time as it is very likely that they will never work again, without the possibility of recovering them in any way.

When the camper is not being used, the battery must be recharged for about 36/48 hours every 60 days, so as to keep it always charged and extend its life over time.

To remedy the oversights that each of us can have in a very long period in which we do not go out with the camper, we can install a solar panel that will recharge the battery for us without damaging it and always keeping it in optimal conditions. This remedy is only effective if you do not leave the camper in a garage or away from direct sunlight.

Tip N 2 : disconnect the negative cable (-)

When the camper is not being used for medium/long periods, it is advisable to disconnect the negative cable of the battery so as to prevent it from discharging due to small absorptions which, prolonged over time, cause the battery to lose its charge.

Tip N 3: A very short trip fails to recharge the batteries 100%

To fully recharge the batteries, you need to make a very long journey as it takes about 24 hours even if the display inside the camper indicates that the battery is fully charged.

So, it is recommended to charge the battery once you get home in order to bring the battery back to 100% charge.

RV camper repair on the road

While it's best to address significant RV camper repairs at a professional service center, there are certain minor repairs that you can handle on the road. Here are some tips for RV camper repairs on the road:

- Carry a basic toolkit: Keep a well-equipped toolkit with essential tools such as screwdrivers, wrenches, pliers, duct tape, electrical tape, and a multimeter. This will enable you to tackle basic repairs and address minor issues.
- Address electrical issues: If you encounter electrical problems, such as a non-functional light or a blown fuse, check the fuse box and replace any blown fuses. Ensure you have spare fuses of the appropriate sizes. If you identify a specific electrical component causing the issue, you can attempt to troubleshoot or replace it.
- Fix plumbing leaks: If you discover a minor plumbing leak, you can use a patch kit or plumber's tape to temporarily seal the leak until you can reach a service center. If the issue is with a faucet or showerhead, tightening the connections might help.
- Repair minor exterior damage: If you notice small scratches or dings on the exterior of your RV camper, you can use touch-up paint or a repair kit specifically designed for your RV's surface material to address the damage temporarily.
- Secure loose components: While on the road, vibrations and movement may cause screws, nuts, or bolts to loosen. Regularly inspect and tighten any loose components, such as handles, knobs, or brackets, to prevent further damage.
- Handle tire issues: If you find yourself on the road with a flat tire, use your spare tire to replace the flat one. Ensure you have the necessary tools, such as a lug wrench and jack, to perform the tire change safely. If you encounter minor punctures, you can use a tire repair kit to temporarily patch the tire until you can reach a tire repair shop.
- Temporarily fix slide-out issues: If your RV camper has a slide-out that is not functioning properly, check for any obstructions or debris preventing its movement. In some cases, manually assisting the slide-out by pushing or pulling while someone operates the controls may help. However, it's essential to address slide-out issues at a professional service center as soon as possible.
- Seek assistance from RV parks or campgrounds: When faced with significant repairs that you cannot handle on your own, consider reaching out to nearby RV parks or campgrounds. They might have recommendations for local repair services or onsite technicians who can assist you.

Remember, safety should be your top priority. If you are unsure about a repair or lack the necessary skills and tools, it's best to consult a professional RV technician or visit a specialized RV service center. They have the expertise and equipment to handle complex repairs and ensure your RV camper is in optimal condition.

Winter in a camper: how to maintain your DIY camper heater?

To fully enjoy the winter in a camper, the heating system must work properly.

It is therefore very important to pay attention to this aspect and carry out periodic checks, in order to act promptly in the event of a malfunction and avoid freezing.

Many campers search for RV heater maintenance news on online forums. The most frequently asked questions concern the methods of do-it-yourself maintenance.

In fact, if you are sufficiently familiar, personally taking care of the maintenance of your camper is not impossible.

However, whatever your experience in this regard, it is always necessary to have the heating system checked by a technician or a specialized workshop, to verify that combustion takes place properly.

Anyway, if you want to try it yourself, here are the checks to carry out:

- Boiler control
- Control of exhaust chimneys
- Thermostat
- Management software and hardware
- Stoves.

Regarding the stoves, there are specific checks to be made based on the type of heating installed on the camper.

For example, if your RV's heating is forced air, you need to check the fan motor and verify that it is adequately carrying heat throughout the RV.

On the contrary, if the heating is of the Alde type, in this case it is necessary to check the glycol level inside the pipes and make the system air-free.

In fact, even just one air bubble in the radiator system could block the heating.

Checking the boiler of a camper: how to do it?

Along with the heating system, the campers are also equipped with a hot water boiler.

Boiler and heating could be together or, in most cases, work independently of each other, so that only the former can be used in the summer.

When periodically checking boiler operation, it is very important to check:

- Gas combustion
- The integrity of the flue, both on the roof and on the wall
- The state of the pot that collects the water inside the boiler.

In fact, the latter tends to get punctured over time, so it must be checked often and, if there are holes or lesions, it must be replaced immediately.

How to check and overhaul a camper stove

Having an intact and tidy stove is the first step for a perfectly efficient heating system. A stove in perfect condition, in fact, not only ensures reliability and maximum heating output, but also guarantees lower fuel consumption.

You can also do it yourself to check the functioning and overhaul of a camper stove, making sure that:

- The burner is completely clean
- The ignition system works properly
- The safety devices are active and functioning properly
- The combustion air intake is not obstructed by obstacles
- The exhaust of the combustion gases is intact, free and protected from the action of atmospheric agents.

CHAPTER 4

RV Troubleshooting. How to Solve Common Problems

RV troubleshooting

When it comes to troubleshooting an RV (Recreational Vehicle), "it" can refer to various issues or symptoms. Without specific details, it's challenging to provide a precise answer. Let's us show you now some information about common RV problems and what they might mean:

- Electrical issues: If you're experiencing problems with the electrical system in your RV, such as lights not working or appliances not functioning, it could indicate a blown fuse, a faulty circuit breaker, a wiring problem, or a battery issue.
- Plumbing problems: Leaks, clogged drains, or malfunctioning toilets can be signs of plumbing issues in your RV. The problem might be related to a faulty pipe, a defective valve, or a water pump failure.
- HVAC (Heating, Ventilation, and Air Conditioning) problems: If your RV's heating or cooling system isn't working correctly, it could mean there's a problem with the thermostat, a clogged filter, a faulty blower motor, or issues with the refrigerant.
- Engine or mechanical issues: If your RV has an engine, transmission, or mechanical components, problems with starting, strange noises, or poor performance may indicate issues like a dead battery, fuel system problems, engine misfire, or worn-out parts.
- Structural or exterior issues: Damages to the RV's body, windows, roof, or slide-outs can cause leaks, drafts, or other issues. These problems could be a result of accidents, wear and tear, or poor maintenance.

This indicated above is just a general overview, and troubleshooting an RV can be complex. If you're experiencing specific issues with your RV, it's best to consult a qualified RV technician or mechanic who can diagnose and address the problem accurately.

RV parts and accessories troubleshooting

When troubleshooting RV parts and accessories, here are some common issues you might encounter and their possible causes:

- Awning problems: If your RV's awning is not retracting or extending properly, it could be due to a faulty motor, a problem with the control switch, a blown fuse, or an issue with the awning's hardware or fabric.
- Refrigerator issues: If the refrigerator in your RV is not cooling properly or not working at all, it could be caused by a variety of factors, including a tripped circuit breaker, a faulty thermostat, a blocked ventilation system, or a problem with the cooling unit.

- Water heater malfunctions: If your RV's water heater is not providing hot water, the causes can be connected to a faulty heating element, a gas supply issue, an issue with the ignition system, or a malfunctioning thermostat.
- Slide-out problems: If the slide-out mechanism is not operating correctly, it could be caused by a low battery charge, a blown fuse, a faulty motor or gearbox, an obstruction in the slide-out's path, or issues with the slide-out's control module.
- Electrical accessory failures: If various electrical accessories like lights, fans, or power outlets are not working, it could be due to a blown fuse, a tripped circuit breaker, a faulty switch or wiring connection, or a problem with the RV's electrical system.
- Plumbing accessory issues: Problems with plumbing accessories such as faucets, sinks, or toilets could be caused by clogs in the plumbing lines, leaky connections, faulty valves, or a malfunctioning water pump.

When troubleshooting RV parts and accessories, it's often helpful to consult the specific manuals or documentation provided by the manufacturer. Additionally, reaching out to an RV service center or technician with expertise in RV repairs can provide valuable assistance in diagnosing and resolving the issues you are facing.

RV camper: how to solve common problems

To end this chapter, here are some solutions for common problems you may encounter with an RV camper:

Battery issues

- Check the battery connections for corrosion or loose cables and clean/tighten them if necessary.
- Test the battery voltage with a multimeter to ensure its adequately charged. Recharge or replace the battery as needed.
- Consider investing in a battery maintenance system to keep the battery charged during storage periods.
- Water system problems:
- If you have no water flow, check if the water pump is running and the water tank is filled.
- If you have low water pressure, check for clogs or debris in the water lines, filters, or faucets. Clean or replace them as necessary.
- If you have leaks, inspect all connections, fittings, and fixtures. Tighten or replace any faulty components.

Awning difficulties

- Ensure there's no obstruction preventing the awning from retracting or extending fully.
- Inspect the awning fabric for tears or damage. Replace if necessary.
- Check the awning's motor or manual crank mechanism for any faults. Repair or replace as needed.
- Refrigerator not cooling:
- Check for obstructions in the refrigerator vents that may hinder airflow.
- Verify that the propane or electric power supply is functioning properly.
- Clean the refrigerator's condenser coils to improve cooling efficiency.

HVAC problems

- Be certain the thermostat is connected to the desired temperature and mode.
- Check the air filters and clean or substitute them.
- Check the HVAC unit's components for any damage or loose connections.

Slide-out malfunctions

- Verify that the battery is fully charged or connected to shore power.
- Look for any obstructions or debris that can prevent the slide-out from moving smoothly. Clear them away.
- Inspect the slide-out mechanism for loose or damaged components.

Remember, if you encounter more complex or persistent issues, it's advisable to consult a professional RV technician who can provide specific guidance and assistance based on your camper's make and model.

Camper Stove Problems: What to do if it doesn't turn on?

The advantages of a heating system with a stove are many, from reduced consumption to a reasonable price, up to the simplicity of maintenance.

Although stove heaters are quite reliable, problems may still arise regarding their correct functioning, especially the older models.

One of the most common problems is that the stove does not light. It may happen that by pressing the piezoelectric of the stove, the blue pilot flame lights up but after a few seconds, when you release the regulator, it begins to fade until it goes out.

Or it may happen that no gas reaches the pilot flame at all and that the stove cannot start. What can be done in these cases?

- Check that there is gas in the cylinder
- Check the condition of the ignition wires
- Clean the internal burner
- Remove the chimney pipe, clean it and place it in the same position as before, however replacing the sealing gasket
- Check the functioning of the gas lighter battery, if you have a piezo battery, and replace it if necessary.

If, despite these checks, the stove still does not light up, our advice is to contact a mechanical workshop specialized in the repair of motorhomes and its components.

CHAPTER 5

Storing Your RV. Tips for a Perfect Storage

What to do before storing your RV and types of storing

Storing your RV typically refers to the act of safely parking and securing your recreational vehicle (RV) when it is not in use. RVs are large vehicles designed for travel and leisure, such as motorhomes, campervans, travel trailers, or fifth-wheel trailers. Storing an RV properly is essential to protect it from the elements, theft, and damage, and to ensure its longevity.

RV storage options can vary depending on individual needs and circumstances. So, let's see, at this point, some common methods of storing an RV:

- Residential Storage: If you have enough space on your property, you can store your RV at home. This can involve parking it in your driveway, backyard, or a designated parking area.
- RV Storage Facilities: Many areas have dedicated storage facilities designed specifically for storing RVs. These facilities offer secure parking spaces with various amenities, such as surveillance systems, gated access, and sometimes even electricity hookups.
- RV Covers: If you have limited space or can't access storage facilities, you can consider using RV covers. These large, weatherproof covers protect your RV from sun exposure, rain, snow, and other environmental factors. They are typically made of durable materials and provide an extra layer of protection against dust, debris, and UV rays.
- Indoor Storage: Some storage facilities or warehouses offer indoor RV storage options. Indoor storage protects your RV from extreme weather conditions, direct sunlight, and potential vandalism. It often provides more security, climate control, and additional services, but it can be more expensive than outdoor storage options.

Before storing your RV, it's important to prepare it properly:

- Clean your RV thoroughly, both inside and out, to remove dirt, dust, and any food particles that may attract pests.
- Empty and clean all tanks, including the freshwater, gray water, and black water tanks, to prevent odors and damage from stagnant water.
- Turn off and disconnect all utilities, such as electricity, gas, and water, to avoid potential hazards and conserve resources.
- Check the tires and inflate them to the recommended pressure. Take into consideration the utilization of tire covers as a means of shielding them from sun damage.
- Close and secure all windows, doors, vents, and other openings to prevent water leaks, pests, and unauthorized access.

By properly storing your RV, you can help maintain its condition, prolong its lifespan, and be ready for your next adventure when the time comes.

How to properly store your RV

Storing your RV properly is crucial to ensure its longevity and protect it from damage. Below we will show you some useful steps to follow when storing your RV:

- Clean the RV: Remove any food items, clean the kitchen appliances, and wipe down all surfaces. Clean the bathroom, including the toilet, shower, and sink. Vacuum or sweep the floors and consider using moisture-absorbing products to prevent mold and mildew.
- Empty and clean tanks: Empty the freshwater, gray water, and black water tanks completely. Flush and sanitize the tanks according to the manufacturer's instructions to prevent odors and bacteria growth. Leave the tanks dry to avoid any damage.
- Remove perishables: Take out any perishable items from the refrigerator and pantry.
- Disconnect utilities: Turn off and disconnect all utilities, including electricity, gas, and water. Shut off the main power supply and unplug all appliances to prevent any electrical issues or energy drain. Drain the water lines and water heater to avoid freezing and potential damage.
- Protect against pests: Seal any openings or gaps where pests could enter, such as vents, exhaust pipes, and access panels. Consider using pest repellents or traps to discourage insects and rodents from entering the RV. Place mothballs or dryer sheets inside the RV to deter pests.
- Cover the RV: If storing the RV outdoors, consider using a breathable, weatherproof cover to protect it from the elements. Ensure the cover fits properly and is securely fastened to prevent damage from wind or moisture.
- Tire care: Place tire covers to protect them from sunlight and reduce the risk of cracking. If possible, occasionally move the RV slightly to avoid flat spots on the tires.
- Secure the RV: Lock all doors, windows, and storage compartments to ensure the RV is secure.
- Choose a suitable storage location: If storing the RV outdoors, look for a secure and level area away from trees or falling debris. If possible, park it on a gravel or concrete surface rather than grass or soil. If using an indoor storage facility, ensure it has appropriate security measures and climate control.
- Regular maintenance: Even during storage, it's important to perform regular maintenance checks. Visit the RV periodically to inspect for any issues, check the tire pressure, and ensure everything is in proper working condition.

Following these steps will help ensure that your RV is stored properly and ready for use when you're ready to hit the road again.

Tips for a perfect RV storage

To achieve a perfect RV storage experience, here are some additional tips to consider:

- Choose the right storage option: Assess your needs and budget to determine the most suitable storage option for your RV.
- Prepare the exterior: Before storing, wash and wax the exterior of the RV to protect the paint and finish. Inspect for any cracks, damages, or loose parts and address them promptly.

- Protect the tires: In addition to inflating the tires to the recommended pressure, place the RV on blocks or use tire cradles to take the weight off the tires. This helps prevent flat spots and uneven wear. Consider covering the tires to shield them from the sun's harmful rays.
- Battery maintenance: If storing your RV for an extended period, it's advisable to remove the battery and store it separately in a cool, dry place.
- Use RV covers or tarps: Invest in a quality RV cover that fits your vehicle properly. A breathable cover will protect the RV from dirt, dust, UV rays, and moisture.
- Ventilation: Ensure proper ventilation inside the RV by leaving vents slightly open or using vent covers. This helps prevent humidity build-up, condensation, and musty odors.
- Pest prevention: Take measures to deter pests from entering your RV. Use mouse traps or repellents and seal any openings where pests could gain access. Avoid storing food or attracting pests with crumbs or spills.
- Fuel and propane considerations: If storing the RV for an extended period, it's best to drain the fuel tank or use a fuel stabilizer to prevent fuel degradation. If you have propane tanks, shut off the valves and secure them properly.
- Regular inspections: Visit your stored RV periodically to inspect for any issues. Check for leaks, pests, or signs of damage. Run the engine and generator for a short time to keep them in good working condition.
- Documentation and insurance: Keep a record of your RV's storage location, any maintenance or repairs performed, and your insurance coverage. Ensure your insurance policy covers your RV during storage and adjust it accordingly.
- Plan for reactivation: As your storage period comes to an end, plan ahead for reactivating your RV. Schedule a thorough inspection, maintenance, and any necessary repairs before your next adventure.

These was our general storing tips, which will be useful for you to be certain that your RV remains in excellent condition while in storage and is ready for your next trip.

BOOK 5

MAKING THE MOST OF YOUR RV CAMPING EXPERIENCE

CHAPTER 1

Camping Activities: Fun things to Do while Camping

Whether you are near water, the woods, or spending time with kids or pets, there are plenty of enjoyable activities to do while camping that will keep you busy as you enjoy the wonder of nature outdoors.

There are people who, as soon as they plan their camper trip, also plan the activities to be carried out, while there are other more spontaneous people who decide what to do once they arrive on site.

Activities to be done in or near the water

1. Go fishing. Whether you are an experienced fisherman or a beginner, this activity offers you the chance to connect with nature and completely relax. Pack your fishing gear, put on your sunglasses, and spend some quiet time with friends and family along the water's edge.

2. Swim. Use the opportunity to swim during your campsite by donning your bathing suit and heading to the lake or ocean shores. Feel free to jump off the dock or jetty, or just dip into the refreshing water. Swimming allows you to relax, enjoy the thrill of the water around you and enjoy a recreational activity that gives you a feeling of lightness and joy.

3. Go snorkeling. Snorkeling is a perfect activity to enjoy while camping on the beach, as it requires bodies of water that are clear and not too murky. The coast and the transparent waters offer the perfect environment to explore the seabed, observe the marine life and enjoy the experience of swimming and diving. Whether you are exploring coral reefs, spotting colorful tropical fish, or simply marveling at the underwater beauty, snorkeling while beach camping is an exciting and relaxing activity.

4. Canoeing, tubing, kayaking and other water sports. While camping on the beach, you will have the opportunity to participate in a variety of local water sports that will make your experience even more adventurous and fun. You can try activities such as canoeing, tubing and kayaking, which will allow you to explore the surrounding waters and admire the coastal landscape from an unfamiliar perspective. If you are a thrill seeker, you might want to try bodyboarding, surfing, jet skiing or kite surfing, all of which offer the chance to ride the waves and experience the adrenaline rush of the water. If you prefer a more relaxed experience, stand-up paddleboarding allows you to glide gently through the water standing up on a board. Choose the water sport that fascinates you the most and have fun practicing it during your camping on the beach.

5. Try to jump the rocks. Skipping rocks is a fun and challenging activity to do while camping by the ocean or near a lake or river. No matter the age, it is an exciting way to challenge yourself and enjoy being in nature. You can try jumping rocks so that they bounce off the water, trying to get as many jumps as possible or the greatest distance. It can also be an enjoyable competition

between friends or family to see who can get the best results. Even though exact numbers can fade over time, the important thing is to enjoy the fun and challenge that this activity offers. Next, take a smooth, flat stone, focus your energy, and throw it across the water to see how far it can go.

Activities to do on land

1. Go hiking. Hiking presents an incredible opportunity to fully immerse yourself in nature and explore scenic trails, awe-inspiring viewpoints, and enchanting waterfalls. Embarking on these trails allows you to appreciate the diverse range of flora and fauna, offering a serene experience that can last for hours as you revel in the natural beauty that surrounds you. Also, exploring the city or town nearby can offer you a unique experience. You can visit the local shops, try the typical restaurants of the area and perhaps discover the local craft breweries, if you are passionate about beer. Supporting the local economy is a wonderful way to connect with the community and discover its quirks. Alternatively, if you prefer a more relaxing experience, you can opt for a scenic journey by car, taking in the stunning scenery along the way. Then, put on your hiking boots or hop in your car and head out on an adventure, exploring everything the area has to offer during your camping trip.

2. Go bird watching. Bird watching is a very popular activity while camping, especially if you are in an area rich in birdlife. You can bring along binoculars and a bird guide to identify the species you encounter along your route. Find a quiet spot, such as a nature trail or wooded area, and observe the birds in their natural habitat. Take the time to appreciate their behaviors, songs, and unique characteristics. You may spot common species such as blackbirds, robins and goldfinches, or you may be lucky enough to see rarer and more colorful birds. Remember to respect your surroundings and observe the birds from a safe distance so as not to disturb them. Birdwatching can offer a special connection to nature and a heightened awareness of the importance of conserving birds and their habitat.

3. Play horseshoes. The game of "Horseshoes" is a traditional game involving throwing horseshoes so that they land around a metal stake driven into the ground. It's a popular game to play outdoors, especially during camping trips. Find an open area and drive a metal stake into the ground. Usually, the stake has a U shape, and players will have to try to land the horseshoes around it. Draw a throwing line at an appropriate distance from the stake. Each player throws their horseshoes towards the post, trying to land them as close to the post as possible. Players can throw one iron at a time or both together, depending on the established rules. Assign points based on the position of the horseshoes in relation to the stake. Usually, an iron that comes to rest around the post without touching it (literally forming a "horseshoe") is considered the best pitch and can be awarded the maximum score. Throws that come close to the stake may be awarded a lower score. Players alternate throwing the horseshoes until a pre-set score is reached or until all players have completed a pre-determined number of throws.

4. Play cornhole. Cornhole is a fun and addictive game to play while camping. It's a game of skill that involves throwing bags of corn at a pole or sloping platform with holes. You can play in pairs or individually and try to get the maximum score by throwing the bags in the hole or on the table. You can organize tournaments with other campers or just have fun with friends and family. Just make sure you have enough open space and consider the safety rules when playing.

Activities to do during the evening

1. Watch the sunset. Watching the sunset while camping can be a magical and evocative moment. Look for a vantage point with an open view, such as a beach, hill or clearing, where you can watch the sunset without obstructions. Invite your camping mates to join you to enjoy the sunset together. It can be a special moment to share with friends or loved ones. Remember that every sunset is unique and offers different shows. Take the time to appreciate the beauty of nature and recharge your batteries for the evening of fun that awaits you while camping.

2. Tell each other stories around the fire. Storytelling is a classic camping tradition that can create an engaging and fun atmosphere. Whether you want to tell scary or funny stories, take some time to prepare your stories in advance. You can search online for ready-made stories or create your own. Choose a suitable place to tell the stories, such as by the fire or under the stars. Adjust the lighting and create an atmospheric atmosphere with lanterns or candles. You can also consider using sound or special effects to increase engagement. Engage with the audience as you tell the story. Ask questions, involve people in the descriptions, or let them actively participate in the storytelling. You can ask them to imagine what will happen next or to make appropriate noises during the story. Remember, the main goal is to have fun and create a pleasant atmosphere. It doesn't matter if you are a skilled storyteller or not, the important thing is to share moments of entertainment and lightness with friends or family while camping.

3. Take out a musical instrument and enjoy playing and singing. Bringing out a musical instrument while camping can add a special and immersive atmosphere. Whether you play guitar, harmonica or another instrument, you can create memorable musical moments and have fun with friends around the fire or in a cozy common area of the campsite. The acoustic guitar is a classic camping instrument because it's portable and can be played in a variety of musical styles, from folk to rock to country. But don't worry if you're not a big fan of the acoustic guitar or if you can't play an instrument yourself. You can always join other musicians or enjoy the show of other campers' musical talents. The harmonica is another popular camping instrument because it is small, easy to carry, and can create a powerful, immersive sound. Bluesy or folk tunes played on the harmonica can add a special touch to camping evenings. If you're not sure which instrument to play, you can also consider the ukulele, tambourine, percussion, or any other instrument that inspires you.

4. Play cards. Card games are classic camping entertainment and can be fun for the whole family or a group of friends. Poker is definitely one of the most popular card games to play while camping. You can organize a poker tournament with friends around the camping table and have fun bluffing and betting your chips. If you are not a poker expert, don't worry, there are many variations of the game that you can easily learn and enjoy playing. Other classic card games to try including Go Fish, War, and more. You can also look for new card games that you have never played before and try something different. Remember that card games can be a great way to socialize, laugh, and make memories while camping. Make sure you have a deck of cards with you and take time to play and have fun with the other campers. So, don't forget to pack a deck of cards in your camping gear and get ready to spend pleasant evenings playing cards under the stars.

5. Play hide and seek in the dark. Playing hide and seek in the dark while camping can be a fun and adventurous activity, especially at night. Make sure you choose a safe and unobstructed area to play hide and seek in the dark. Avoid areas with rough or dangerous terrain. Set the boundaries

of the play area so that all players know how far they can go in an attempt to hide. Choose one of the participants as a finder. He will be in charge of closing his eyes and counting to a pre-set number to give the other players time to hide. Make sure the area is dark enough to make the game more challenging. You can turn off the lights or, if possible, play in a darker natural area away from artificial lights. The seeker closes his eyes and counts to a predetermined number (for example, 20 or 30) while the other players try to hide in the designated area. After finishing counting, the seeker looks for the other players hiding in the dark. He moves around the area, trying to spot the participants who have hidden. If the finder spots a hidden player, he may call his name or say "I found you!" The discovered player comes out of hiding and joins the finder in trying to find the other players. The game continues until all players have been face up or until the pre-set time for the game has expired. You can play multiple games or rotate the seeker's role to give everyone the opportunity to hide and seek.

Activities to do with children

1. Collect the leaves. Collecting leaves is one of the most classic and fun activities you can do while camping, especially if you are in an area full of trees and vegetation. Wax paper books are perfect for storing collected leaves. You can place the leaves between the pages of the book and leave them pressed together for some time. In this way, the leaves will dry and remain well preserved in the book. This allows you to have a collection of leaves that you can keep over time and enjoy looking at on future camping trips. You can identify the collected leaves, observe their shapes, colors and distinctive characteristics, and even learn to recognize the trees from which they came. It's a fun and educational way to learn more about the local flora.

2. Put the fireflies in a jar. Collecting fireflies in a jar is a magical activity that can take us back to childhood and immerse us in the wonder of nature. These little nocturnal creatures, with their bioluminescence, create a dazzling and mesmerizing display on warm summer nights. To harvest fireflies safely and respectfully, follow these guidelines:

- Choose a clear jar with a lid that is perforated to allow air to enter. Make sure the jar is large enough for the fireflies to move freely without harming them.

- Wait until dark and look for an area where you know there are fireflies. They are usually found in grassy areas or near ponds, rivers or woods. Remember that fireflies are delicate creatures, so try to disturb their natural environment as little as possible.

- Turn on a dim light to attract fireflies and slowly approach the jar without making sudden movements. Gently place the jar on top of the firefly and close the lid quickly when it is close to the lid.

- Observe the fireflies in the jar for a short time, admiring their sparkling light. Make sure you don't keep the fireflies trapped in the jar for too long, as it could cause them stress or harm.

- After enjoying the experience, open the lid of the jar and release the fireflies to return to their natural environment.

3. Play treasure hunt. Treasure hunting is a fun and engaging activity that can keep kids busy while camping. Here's how to organize a scavenger hunt:

- Make a list of items to find: You can include a variety of items such as leaves of different shapes and colors, pinecones, feathers, rocks of specific sizes, sticks shaped like letters of the alphabet, and more. Make sure the objects are appropriate to their surroundings.

- Before the kids start the treasure hunt, hide the items in different areas of the campsite. Make sure you choose locations that are accessible and safe for children.

- Explain the rules of treasure hunting to the children. Tell them what items they need to find and provide them with a list or card with pictures or names of items to look for. You can also add clues or puzzles to make the treasure hunt more intriguing.
- Establish a specific time frame for the treasure hunt. This will add some challenge and keep the kids active and focused while searching.
- Once the treasure hunt is completed, collect the items found by the kids and check if they found everything according to the list. You can reward the winners with small prizes or simply compliment everyone for taking part.
- Treasure hunting is a fun way to get kids involved and explore their surroundings while camping. Make sure you supervise the children during the activity and promote respect for nature and the environment in which they find themselves.

CHAPTER 2

Outdoor Fire: Recipes and Tips for Cooking Around the Campfire

One of the most delightful aspects of camping is the camaraderie of gathering around the crackling fire with your loved ones, savoring a delectable meal prepared amidst the dancing flames. This cherished tradition creates a warm and inviting atmosphere, fostering memorable moments and fostering a sense of togetherness in the great outdoors. Below you will find all the methods and tips for cooking properly during your camping trip.

Cooking food over a fire pit

It is possible to cook over a fire pit while camping. Cooking over a fire pit is a traditional and charming method that allows you to prepare delicious meals outdoors. Here is some helpful information and tips for cooking over a fire pit:

Dig a shallow hole in the ground next to the fire. You can use special pots, pans or grills for cooking over a fire. Choose heat and flame-resistant containers. You can use cast iron pans, heavy aluminum pans, or camping-specific pans that are suitable for cooking over an open flame.

Light the fire in the pit and let it burn until it burns to smoldering embers. You can adjust the intensity of the heat by moving the vessels closer or further away from the embers. If you need direct heat, place the container directly over the coals. If, on the other hand, you need slower cooking or less heat, place the container further away from the embers.

Remember that the heat can be more intense than cooking over a domestic flame; therefore, it may take some practice to achieve the desired cooking times.

Be sure to operate safely when cooking over the fire pit. Use long cooking utensils to avoid getting too close to the fire. Wear heat resistant gloves to protect your hands when handling hot containers.

Cooking over a fire pit offers many creative possibilities. You can make roasts, soups, stews, pancakes, grills and so much more.

How to cook on a campfire

Cooking over a campfire can be a rewarding and tasty camping experience.

While associations with s'mores and hot dogs are common when thinking of campfire food, a wide variety of dishes can be prepared by using the appropriate tools to place on the fire.

Decide which dishes you want to prepare and organize the ingredients so that they are close at hand. You can cut vegetables, marinate meat or prepare the main ingredients before arriving at the campsite.

Be sure to bring essential utensils for cooking on the campfire. These can include tongs, spatulas, camping grills or grills, cast iron pots, pans, baking trays and stainless-steel cutlery. It's also helpful to have heat resistant gloves to protect you when cooking and handling hot utensils.

Depending on the dish you want to prepare, you can use different cooking methods on the campfire. You can cook directly over glowing embers, use a grill or camping grill, wrap food in aluminum foil and place it in the embers, or use pots and pans designed for cooking over an open fire.

Don't limit yourself, as we've already said, to the usual s'mores and hot dogs (although they are delicious). Experiment with creative recipes such as camping omelets, grilled pancakes, stews, meat and vegetable kebabs, smoked fish, jacket potatoes, grilled fruit and much more. Cooking on the campfire offers endless possibilities.

Have fun exploring new recipes and enjoy the process of cooking outdoors with the warmth and cozy atmosphere of the fire.

Camping cooking equipment

Now let's see what equipment you must necessarily have in order to cook outdoors.

Let's start with the pans

Cast iron camping cookware is considered an essential item for a camping trip. Unlike wrought iron equipment, which uses a different manufacturing method, you're unlikely to find wrought iron cookware while camping. However, titanium, steel, and aluminum cookware are common materials used for camping cookware.

Cast iron grills and plates

A cast iron grill and griddle are ideal tools for preparing a variety of delicious meals while camping. The cast iron grate allows you to cook pancakes, eggs and steaks with ease. You can prepare a hearty breakfast with fluffy pancakes and scrambled eggs right on the grill. For a more substantial meal, you can grill succulent steaks for even cooking and a delicious crust on the surface.

If you're looking for a sweet twist, grilling pineapple slices is a great choice. Caramelized pineapple on the grill develops a sweet and juicy taste that can be served as a dessert or as an accompaniment to other dishes. Whether you want to prepare a savory meal or something sweet, the cast iron grill and griddle are versatile tools that allow you to experiment with a wide range of recipes during your camping trip.

Dutch oven

The Cast Iron Dutch Oven is a versatile and indispensable tool for camping cooking. With a Dutch oven, you can prepare a variety of delicious recipes. You can cook succulent stews, warm and comforting soups, classic baked beans, and even boil water for pasta right over the stove. In addition, the Dutch oven allows you to bake the bread, creating a crispy crust and a soft, fragrant interior.

Rotisserie and spit

If the idea of a chicken roasted over a fire makes your mouth water, you may want to consider using a rotisserie and spit for your camping kitchen. A combined rotisserie and spit allow you to cook items such as corn on the cob or grilled potatoes on the grill itself, while at the same time you can cook a chicken or other food on the spit placed above the grate. This cooking method offers a delicious alternative to enjoying camping-style roasted meats.

Dutch oven stand

A Dutch oven stand is a useful accessory that lifts cookware off the ground and places it in close proximity to the heat source while cooking. This stand allows for even heat distribution and allows you to cook with a dutch oven effectively. Also, raising the Dutch oven off the ground helps protect your food from unwanted burns or debris on the floor. It's a practical option for cooking succulent dishes over the fire while camping.

Cast iron tripod

A cast iron cooking tripod is a fantastic option for cooking over a fire while camping and can definitely make you feel like you're in the Old West. With a tripod, you can hang the Dutch oven over the fire, keeping it off the ground. This not only creates an atmospheric atmosphere, but also allows for even and controlled cooking. You can experiment with a variety of recipes in your hanging Dutch oven, creating delicious meals that fit right into the country setting.

Tools

Once you've acquired the essential cookware, it's important to have the necessary firewire on hand to ensure the success of your cooking and the safety of your hands. Here are some recommended tools for flipping, turning, stirring, and serving your delicious fireside dishes:

- Folding grill tool. A handy option for campers is a three-in-one folding grill tool. This tool takes up little space but offers several essential functions. It features a grilling spatula, grilling fork, and knife all packed into one foldable piece. This allows you to have the utensils you need to turn, flip and serve food on the grill, without having to carry around a separate set of utensils. The three-in-one folding grill tool is a convenient option that offers multiple functions, saving space and making it easier to prepare meals while camping.
- Steel pliers. A staple for any camping chef is a solid pair of stainless-steel tongs. These tongs provide a secure grip when you need to turn or remove food from the grill and protect your hands from burns. They come in different lengths, so you can choose between nine-inch or 16-inch tongs, depending on your personal preferences and the specific needs of your cooking setup. The steel tongs are durable and strong, making them ideal for use over an open fire. Make sure you have a high-quality pair of tongs in your camping utensil set to ensure safe and precise handling of your foods when preparing meals in the great outdoors.
- Long handle spoon. A long-handled spoon is an indispensable tool for stirring soups, stews or oatmeal when preparing meals on a camping trip. You can opt for a wooden spoon, which is durable and doesn't react with food. Stainless steel spoons are also a popular choice as they are durable and easy to clean. Alternatively, you can use an aluminum spoon, which is light and easy to handle. Choose the material that feels most comfortable to you, and make sure you have a long-handled spoon on hand to make it easier to prepare and mix your meals while camping.

How to build the perfect camping fire for cooking

Once you have your cooking utensils at your disposal, it's time to create the perfect fire for even cooking. This is obtained by burning the wood until it is transformed into glowing embers. Before we begin, it's important to consider a few key factors.

One of the primary considerations is the selection of suitable wood. It is crucial to choose dry and seasoned wood, indicating that the moisture has been effectively removed. Opting for such wood ensures a more efficient and enjoyable fire, as it ignites easily, produces less smoke, and generates a consistent and pleasant heat. This type of wood is ideal for clean and efficient combustion. You can look for seasoned wood from specialized suppliers or collect it in advance and season it yourself. Also, if you want to add a touch of extra flavor to your food, you can opt for aromatic woods like oak or mesquite, which will lend a delicious smoky aroma while cooking.

Next, it is essential to meticulously choose a safe location for your fire. Whenever possible, opt for pre-built fire pits as they are specifically designed to offer a stable and secure foundation for your fire. These fire pits minimize the risk of spreading flames, provide containment for the fire, and offer an added layer of protection against accidental mishaps. If there are no fire pits available, choose an area free of grass, tree roots, loose earth, and other debris that could pose a fire risk. Make sure there are no tree branches or other structures above the fire that could be caught by the flames. Safety is paramount when preparing a fire, so always take the necessary precautions to avoid dangerous situations.

To ensure maximum safety, it is advisable to select a fire site that is at least eight feet away from bushes or anything else that is easily flammable.

Next, it is advisable to establish a perimeter around the fire by utilizing rocks or green logs. When we refer to green logs, we mean fresh wood that still retains moisture, in contrast to dry and dead logs. Creating this perimeter acts as a preventive measure, reducing the risk of unintentional fire spread and providing an additional layer of protection. Finally, place a large rock at the back of the fire pit to act as a natural "chimney" and direct the smoke upward, reducing smoke buildup around the fire area. Always remember to take extra safety precautions and abide by local rules regarding open fires when camping.

To start a fire, you can start by filling the fire area with tinder such as crumpled up newspaper. Make sure the bait is well distributed evenly. Next, place a layer of thin pieces of wood or small dry branches on top of the tinder, so that they form a vertical layer.

Finally, light the fire by lighting the tinder paper using a flame or lighter. Be sure to monitor the fire closely and keep it under control throughout the lighting and cooking process.

Once the kindling is ablaze and well underway, you can add firewood to the fire. Place the wood over the kindling evenly, making sure to create a stable, well-ventilated arrangement. As the kindling burns and the flames diminish, the logs will catch fire and turn to coals. This process will take some time, usually between 30 and 45 minutes; therefore, be patient and let the fire develop naturally. During this time, be sure to monitor the fire closely to ensure it is under control and that the temperature is adequate for cooking your food.

Once you have a good base of glowing embers, you can place the grate on the structure of rocks or logs above the embers. Make sure the grill is stable and well positioned so you can cook safely and evenly. You are now ready to cook directly on the grill or use the pots and pans above it to prepare your meals over the fire. Make sure you adjust the distance between the grate and the embers according to the temperature needed to cook your food. Always remember to use the proper tools for turning and handling food while cooking to avoid burns.

Always keeping a bucket of water or sand nearby is an essential precaution to extinguish the fire in case of need. After extinguishing the flames, stir the ashes and pour in additional water or sand to ensure they are completely covered. This will help avoid the risk of accidentally reignited fires.

If you feel less confident cooking with wood, you can opt for using charcoal instead. It's important to choose charcoal that doesn't contain lighter fluid or chemicals that could affect the flavor of your foods.

Tips on how to cook outdoors

Cooking on the fire and in the open air is a unique and unrepeatable experience. Sharing this experience with friends and family makes it all the more special. To ensure the success of this culinary adventure, here are some tips to keep in mind.

- Choose the right cooking method and the most appropriate tools. Adapt the cooking method to your needs. If you're planning a simple afternoon picnic of hot dogs and marshmallows, you might not need to bring a heavy Dutch oven. Instead, make sure you have skewers and fire-starting gear. However, if you plan to spend several days camping and have a number of Dutch oven recipes planned that you can't wait to try, then it might be worth bringing along a cast iron pot.
- Try to maintain proper food safety. Pay attention to food safety during your camping trip to avoid illness. Keep food fresh by storing raw meat on ice until ready to cook, as bacteria tend to thrive between 40- and 140-degrees Fahrenheit. Make sure you put away any leftovers within two hours, and in very hot conditions, don't leave food out for more than an hour. By following these precautions, you can enjoy your meal without worrying about food safety. To store food safely on your camping trip, it's best to use airtight bags or containers and keep them refrigerated. Be sure to bring separate coolers for drinks and perishables and fill them adequately. You can use frozen gel packs, ice cubes or frozen water bottles to keep your core temperature cool. Also, remember to keep your hands clean by using disposable wipes or eco-friendly soap to avoid food contamination. These precautions will help keep your food fresh and safe on your camping trip.
- Do not light fires that are too large for cooking. Large fires tend to burn wood quickly and may not provide even or controlled cooking. It is advisable to spend your wood wisely, using only what is necessary to maintain a constant and controlled ember. That way, you'll have enough wood on hand to extend the life of the fire, creating the perfect atmosphere for campfire stories and post-dinner snacking.
- Prepare yourself in advance. To get the best results when cooking on a campfire, it's important to prepare properly. Light the fire at least an hour in advance to allow the flames to go out and the coals to reach an ideal temperature for cooking. Keep in mind that cooking over a campfire takes longer than cooking at home, so be patient and take your time to get even cooking. When cooking, be sure to turn the food regularly to ensure even cooking from all sides. Use a food thermometer to check that food reaches safe doneness levels.

Download 15 Easy Recipes to Enjoy While Camping in Your RV

CHAPTER 3

Travel Photography: Tips and Techniques for Capturing Your RV Adventures

Most of us love to travel and take countless photos during our travels. Travel photography has a unique potential to connect us with the beautiful world around us, both consciously and subconsciously.

Travel photos allow us to capture special moments, evocative places and different cultures. Each photo can tell a story and convey emotions, allowing us to relive those precious moments even when we are back home.

Also, travel photos can be an opportunity to explore and appreciate the world around us more attentively. As we look for the best angle or the right light to take a picture, we become more aware of the details and beauties that surround us. We can notice architectural details, vibrant colors, breathtaking landscapes and unique moments that we might otherwise overlook.

Below you will find some tips for taking the perfect souvenir photos of your travels.

Pack the right equipment

To get a variety of shots while traveling, it might be helpful to have a set of lenses that allow you to adapt to different photographic situations. However, if you have to limit yourself to just one lens, it's wise to choose one that offers a versatile range of focal lengths to cover your needs.

A zoom lens can be a smart choice in these cases, as it allows you to adjust the focal length to achieve different photographic effects. For example, a zoom lens with a wide-angle to telephoto focal length range may be suitable for most travel situations. It allows you to capture breathtaking landscapes with the wide angle and get closer to distant subjects with the telephoto.

If, on the other hand, you have a particular interest in landscape or architectural photography, you might opt for a wide-angle lens, which allows you to capture wide panoramas and emphasize perspective. If, on the other hand, you prefer to portray details or distant subjects, you may want to consider a telephoto lens to get you closer to your subjects.

A sturdy tripod is definitely another must-have accessory for getting sharp, stable shots while traveling. Its solidity and stability are more important than the specific brand; therefore, you can find great options even with lesser-known brands.

When choosing a tripod, it is important to consider several factors. First, make sure it's made of quality materials and that it's well built to withstand frequent use and the changing environments of travel. An aluminum or carbon fiber tripod is usually a good choice due to its strength and light weight.

Another factor to consider is the portability of the tripod. If you plan to take it with you on trips, make sure it's lightweight and easy to store in a purse or backpack. Ease of use is also important, so look for a tripod with intuitive, stable locking mechanisms for adjusting height and angle.

Practice the settings to work them to your advantage

The three main factors that influence the exposure of photographs: aperture, shutter speed and ISO. By adjusting these three factors, you can control the exposure of your photographs based on the lighting conditions you're shooting in and the creative result you want to achieve.

Experimentation is key to improving your photography skills. Experimenting with different aperture and shutter speed settings will allow you to explore various depths of field, resulting in creative and interesting results.

Taking multiple photos of the same scene with minor tweaks to the settings will give you a chance to compare the results and figure out which combination works best for the desired effect. This trial-and-error process is an excellent way to develop your photographic eye and hone your composition skills.

Experiment with different aperture and shutter speed combinations to discover new perspectives and styles of photography. Every shot is an opportunity to learn and improve, so have fun and let your creativity flow.

Choose your location

Once you've selected the location, it's important to do some preliminary preparation. This is especially useful when you want to capture sunrises and sunsets, as it's important to know the time and direction of the sun in advance. Also, the advice is to use a tripod to avoid unwanted blurring in your photos.

Avoid taking pictures of the sun directly. Instead, point the camera at wide landscapes to capture the full color spectrum of the sky during sunrise or sunset. You can add interest to your photo by choosing a foreground landmark, such as a tree or stream, but be careful not to distract from the main effect of the sunset.

To capture breathtaking sunrises, start shooting as soon as the sun begins to peek over the horizon. At that time, the colors will be more vivid and will gradually fade as the sun rises. For sunsets, the best time for intense colors is right after the sun has completely set. You'll only have a short window of time before it gets completely dark, so make sure you're ready to shoot by then.

Be aware of everything around you

Life is in constant motion around us, with people interacting with each other and with nature, and nature itself offering us wonderful shows, such as sunrise, sunset or a thunderstorm. However, don't wait for the perfect moment or have a preconceived idea of when and how to take your travel photos.

At the same time, don't just see the world through your camera's viewfinder. Take the time to observe the scene, anticipate the shot you really want to capture, and prepare yourself for that moment. Don't take photos in every situation only to realize you completely missed the very moment you wanted to capture.

The key is to find a balance between being ready to seize the opportunity and carefully observing the world around you. Be aware of the details, emotions and interactions unfolding before you.. Don't be afraid to wait for the perfect moment, but also be ready to catch the unexpected moment that could give you an extraordinary photo.

Remember that travel photography isn't just about the final image, it's also about the experience itself. It's a way to explore the world, appreciate the beauty around us, and connect with people and nature. Whether it's a chance meeting, a moment of serenity or a spectacular event, try to capture the essence of the moment and share it with others through your travel photos.

Have confidence in your skills as a photographer

Travel photography is often a fast-paced and dynamic activity, as you try to capture a scene as it unfolds in front of you. In these cases, you may not have the time or opportunity to carefully compose and plan the shot. However, that doesn't mean you should just snap a series of photos at your camera's full shutter speed and hope one of them is the right one.

Instead, it's important to use your technical and artistic skills to read the scene, evaluate the available light, adjust the camera settings correctly, and imagine the end result before taking the shot. This takes practice and observation skills, but over time you'll get better at both capturing key elements of a scene and predicting decisive moments.

Good travel photography requires a balance of responsiveness and planning. You have to be ready to seize the moment without hesitation, but at the same time you have to be aware of the technique and composition to get a quality photo. Observe the scene carefully, evaluate the opportunities for light and shadow, identify the elements that make the situation unique and take the photo at the right moment.

As you develop your observation and travel photography skills, you'll notice an improvement in the way you read scenes and capture decisive moments. Constant practice and experience will allow you to achieve ever better results and to create travel photographs that tell memorable stories.

CHAPTER 4

Relaxing and Unwinding: Tips for Enjoying Your Downtime While RV Camping

Camping is an extremely relaxing activity that offers multiple ways to find tranquility and peace. You can enjoy moments of relaxation sitting around the fire or immerse yourself in pleasant excursions in the woods. While camping, there are plenty of opportunities to engage in relaxing and rejuvenating activities.

Here are some of the relaxing activities you can enjoy while camping.

Watch the sunset

Sunsets while camping provide a nice and relaxing experience to end the day. The beauty of being surrounded by nature while camping is that you are always outdoors, making it hard to miss an opportunity to watch the beautiful sunsets. The best campsites are often located near enchanting places where it is possible to enjoy spectacular sunsets. Whether you are camping on the beach, in the forest, in the desert or anywhere else, surely you will find an ideal place to enjoy a magnificent sunset and relax while camping.

Wait for the sun to come up

Just like watching the sunset, watching the sunrise can also be a relaxing and awe-inspiring experience. It's true that this activity is best suited for those who like to get up early in the morning, as it requires waking up in time to witness the sunrise show. However, the beauty and serenity that can be experienced are often values that amply repay the effort. If you're fascinated by the sun and its play of light, I highly recommend trying to capture a sunrise the next time you're looking for a relaxing camping activity. It will be an unforgettable experience.

Take a relaxing nap in a hammock

Hammocks can be a great way to relax and take a nap, even for people who are already rested. The gentle swing of the hammock can promote a sense of calm and tranquility, creating an ideal environment for rest.

Taking a nap while camping can be especially nice, as it allows you to enjoy your natural surroundings while relaxing. However, it's important to keep in mind that the length and timing you take a nap can affect the quality of your night's sleep.

To get the most benefit from a nap, try to limit it to around 20-30 minutes and make sure you do it during the early afternoon. This way, you'll avoid interfering with your nightly sleep cycle and you'll be able to enjoy greater energy and focus later in the day.

Relax by soaking in a hot spring

The idea of soaking in a hot spring while camping can be quite fascinating. The natural thermal springs offer numerous benefits for the body and mind, thanks to the healing properties of the mineral-rich hot waters.

The experience of soaking in a hot spring can promote muscle relaxation, relieve stress, and promote a feeling of overall well-being.

If you want to find a campground near hot springs, I recommend researching the areas you want to go to and see if there are any hot springs nearby. You can consult local tourist guides, websites or ask local authorities or other campers for information. Be sure to abide by local rules and regulations regarding access and use of the hot springs.

Relax by soaking up some sun

The sun can offer many benefits for our well-being. Moderate exposure to the sun can help regulate circadian rhythms, stimulate vitamin D production and improve our mood.

Read

Reading while camping can be an enjoyable and rewarding activity. It lets you immerse yourself in engaging stories, expand your knowledge, or simply enjoy hours of entertainment.

If you have access to a local library near the campsite, you can rent a variety of books to take with you. This allows you to have a large selection of titles to explore during your stay outdoors.

Additionally, the growing popularity of e-books offers a convenient and portable alternative for reading while camping.

Whichever format you prefer, make sure you have an adequate light source, such as a camping lamp or flashlight, for comfortable reading during the evening hours or in low-light conditions.

Relax with meditation

Camping can provide an ideal environment for meditation practice. Finding a lonely, peaceful spot in nature can foster concentration and inner calm.

Look for a secluded area on the campsite where you can be surrounded by nature and away from distractions. It can be a vantage point with a breathtaking view, a lake shore, or a quiet corner in the trees.

Choose a time of day that works best for you and create a meditation routine. It can be in the early morning to start the day calmly, during sunset to reflect on the day, or at bedtime to unwind before sleep.

You can choose a meditation practice that you prefer, such as focused breathing meditation, body awareness, or walking meditation. Choose a practice that helps you center and connect with the present moment.

As you meditate, try to be aware of the sensations you experience. Notice the sound of birds, the feel of the wind on your skin, or the smell of the surrounding nature. This helps you stay in the present moment and deepen your meditation experience.

BOOK6

RV CAMPING RESOURCES AND TOOLS

CHAPTER 1

RV Camping Apps and Websites

The Best Trip Planner Apps

There are many functional and amazing RV trip planner apps available that can be really useful to you on planning and organizing your next adventure. Let's see some of the best RV trip planner apps:

- Roadtrippers: Roadtrippers is a popular app that allows you to plan your route, discover attractions, and find campgrounds along the way. It also provides information on points of interest, hotels, restaurants, and more.

- RV Trip Wizard: RV Trip Wizard is a comprehensive trip planning tool specifically designed for RVers. It helps you plan your route, find campgrounds, and calculate driving distances and fuel costs. It also offers campground reviews and integrates with other RV tools.

- RV Parky: RV Parky is a user-friendly app that provides information on RV parks, campgrounds, rest areas, and overnight parking locations.

- Campendium: Campendium is a popular app among RVers for finding campgrounds, RV parks, and boondocking spots. It provides detailed information, user reviews, photos, and a map-based interface.

- AllStays Camp & RV: AllStays Camp & RV represents a complete app that gives information on campgrounds, RV parks, rest areas, and other accommodations. It includes filters for amenities, pricing, and reviews, making it easy to find suitable options.

- CoPilot RV: CoPilot RV is a navigation app specifically designed for RVers. It offers RV-specific routing, which takes into account the size and weight of your RV, and provides turn-by-turn directions, offline maps, and real-time traffic updates.

- iOverlander: While not exclusively for RVs, iOverlander is a great app for finding free camping spots, boondocking locations, and places to park overnight. It relies on user-generated data, so it's constantly being updated with new spots.

Apps for Finding Activities

When planning an RV trip, it's essential to find activities and attractions along your route to enhance your travel experience. Here are some apps that can help you find RV trip activities:

- Roadtrippers: Roadtrippers, mentioned earlier as a trip planner app, also offers a wide range of attractions and activities along your route. You can discover popular landmarks, scenic spots, hiking trails, museums, and other points of interest.

- TripAdvisor: TripAdvisor is a well-known app that provides user reviews, ratings, and recommendations for activities, attractions, and things to do in various locations. You can browse through categories like outdoor activities, tours, museums, and more.

- Yelp: Yelp is a popular app for finding restaurants, cafes, and local businesses. It can be handy when you're looking for places to eat or unique local experiences along your RV journey.
- Atlas Obscura: Atlas Obscura is an app dedicated to showcasing unusual and hidden attractions worldwide. It highlights offbeat locations, quirky museums, unique landmarks, and other interesting points of interest that you may not find on traditional travel apps.
- Eventbrite: Eventbrite is a platform that allows you to discover and book tickets for local events, festivals, concerts, workshops, and more. It's an excellent resource for finding entertainment and community events happening near your RV travel destinations.
- National Park Service Apps: If you plan on visiting national parks during your RV trip, many of them have their own dedicated apps. For example, the National Park Service offers apps for parks like Yellowstone, Yosemite, Grand Canyon, and more, providing information on trails, activities, maps, and park highlights.
- Local tourism apps: Depending on the regions you'll be visiting, many cities, states, and tourist destinations have their own official apps. These apps often feature comprehensive information on local attractions, events, outdoor activities, and cultural experiences.

Remember to check app reviews, update frequency, and accuracy of information to ensure you have the best experience while finding activities for your RV trip.

Perfect Apps to Use While Driving

When driving an RV camper, it's essential to have apps that assist you in navigation, finding RV-friendly amenities, and ensuring a safe and enjoyable journey. Here are some useful apps to consider

- Google Maps: Google Maps is a widely used navigation app that offers real-time traffic updates, turn-by-turn directions, and voice-guided navigation. It's particularly useful for RV travel as it allows you to input the dimensions of your RV and avoid low clearance bridges or narrow roads.
- Waze: this represents i a community-based navigation app that gives you some real-time traffic information, accident reports, and road hazards. It's helpful for RV travel as it helps you avoid heavy traffic and find the most efficient routes.
- iExit: iExit is an app designed for road trips, specifically to help you locate amenities and services at upcoming highway exits. It provides information on gas stations, rest areas, restaurants, hotels, and more. This app is useful for finding RV-friendly stops along your route.
- GasBuddy: GasBuddy is a mobile application designed to assist you in locating the most affordable fuel prices in your vicinity.. It can be particularly helpful during long RV trips to save money on fuel expenses.
- Campground Apps: Many RVers rely on campground-specific apps like KOA, ReserveAmerica, or Campendium (mentioned earlier) to find and book RV campsites. These apps provide information on campsite availability, amenities, reviews, and pricing.
- Weather Apps: Weather apps like AccuWeather or The Weather Channel can help you stay updated on current weather conditions and forecasts along your RV route. This information is crucial for planning stops, avoiding severe weather, or adjusting your travel plans if necessary.
- RV Parky: RV Parky, mentioned earlier as a trip planner app, also provides valuable information for RVers on-the-go. You can use it to find RV parks, campgrounds, rest areas, dump stations, and overnight parking locations as you travel.

It's so essential to remind to use these apps responsibly and ensure that you operate your RV camper safely. Prioritize safe driving practices and avoid interacting with your phone while riving. Consider using voice commands or having a co-pilot handle the apps to minimize distractions.

CHAPTER 2

Joining RV Clubs and Online Communities

Why joining to RV clubs

Joining RV clubs can offer several benefits for RV enthusiasts. We want you to know some reasons why people choose to join RV clubs:

- Community and Networking: RV clubs provide a sense of community and a chance to connect with fellow RVers who share similar interests. It's an opportunity to meet like-minded people, make friends, and exchange valuable information and experiences.

- Organized Group Activities: RV clubs often organize group activities, such as camping trips, rallies, educational seminars, and social events. These events can give you the real chances to socialize, learn new skills, and explore new destinations together.

- Discounts and Deals: Many RV clubs offer members exclusive discounts on various RV-related products and services. These can include discounts on campsite fees, RV park memberships, fuel, RV accessories, insurance, and more.

- Access to Resources: RV clubs typically provide members with access to resources like online forums, newsletters, and educational materials. These resources can be valuable for learning about RV maintenance, troubleshooting common issues, discovering new travel destinations, and staying updated on the latest RV trends and technologies.

- Advocacy and Support: Some RV clubs advocate for RVers' rights and work towards improving the RVing experience. They may address issues related to RV regulations, campground accessibility, and other matters that affect the RVing community. Being part of such a club can offer a sense of support and empowerment.

- Expertise and Advice: RV clubs often have experienced members who can provide valuable advice and guidance to newer RVers. Whether you need recommendations for campgrounds, tips for RV maintenance, or assistance with trip planning, these experienced RVers can be a valuable resource.

- Safety and Security: Joining an RV club can enhance safety and security while on the road. Some clubs have programs that provide emergency assistance, roadside services, or access to a network of fellow members who can offer help or guidance if needed.

It's important to research different RV clubs to find one that aligns with your interests and offers the specific benefits you're looking for. Consider factors such as membership fees, club rules and regulations, geographic focus, and the overall culture and atmosphere of the club before making a decision to join.

Why joining RV online communities

Joining RV online communities can be beneficial for several reasons. Here are some advantages of becoming part of RV online communities:

- Knowledge Sharing: RV online communities are vibrant hubs of information and experience. By joining these communities, you gain access to a wealth of knowledge shared by experienced RVers. You can ask questions, seek advice, and learn from the collective wisdom of the community. Whether you have inquiries about RV maintenance, travel destinations, or RV lifestyle tips, there will likely be someone in the community who can provide valuable insights.
- Problem Solving: RVing can come with its fair share of challenges, from mechanical issues to troubleshooting equipment problems. In online communities, you can seek help when you encounter difficulties. Members can offer suggestions, share their own experiences with similar problems, and provide step-by-step guidance to help you resolve issues more efficiently.
- Community Support: RV online communities provide a sense of camaraderie and support. You'll connect with other RV enthusiasts who understand the joys and challenges of RVing. It's a space to share your experiences, celebrate your successes, and find encouragement during challenging times. The community can offer emotional support and practical advice, making you feel part of a larger network of like-minded individuals.
- Trip Planning and Recommendations: RV online communities can be excellent resources for trip planning. Members often share their favorite camping spots, scenic routes, and hidden gems that you might not find in traditional travel guides. By tapping into the collective knowledge of the community, you can discover new destinations, receive campground recommendations, and benefit from insider tips that can enhance your travel experiences.
- Stay Updated: RV online communities are great sources for staying up to date with the latest news, trends, and developments in the RVing world. Members often share information about new RV models, technological advancements, campground reviews, and relevant industry updates. This ensures that you're aware of the latest innovations and can make informed decisions regarding your RV and travel plans.
- Virtual Connections: Online communities provide an opportunity to connect with RVers from all over the world, transcending geographical boundaries. You can engage in conversations, share stories and photos, and develop friendships with people who share your passion for RVing. These connections can lead to real-life meetups and travel companionship, creating a rich social network of fellow RV enthusiasts.

When joining RV online communities, it's important to maintain online etiquette, follow community guidelines, and respect the opinions and experiences of others. Actively participating in discussions, contributing valuable information, and offering support to fellow members can help foster a positive and engaging community experience.

7 camper clubs and organizations you should take into consideration

To end this second chapter, we want you to know seven popular camper clubs and organizations that you should join:

- Good Sam Club: Good Sam Club is one of the hugest RV clubs in North America. They offer a wide range of benefits, including campground discounts, fuel savings, RV insurance, roadside assistance, and a subscription to the Highways magazine. They also organize rallies and events for members to socialize and network with other RVers.
- Escapees RV Club: Escapees RV Club is focused on providing support and resources to full-time RVers. They offer educational programs, mail forwarding services, advocacy, and a network of RV parks and campgrounds. Escapees also have an active online community and organize rallies and gatherings for members.
- Family Motor Coach Association (FMCA): FMCA represent a true international organization for motorhome owners. They provide resources, exclusive member benefits, and a community for motorhome enthusiasts. Membership benefits include access to FMC Assist Medical Emergency and Travel Assistance program, RV insurance discounts, and a subscription to Family Motor Coaching magazine.
- Airstream Club International (ACI): ACI is dedicated to Airstream trailer owners and enthusiasts. They organize rallies, caravans, and social events specifically for Airstream owners. Members gain access to exclusive Airstream-related resources, forums, and a subscription to Airstream Life magazine.
- Thousand Trails: it represents a membership-based campground network with locations across North America. By joining Thousand Trails, you gain access to a network of campgrounds where members can stay for extended periods at no additional cost. They offer different membership tiers to suit various camping preferences.
- National African American RVers Association (NAARVA): NAARVA is a community-focused organization dedicated to African American RVers. They provide support, education, and opportunities for fellowship among African American RV enthusiasts. NAARVA organizes annual rallies, caravans, and local chapter events.
- Loners on Wheels (LoW): LoW is a club specifically for single RVers who enjoy traveling and camping independently. They offer a supportive network for solo RVers, organizing events, trips, and providing resources for those who prefer to travel alone or in smaller groups.

Remember to research each club or organization thoroughly to determine if their offerings, membership fees, and community align with your preferences and interests.

CHAPTER 3

Must-Have RV Camping Equipment, Electronics, and More

RV camping equipment

When we are dealing with RV camping, it is right to have the right equipment can make your trip more enjoyable and comfortable. We want to show you some essential items to consider for your RV camping equipment list:

- RV: The first and most important piece of equipment is, of course, the RV itself. Choose a size and type of RV that meets your needs and preferences.
- Camping Chairs and Table: Comfortable folding chairs and a sturdy camping table are essential for outdoor relaxation and dining.
- Bedding and Linens: Pack sheets, blankets, pillows, and towels to ensure a cozy and comfortable sleeping experience.
- Kitchen Supplies: Stock your RV kitchen with cooking utensils, pots and pans, dishes, cutlery, cups, and mugs. Don't forget essentials like a can opener, peeler, and cutting board.
- Camping Stove/Grill: While RVs often have built-in stoves, having a portable camping stove or grill can expand your cooking options when you want to cook outdoors.
- Cooler or Refrigerator: Depending on the size of your RV, you may have a refrigerator, but it's always a good idea to have a cooler for extra storage and to keep beverages cold during outdoor activities.
- Basic Tools: Carry a toolbox with essential tools such as screwdrivers, pliers, wrenches, and a multi-tool for minor repairs and adjustments.
- First Aid Kit: A well-stocked first aid kit should include bandages, antiseptic ointment, pain relievers, adhesive tape, tweezers, and any necessary prescription medications.
- Flashlights and Lanterns: Make sure you have reliable lighting options for nighttime activities or emergencies. LED flashlights and lanterns are energy-efficient and provide bright illumination.
- Camping Gear: Depending on your preferences, you may want to bring camping gear such as tents, sleeping bags, and camping mattresses for additional sleeping space or outdoor adventures.
- Outdoor Equipment: If you plan on engaging in outdoor activities, consider bringing items like hiking boots, backpacks, binoculars, fishing gear, bikes, or kayaks.
- RV Accessories: Don't forget to bring essential RV accessories like leveling blocks, chocks, sewer hose, water hose, and electrical adapters to ensure a smooth camping experience.

- Personal Items: Pack toiletries, medications, sunscreen, bug repellent, and any other personal items you may need during your trip.

For having all you will need in your RV trip is essential to check the specific amenities provided by your RV rental or campground to avoid duplicating items unnecessarily. Additionally, always consider the climate and location of your camping destination when packing your RV camping equipment.

RV camping electronics

Let's move on the "electronic side". When it comes to electronic equipment for RV camping, here are some items you may want to consider:

- GPS Navigation System: A GPS navigation system designed for RVs can help you navigate unfamiliar roads, find campgrounds, and avoid low bridges or narrow routes that may be unsuitable for your RV.
- Mobile Phones and Chargers: Bring your mobile phones for communication and emergencies. Make sure to pack chargers and consider portable power banks for recharging when electricity is not readily available.
- Portable Wi-Fi Hotspot: If you need internet access during your trip, a portable Wi-Fi hotspot or a mobile data plan with tethering capabilities can keep you connected.
- Entertainment Devices: Depending on your preferences, you may want to bring devices like a portable DVD player, tablets, or a laptop for watching movies, playing games, or streaming content during downtime.
- Portable Speakers: Enjoy your favorite music or podcasts while relaxing outside your RV with portable Bluetooth speakers.
- Camera and Accessories: Capture your camping memories with a digital camera or a smartphone with a good camera. Consider bringing extra memory cards, batteries, and a tripod for stable shots.
- Power Surge Protector: Protect your RV's electronic devices from power surges by using a power surge protector. This is particularly important when connecting to campground electrical hookups.
- Weather Radio: Stay informed about weather conditions in the area by bringing a weather radio that can receive emergency alerts and provide forecasts.
- Portable Generator: If you plan to camp in areas without electrical hookups, a portable generator can offer you the necessary electrical power for your RV's. Make sure to check campground regulations regarding generator usage.
- Solar Panels: Consider installing solar panels on your RV's roof to harness solar energy and charge your batteries, reducing the reliance on generators or electrical hookups.

Remember to take precautions when using electronic equipment in your RV, such as being mindful of power consumption and ensuring proper ventilation for devices that generate heat.

RV Accessories and their usefulness

Here are 10 useful RV accessories that can enhance your camping experience:

- Leveling Blocks: Leveling blocks help you stabilize your RV and be certain about the fact that it is level. They are essential for setting up your RV on uneven ground, providing stability and preventing appliances from being off balance.
- RV Awning: An RV awning extends the living space outside your RV, providing shade and protection from the sun or light rain.
- RV Surge Protector: A surge protector is crucial for protecting your RV's electrical system from power fluctuations and surges. It safeguards your appliances, electronics, and wiring, preventing potential damage.
- RV Water Filter: Installing a water filter for your RV's fresh water system ensures that the water you use for drinking, cooking, and showering is clean and free from impurities.
- RV Tire Pressure Monitoring System (TPMS): A TPMS constantly monitors the tire pressure and temperature of your RV's tires, providing real-time alerts if there are any abnormalities. It helps improve safety and prevents tire blowouts or damage.
- RV Backup Camera: A backup camera helps you maneuver your RV more safely and effectively. It provides a clear view of what's behind your RV, assisting you during parking, backing up, and lane changes.
- RV GPS Navigation System: A GPS navigation system designed specifically for RVs provides RV-friendly routing, highlighting low-clearance bridges, narrow roads, and RV campgrounds. It helps you navigate with confidence, avoiding potential hazards.
- RV Vent Covers: Vent covers allow you to keep your RV's roof vents open even during rainy weather. They promote ventilation inside your RV, preventing condensation buildup and maintaining a comfortable indoor environment.
- RV Portable Waste Tank: A portable waste tank enables you to empty your RV's gray and black water tanks without having to move your entire RV to a dump station. It is especially useful when camping in areas without sewer hookups.
- RV Patio Mats: Patio mats are designed to be placed outside your RV's entrance, providing a clean and comfortable outdoor space. They help keep dirt and debris outside, allowing you to enjoy a tidy and inviting camping area.
-

10 General RV Camping Accessories – Technology

To conclude this chapter, here are 10 general RV technology camping accessories that can enhance your camping experience:

1. Solar Panels: Solar panels harness the power of the sun to generate electricity, allowing you to charge your RV's batteries and run appliances without relying solely on electrical hookups or generators.
2. Portable Wi-Fi Extender: A portable Wi-Fi extender boosts the signal strength of existing Wi-Fi networks at campgrounds, ensuring a more reliable and stronger internet connection inside your RV.

3. Cell Phone Signal Booster: In areas with weak cell phone reception, a cell phone signal booster amplifies the signal strength, allowing for better call quality, faster data speeds, and improved connectivity.

4. RV Monitoring Systems: These systems provide real-time monitoring of various aspects of your RV, such as battery levels, propane levels, temperature, and security. They often come with mobile apps for convenient access to the information.

5. RV Entertainment System: An RV entertainment system combines a TV, speakers, and a media player, allowing you to enjoy movies, TV shows, music, and streaming services while on the road.

6. RV GPS with Traffic Updates: A GPS system specifically designed for RVs can provide navigation guidance, considering the size and weight of your RV. Additionally, with traffic updates, it helps you avoid congested areas and find the best routes.

7. Smart Thermostat: A smart thermostat enables you to control the temperature inside your RV remotely. You can adjust the heating or cooling settings using a smartphone app, ensuring a comfortable environment upon your arrival.

8. RV Backup Camera with Wireless Monitor: A wireless backup camera with a monitor makes it easier to see what's behind your RV while driving or maneuvering. It enhances safety and simplifies tasks like parking and backing up.

9. Portable Bluetooth Speaker: A portable Bluetooth speaker allows you to enjoy music or podcasts wirelessly from your smartphone or other devices. It's great for outdoor activities or when you want to create a surround sound experience inside your RV.

10. Portable Projector: A portable projector lets you turn any surface into a screen for outdoor movie nights. You can connect it to your smartphone or media player and enjoy a cinematic experience under the stars.

These RV technology camping accessories can add convenience, entertainment, and connectivity to your camping adventures, making your RV experience even more enjoyable.

CHAPTER 4

RV Maintenance Tools. Essential Tools and Equipment for DIY Repairs

Necessary RV repairs equipment

If you're planning to do DIY repairs on your RV, there are several essential tools and equipment you should consider having on hand. Below you may find a full list of any normally utilized tool for RV repairs:

- Screwdrivers: A set of screwdrivers with various sizes and types (Phillips, flathead) will be useful for removing screws and accessing different parts of your RV.
- Pliers: Pliers are versatile tools that can help you grip, twist, and cut wires, as well as handle various fasteners.
- Adjustable wrench: An adjustable wrench permits you to operate with different sizes of nuts and bolts.
- Socket set: A socket set with a range of sizes will come in handy for loosening or tightening bolts and nuts on your RV.
- Multimeter: A multimeter is used to measure electrical voltage, current, and resistance. It can help you diagnose and troubleshoot electrical issues in your RV.
- Electrical tape: Electrical tape is essential for insulating and securing electrical connections.
- Wire cutters and strippers: These tools are useful for cutting and stripping wires when working on electrical systems.
- Silicone sealant: Silicone sealant is great for sealing gaps, cracks, and leaks in your RV, such as around windows or vents.
- Duct tape: Duct tape can be a temporary fix for minor repairs, securing loose items, or patching small holes.
- Lubricants: Having a can of lubricant, such as WD-40 or a silicone-based lubricant, can help free up stuck or squeaky parts.
- Leveling blocks: Leveling blocks are handy for leveling your RV when parked on uneven ground.
- RV sealant and adhesive: These specialized sealants and adhesives are designed specifically for RVs and can be used for repairs on roofs, windows, and other parts of your RV.
- Safety gear: Don't forget to wear appropriate safety gear, such as gloves, safety glasses, and a dust mask when working on repairs.

Essential repair accessories and their usefulness

In addition to tools, there are various accessories that can be useful for DIY RV repairs. These accessories can assist in specific repair tasks or enhance the functionality and convenience of your RV. Here are some commonly used DIY RV repair accessories and their usefulness:

- RV Repair Manuals: RV repair manuals provide detailed instructions, diagrams, and troubleshooting tips for repairing specific makes and models of RVs. They are valuable resources for DIY repairs, guiding you through the repair process.
- RV Awning Repair Kit: An awning repair kit contains patches, adhesive, and other materials for repairing tears or damage to your RV's awning fabric. It can save you money by allowing you to fix minor issues instead of replacing the entire awning.
- RV Caulking Kit: Caulking kits include various sealants and caulks designed for RV use. They are essential for sealing gaps, cracks, or leaks around windows, doors, roof vents, and other areas susceptible to water intrusion.
- RV Roof Repair Kit: Roof repair kits typically contain sealants, patching materials, and instructions for fixing minor leaks or damage on the RV roof. They are handy for addressing small issues before they become major problems.
- RV Slide-Out Lubricant: Slide-outs are common in many RVs and require regular maintenance to ensure smooth operation. Slide-out lubricants reduce friction, preventing wear and tear on the mechanisms and extending the lifespan of your slide-outs.
- RV Water Pressure Regulator: A water pressure regulator can be useful for you to protect your RV's plumbing system by reducing the water pressure coming into your RV. Excessive water pressure can cause damage to pipes, fittings, and appliances, so a regulator ensures a safe and consistent water flow.
- RV Tire Covers: they help extend the life of the tires and prevent cracking or premature deterioration.
- RV Vent Covers: Vent covers allow you to keep your RV's roof vents open even when it's raining. They promote airflow and ventilation inside the RV while preventing water from entering through the vents.
- RV Battery Monitor: A battery monitor helps you keep track of your RV's battery status, including voltage, charge level, and usage. It allows you to monitor and manage your battery power, ensuring you don't run out of electricity while on the road.

To end this chapter, we just want you to remind that the specific accessories you'll need for DIY RV repairs may vary depending on the make and model of your RV and the type of repairs you plan to undertake. It's always a good idea to research and consult resources specific to your RV and seek professional guidance when needed.

CHAPTER 5

Tips for Finding RV-Friendly Gas Stations

Features that a gas station suitable for refueling RVs must have

A gas station suitable for fueling an RV should have certain features to accommodate the specific needs of RV owners. Here are some important features a gas station should have for RV fueling:

- High Canopy or Clearance: RVs are taller than regular vehicles, so the gas station should have a high canopy or clearance to accommodate the height of RVs. This ensures that the RV can easily access the fueling area without the risk of damaging the vehicle or the structure.
- Pumping Space: The fueling area should have enough space for maneuvering large RVs. There should be ample room for the RV to navigate around the pumps, making it easier to position the vehicle for fueling.
- Multiple Fueling Lanes: Having multiple fueling lanes can accommodate RVs of different sizes and allow for quicker service. It helps reduce wait times and provides flexibility for RV owners to choose a suitable pump.
- Easy Access and Exit: The gas station should have suitable entry and exit points that can comfortably accommodate larger vehicles. Wide driveways, easy turning radius, and clear signage can help RV drivers navigate in and out of the station with ease.
- RV-Specific Fueling Area: Some gas stations have designated RV fueling areas, separate from regular vehicle fueling. These areas often have larger pump nozzles, longer hoses, and additional space to accommodate the size of RVs. Look for gas stations that provide dedicated RV fueling spaces for convenience.
- Propane Refilling: Many RVs use propane for various purposes, such as heating, cooking, and refrigeration. A gas station that offers propane refilling services can be convenient for RV owners who need to top up their propane tanks.
- Dump Stations: RVs have wastewater holding tanks that need to be emptied normally. Some gas stations or truck stops have dump stations where RV owners can empty their gray and black water tanks. This feature is especially useful for longer trips when camping grounds or RV parks may not be readily available.
- Adequate Lighting: Adequate lighting in the fueling area is crucial, especially for RV owners who may need to fuel up during nighttime hours. Well-lit stations provide better visibility, ensuring safe fueling and maneuvering.
- Potable Water Source: Some RVers may need to fill their freshwater tanks while on the road. A gas station that provides access to potable water can be convenient for RV owners to replenish their water supply.

- RV-Friendly Amenities: Gas stations with RV-friendly amenities like air compressors, vacuum stations, and propane bottle exchanges can be an added bonus for RV owners, making it a one-stop location for various needs.

These are the main features but, remember to plan your fuel stops in advance, research RV-friendly gas stations along your route, and consult online resources or RV travel apps that provide information on suitable fueling locations for RVs.

Useful apps for finding RV friendly gas station

There are several useful apps available for finding RV-friendly gas stations along your route. These apps provide information on gas stations that can accommodate the needs of RV owners. So, let's see together what the most popular and useful apps are for finding RV-friendly gas stations:

- AllStays Camp & RV: AllStays already mentioned, is a complete device that gives you a wealth of information for RV travelers. It includes a database of RV-friendly gas stations, campgrounds, rest areas, and other amenities. The app allows you to filter search results based on your specific needs and provides detailed information for each location.
- RV Trip Wizard: RV Trip Wizard is a planning app that helps you map out your RV trips. It includes a feature that shows RV-friendly gas stations along your route. The app also provides information on campgrounds, points of interest, and other useful amenities for RV travelers.
- GasBuddy: GasBuddy is a popular app for finding gas stations with the best prices. While it doesn't specifically cater to RVs, it allows users to filter search results by fuel type, including diesel for RVs. GasBuddy provides user-generated reviews and real-time fuel prices to help you find the most suitable gas station along your route.
- iExit: iExit is an app designed to assist travelers in finding amenities, including gas stations, along highways. It provides information on upcoming exits, including RV-friendly gas stations, food options, rest areas, and more. The app is particularly useful for finding gas stations while on the road.
- Roadtrippers: Roadtrippers is a travel planning app that helps you discover interesting stops and attractions along your route. While it primarily focuses on trip planning, it also provides information on RV-friendly gas stations and other services. The app allows you to customize your route and find gas stations that cater to RVs.
- CoPilot RV: CoPilot RV is a navigation app specifically designed for RV travelers. It offers customizable routing options based on your RV's dimensions and provides information on RV-friendly points of interest, including gas stations. The app helps you plan your route with consideration for RV-specific requirements.

These apps can be downloaded from major app stores and provide valuable information to help you find RV-friendly gas stations during your travels. Remember to check user reviews, update the app regularly, and verify the accuracy of the information provided as gas station amenities can change over time.

BOOK 7

RV CAMPING ACROSS THE USA: BEST PARKS, CAMPGROUNDS AND ATTRACTIONS

Welcome to our chapter on carefully selected campgrounds to meet the diverse needs of RV campers. We have carefully crafted this list to offer options that meet a variety of preferences and needs.

The campgrounds we have listed have been experienced by us directly or by Rv enthusiasts we know and trust.

All paid campsites are equipped with WiFi at Overnite Sites and at Park.

Discover the best campsites thought up specifically to make your RV adventure unforgettable.

RV CAMPING IN THE WEST

A
L
A
S
K
A

Mile Marker 13, Chugach National Forest Hope Hwy.

Hope, AK 99605
Official Website:
https://www.fs.usda.gov/chugach
GPS: 60.9297, -149.5432
Number of Sites: 15
Open Seasonally: April-October
Elevation 1,738 ft / 529 m
Max Stay: 14
Tent Camping: Yes

Deadman Lake Campground, Tetlin National Wildlife Refuge

Deadman Lake Campground Rd.
Northway, AK 99764
907-883-5312
Official Website:
https://www.fws.gov/refuge/tetlin/visit-us/activities/camping
GPS: 62.8889, -141.5415
Number of Sites: 15
Open Seasonally: April-October
Elevation: 1,738 ft / 529 m
Max Stay: 14
Tent Camping: Yes

Cabela's Parking Lot

155 W 104th Ave.
Anchorage, AK 99501
907-341-3400
GPS: 61.1274, -149.8814
Pad Type: asphalt
Elevation: 65 ft / 19 m
Max Stay: 2

Not Free Rv Camping

Diamond M Ranch Resort

48500 Diamond M. Ranch Road
Kenai, Alaska 99611
(907) 283-9424
Official website:
https://diamondmranchresort.com/
Spaces Available: 77
Max Length: 70

Amenities and services:

Restroom and Showers
Laundry
Guest Services
Self-Service RV Wash
Fishing Supplies
Rec Hall
Planned Activities
Playground

Alaskan Angler RV Resort & Cabine

15640 Kingsley Rd
Ninilčik, Alaska 99639
(907) 567-3393
Official website:
https://alaskabestrvpark.com/
Daily/Weekly/Monthly **Rates: From 50 to 103 dollars**
Official website:
https://alaskabestrvpark.com
Spaces Available: 58
Max Length: 60

Amenities and services

Dump Station
Emergency Phone
Folding Tent Campers Allowed
Pets Welcome
Tent Camping Allowed
RV Park Model Rentals (8)
Cabin/Cottage Rentals (2)
Dedicated Tenting Area

iFi at Overnite Sites
58 Sites with WiFi
Restroom/Showers ($)
Laundry
RV Supplies
Metered LP Gas
Firewood & Ice
Guest Services
Self-Service RV Wash
Fishing Guides
Fishing Supplies
Onsite Rentals (10)
Enclosed Dog Run
River (Kenai River)
Rec Hall
Nature Trails
Rec Open to the Public

Eagle's Rest RV Park & Cabins

139 E Pioneer Dr
Valdez, Alaska 99686
(907) 835-2373
Official website: https://eaglesrestrv.com/
Daily/Weekly/Monthly Rates: From 45 to 75 dollars
Spaces Available: 197
Max Length: 80

Amenities and services

197 Sites with WiFi
Restroom and Showers
Laundry
Ocean
Fishing
Body Of Water (Prince William Sound)
Horseshoes
Planned Activities
Pets Welcome
Tent Camping Allowed
Partial Handicap Access
Emergency Phone

Anchorage Ship Creek RV Park

150 N Ingra St

Anchorage, AK 99501
(907) 277-0877
Location: 61.22169, -149.86906
Daily/Weekly/Monthly **Rates: From 65 to 75 dollars**
Official website:
https://www.alaskatraveladventures.com/
Spaces Available: 130
Max Length: 60

Amenities and services

Dump Station; Partial Handicap Access
Emergency Phone
Folding Tent Campers Allowed
Pets Welcome
Tent Camping Allowed
Dedicated Tenting Area
130 Sites with WiFi
Restroom and Showers
Laundry
Horseshoes
Outdoor Games
Nature Trails
Bike Rentals
Rec Open to the Public

Tanana Valley Campground

1800 College Road
Fairbanks, AK 99709
(907) 456-7956
Location: 64.51846, -147.45533
Daily/Weekly/Monthly **Rates: From 35 to 40 dollars**
Official website:
https://www.tananavalleycampgroundandrv.com/
Spaces Available: 29
Max Length: 40

Amenities and services

Dump Station
Emergency Phone
Folding Tent Campers Allowed
Pets Welcome
Tent Camping Allowed
Dedicated Tenting Area

29 Sites with WiFi
Restroom and Showers
Laundry
Firewood
Rec Open to the Public

ARIZONA

Free Rv Camping

Forest Road 302 Dispersed Camping

FR-302
Grand Canyon, AZ 86023
928-635-5600
928-635-8200
Official Website:
https://www.fs.usda.gov/kaibab
GPS: 35.9681, -112.1185
Pad Type: dirt
Elevation: 6,660 ft / 2,029 m
Max Stay: 14 /Tent Camping: Yes

Forest Road 688 Dispersed Camping

FR-688
Grand Canyon, AZ 86023
928-635-5600
928-635-8200
Official Website:
https://www.fs.usda.gov/kaibab
GPS: 35.9262, -112.1245
Pad Type: dirt
Elevation: 6,594 ft / 2,009 m
Max Stay: 14/Tent Camping: Yes

Forest Road 611 East Rim Dispersed Camping

Kaibab National Forest
FR-611
North Rim, AZ 86052
928-643-7395
Official Website:
https://www.fs.usda.gov/kaibab
GPS: 36.4394, -112.0789
Pad Type: gravel
Open Seasonally: Yes
Elevation: 8,202 ft / 2,499 m/Max Stay: 14
Tent Camping: Yes

Not Free Rv Camping

Weaver's Needle RV Resort

250 S Tomahawk Rd
Apache Junction, AZ 85119
(480) 982-3683
Location: 33.41214, -111.52808
Daily/Weekly/Monthly **Rates: 60 dollars**
Official website: https://www-weaversneedle-com.
Spaces Available: 200
Max Length: 40

Amenities and services

Partial Handicap Access
Age Restrictions May Apply
Pets Welcome;
No Tents
200 Sites with WiFi
Restroom and Showers
Laundry

Activities/Sports

- ✓ Heated Pool
- ✓ Hot Tub
- ✓ Swimming
- ✓ Horseshoes
- ✓ Rec Hall
- ✓ Planned Activities
- ✓ Outdoor Games
- ✓ Pavilion
- ✓ Shuffleboard
- ✓ Putting Green

Superstition Sunrise RV Resort

702 S Meridian Rd
Apache Junction, AZ 85120
(800) 624-7027
Location: 33.40206, -111.58125
Daily/Weekly/Monthly **Rates: 56 dollars**
Official website: https://www-superstitionsunrise-com./
Spaces Available: 250

Max Length: 48

Amenities and services

Partial Handicap Access
Emergency Phone
Age Restrictions May Apply
RV Age Restrictions
Pets Welcome
No Tents
250 Sites with WiFi
Restroom and Showers
Laundry
Control Access Gate
Ice
Worship Services
Snack Bar
Cable
Guest Services
Self-Service RV Wash
Dog Park

Activities/Sports

- ✓ Heated Pool
- ✓ Hot Tub
- ✓ Swimming; Rec Hall
- ✓ Game Room
- ✓ Planned Activities
- ✓ Pavilion
- ✓ Shuffleboard
- ✓ Exercise Room
- ✓ Pickle Ball

Sunrise RV Resort

1403 W Broadway Ave
Apache Junction, AZ 85120
(480) 983-2500
Location: 33.40682, -111.56092
Daily/Weekly/Monthly **Rates: From 58 to 72 dollars**
Official website:
https://www.robertsresorts.com/resorts/sunrise
Spaces Available: 145
Max Length: 55

Amenities and services

Partial Handicap Access

Age Restrictions May Apply
Does Not Allow Class B
RV Age Restrictions
Pets Welcome
Pets Restriction on Dize
No Tents
WiFi Hotspots (2)
145 Sites with WiFi
Streaming; Restroom and Showers
Laundry
Control Access Gate
Ice
Worship Services
Self-Service RV Wash
Onsite Rentals (10)
Enclosed Dog Run

Activities/Sports

- ✓ Heated Pool
- ✓ Hot Tub
- ✓ Swimming
- ✓ Horseshoes
- ✓ Rec Hall
- ✓ Game Room
- ✓ Planned Activities
- ✓ Outdoor Games
- ✓ Tennis
- ✓ Shuffleboard
- ✓ Exercise Room
- ✓ Pickle Ball

Butterfield RV Resort & Observatory

251 S Ocotillo Ave
Benson, AZ 85602
(520) 586-4400
Location: 31.96720, -110.30677
Daily/Weekly/Monthly **Rates: From 45 to 60 dollars**
Official website: https://www.rv-resort.com/
Spaces Available: 118
Max Length: 55

Amenities and services

Partial Handicap Access
RV Age Restrictions
Pets Welcome
No Tents

RV Park Model Rentals (2)
118 Sites with WiFi
Restroom and Showers
Laundry
RV Supplies
Metered LP Gas
Ice
Self-Service RV Wash
Onsite Rentals (2)
Enclosed Dog Run

/Sports

- ✓ Heated Pool
- ✓ Hot Tub
- ✓ Swimming
- ✓ Rec Hall
- ✓ Game Room
- ✓ Planned Activities
- ✓ Outdoor Games
- ✓ Pavilion
- ✓ Exercise Room
- ✓ Pickle Ball
- ✓ Putting Green

Vista Del Sol RV Resort

3249 Activities Felipe Dr
Bullhead City, AZ 86442
(928) 754-0182
Location: 35.06531, -114.56924
Daily/Weekly/Monthly Rates: From 50 to 61
Official website:
https://www.robertsresorts.com/resorts/vista-del-sol/
Spaces Available: 89
Max Length: 80

Amenities and services

Partial Handicap Access
Age Restrictions May Apply
Does Not Allow Class B Motorhomes
RV Age Restrictions
Pets Welcome
No Tents;
WiFi Hotspots (3)
89 Sites with WiFi
Restroom and Showers
Laundry

Control Access Gate
Escort to Site
Onsite RV Service
Cable
Self-Service RV Wash
Enclosed Dog Run

Activities/Sports

- ✓ Heated Pool
- ✓ Hot Tub
- ✓ Swimming
- ✓ Rec Hall
- ✓ Game Room
- ✓ Planned Activities
- ✓ Exercise Room
- ✓ Pickle Ball

CALIFORNIA

Lucky 7 Casino

Parking Lot
350 North Indian Rd.
Smith River, CA 95567
707-487-7777
Official Website:
https://www.lucky7casino.com
GPS: 41.958, -124.2033
Number of Sites: 8
Pad Type: gravel
Elevation: 65 ft / 19 m

Owens Gorge Road Dispersed Camping

Inyo National Forest
Owens Gorge Rd.
Mammoth Lakes, CA 93546
760-924-5500
760-873-2500
Official Website:
https://www.fs.usda.gov/inyo/
GPS: 37.6318, -118.6574
Pad Type: dirt
Elevation: 7,545 ft / 2,299 m
Max Stay: 14
Tent Camping: Yes

Joshua Tree South Dispersed Camping

Cottonwood Spring Rd.
Chiriaco Summit, CA 92201
760-833-7100
Official Website:
https://www.blm.gov/office/palm-springs-south-coast-field-office
GPS: 33.6745, -115.8019
Pad Type: dirt
Elevation: 1,771 ft / 539 m
Max Stay: 14
Tent Camping: Yes

Bakersfield River Run

3715 Burr St
Bakersfield, CA 93308
(661) 377-3616
Location: 35.37857, -119.04705
Daily/Weekly/Monthly **Rates: From 48 to 90 dollars**
Official website:
https://www.riverrunrvpark.com/
Spaces Available: 71
Max Length: 60

Amenities and services:

Dump Station
Partial Handicap Access
Pets Welcome
Day Max Stay (28)
No Tents
71 Sites with WiFi
Restroom and Showers
Laundr
RV Supplies
Metered LP Gas
Ice
Groceries
Cable
Self-Service
RV Wash
Near NASCAR® Track (8 mi to Kern County Raceway Park)

Activities/Sports

- ✓ Swimming Pool
- ✓ Hot Tub
- ✓ River
- ✓ Body Of Water (Kern River (seasonal))
- ✓ Rec Hall
- ✓ Game Room
- ✓ Pavilion
- ✓ Exercise Room
- ✓ Nature Trails

The Lakes RV & Golf

5001 E Robertson Blvd

Chowchilla, CA 93610
(866) 665-6980
Location: 37.12714, -120.22880
Daily/Weekly/Monthly **Rates: From 45 to 65 dollars**
Official website: https://thelakesrv.com
Spaces Available: 77
Max Length: 77

Amenities and services

Dump Station
Partial Handicap Access
Emergency Phone
RV Age Restrictions
Pets Welcome
No Tents
77 Sites with WiFi
Restroom and Showers
Laundry
Control Access Gate
RV Supplies
Ice
Restaurant
Cocktail Lounge
Golf Carts
Enclosed Dog Run

Activities/Sports

- ✓ Heated Pool
- ✓ Hot Tub
- ✓ Pond
- ✓ Swimming
- ✓ Horseshoes
- ✓ Rec Hall
- ✓ Outdoor Games
- ✓ Golf
- ✓ Driving Range
- ✓ Tennis
- ✓ Mini Golf
- ✓ Putting Green
- ✓ Pickle Ball

Coachella Lakes RV

44-790 Dillon Rd
Coachella, CA 92236
(442) 325-9292
Location: 33.72765, -116.16411

Daily/Weekly/Monthly **Rates: From 49 to 110 dollars**
Official website:
https://coachellalakesrvresort.com/
Spaces Available: 360
Max Length: 80

Amenities and services:

Pets Welcome
No Tents
Cabin/Cottage Rentals (15)
WiFi at Park Supports Streaming
360 Sites with WiFi
Restroom and Showers
Laundry
Control Access Gate
Ice
Onsite Rentals (15)
Enclosed Dog Run

Activities/Sports

- ✓ Swimming Pool
- ✓ Hot Tub
- ✓ Splash Pad
- ✓ Pond
- ✓ Swimming
- ✓ Fishing
- ✓ Horseshoes
- ✓ Rec Hall
- ✓ Playground
- ✓ Shuffleboard
- ✓ Exercise Room
- ✓ Nature Trails
- ✓ Pickle Ball
- ✓ Putting Green

Village Camper Inn RV Park

1543 Parkway Dr
Crescent City, CA 95531
(707) 464-3544
Location: 41.77362, -124.18248
Daily/Weekly/Monthly **Rates: From 43 to 59 dollars**
Official website:
https://www.villagecamperinn.com
Spaces Available: 70
Max Length: 60

Amenities and services

Dump Station; Emergency Phone
Folding Tent Campers Allowed
Pets Welcome
Tent Camping Allowed
Cabin/Cottage Rentals (2)
Overflow Area
Dedicated Tenting Area
WiFi at Park Supports Streaming
On-Site WiFi Tech Support
70 Sites with WiFi
Restroom and Showers
Laundry
Onsite RV Service
Self-Service RV Wash
Onsite Rentals (2)
Horseshoes

Activities/Sports

- ✓ Outdoor Games
- ✓ Tennis
- ✓ Pickle Ball

Pomo RV Park & Campground

17999 Tregoning Lane
Fort Bragg, CA 95437
(707) 964-3373
Location: 39.40455, -123.80663
Daily/Weekly/Monthly Rates: 51 dollars
Official website: https://pomorv.com
Spaces Available: 96
Max Length: 60

Amenities and services:

Dump Station
Emergency Phone
Folding Tent Campers Allowed
Pets Welcome
Tent Camping Allowed
Overflow Area
Dedicated Tenting Area
96 Sites with WiFi
Restroom and Showers
Laundry
RV Supplies
Metered LP Gas

Firewood
Ice
Cable

Activities/Sports

- ✓ Fishing Guides
- ✓ Fishing Supplies
- ✓ Horseshoes
- ✓ Rec Hall
- ✓ Outdoor Games
- ✓ Pavilion

COLORADO

Free Rv Camping

Not Free Rv Camping

Glacier View Overlook Dispersed Camping

Roosevelt National Forest
18851 S St Vrain Dr.
Lyons, CO 80540
303-541-2500
GPS: 40.1659, -105.4581
Pad Type: dirt
Open Seasonally: Yes
Elevation: 8,070 ft / 2,459 m
Max Stay: 14
Tent Camping: Yes

Lake Meredith Reservoir Dispersed Camping

County Park
County Lane 21
Sugar City, CO 81076
Official Website:
https://crowleycounty.colorado.gov/
GPS: 38.2119, -103.6925
Pad Type: dirt
Elevation: 4,232 ft / 1,289 m
Max Stay: 14
Tent Camping: Yes

Madden Peak Road Dispersed Camping

San Juan National Forest
FR-316
Hesperus, CO 81326
970-247-4874
Official Website:
GPS: 37.3476, -108.2016
Pad Type: dirt
Open Seasonally: Late April - December
Elevation: 8,103 ft / 2,469 m
Max Stay: 14
Tent Camping: Yes

Oasis Durango RV Resort

30090 Hwy 160 E
Durango, CO 81303
(970) 247-0783
Location: 37.22839, -107.80282
Daily/Weekly/Monthly **Rates: From 69 to 111 dollars**
Official website:
https://www.robertsresorts.com/resorts/oasis-durango
Spaces Available: 99
Max Length: 80

Amenities and services:

Dump Station
Partial Handicap Access
Limited Facilities – Winter
Folding Tent Campers Allowed
Pets Welcome
Pets Restriction on Size
Tent Camping Allowed
Cabin/Cottage Rentals (27)
Dedicated Tenting Area
99 Sites with WiFi
Restroom and Showers
Laundry
RV Supplies
Metered LP Gas
Ice
Snack Bar
Groceries
Escort to Site
Onsite RV Service
Cable
Onsite Rentals (27)
Enclosed Dog Run

Activities/Sports

✓ Heated Pool
✓ Swimming; Rec Hall
✓ Playground
✓ Pavilion
✓ Pickle Ball
✓ Mini Golf

Sky Ute Fairgrounds & RV Park

200 E Hwy 151
Ignacio, CO 81137
(970) 563-5540
Location: 37.11378, -107.63030
Daily/Weekly/Monthly **Rates: 40 dollars**
Official website:
https://www.skyutefairgrounds.com/
Spaces Available: 60
Max Length: 64

Amenities and services:

Dump Station; Partial Handicap Access
Folding Tent Campers Allowed
Pets Welcome
Tent Camping Allowed
Dedicated Tenting Area
64 Sites with WiFi
Restroom and Showers
Laundry
Onsite RV Service
Self-Service RV Wash
River
Body Of Water (Los Pinos River)

Loveland RV Resort

4421 E Hwy 34
Loveland, CO 80537
(970) 667-1204
Location: 40.40789, -105.01328
Daily/Weekly/Monthly **Rates: From 65 to 82 dollars**
Official website:
https://www.lovelandrvresort.com/
Spaces Available: 156 / Max Length: 60

Amenities and services:

Dump Station
Folding Tent Campers Allowed
Pets Welcome
No Tents
WiFi at Park Supports Streaming
156 Sites with WiFi
Restroom and Showers
Laundry

RV Supplies
Metered LP Gas
Ice
Groceries
Escort to Site
Onsite RV Service
Self-Service RV Wash
Enclosed Dog Run

Activities/Sports

- ✓ Heated Pool
- ✓ Swimming; Horseshoes
- ✓ Rec Hall
- ✓ Game Room
- ✓ Planned Activities
- ✓ Playground
- ✓ Pavilion
- ✓ Mini Golf

Sleeping Ute RV Park

3 Weeminuche Drive
Towaoc, CO 81334
(970) 565-6544
Location: 37.20642, -108.68837
Daily/Weekly/Monthly Rates: From 46 to 55 dollars
Official website:
https://utemountaincasino.com
Spaces Available: 61
Max Length: 62

Amenities and services

Dump Station;
Folding Tent Campers Allowed
Pets Welcome
Tent Camping Allowed
Dedicated Tenting Area
Covered Area w/Picnic Table
61 Sites with WiFi
Restroom and Showers
Laundry
ATM
Machine
RV Supplies
Ice
Snack Bar
Groceries
Restaurant

Cable
Enclosed Dog Run

- ✓ Playground
- ✓ Outdoor Games
- ✓ Pavilion
- ✓ Nature Trails

Activities/Sports
- ✓ Heated Pool
- ✓ Swimming
- ✓ Pavilion
- ✓ Sauna
- ✓ Exercise Room
- ✓ Casino

HTR Durango Campground

1567 CR-207
Durango, CO 81301
(970) 247-5406
Location: 37.29368, -107.94747
Daily/Weekly/Monthly Rates: From 70 to 131 dollars
Official website:
https://www.htrresorts.com/destinations/durango
Spaces Available: 62
Max Length: 50

Amenities and services
Dump Station
Partial Handicap Access
Pets Welcome
Tent Camping Allowed
Cabin/Cottage Rentals (12)
Dedicated Tenting Area
WiFi Hotspots (16)
62 Sites with WiFi
Restroom and Showers
Laundry
RV Supplies
Ice
Groceries
Escort to Site
Onsite Rentals (12)
Enclosed Dog Run
Dog Park

Activities/Sports
- ✓ Heated Pool
- ✓ Stream
- ✓ Swimming
- ✓ Body Of Water (Lightner Creek)

HAWAII

Hawaii offers various options for camp parking, allowing visitors to enjoy the beautiful landscapes and outdoor activities that the islands have to offer. There are several campgrounds and parks across the different islands where you can park your campervan or set up a tent for camping. However, camping in Hawaii does not allow for free camping. To camp in designated areas, a camping permit must be purchased. You can obtain a camping permit for Hawaii County through their official website, Hawaii County Camping Reservation. It is important to plan ahead and purchase your permit in advance. Remember to print out the permit and have it ready to present to park rangers or patrols during your camping trip.

MONTANA

Free Rv Camping

Not Free Rv Camping

Confederate Campground

Canyon Ferry Lake USBR
Lower Confederate Ln
Townsend, MT 59644 /406-475-3921
Official Website:
https://www.usbr.gov/gp/mtao/canyonferry
GPS: 46.4896, -111.5154
Number of Sites: 34
Pad Type: dirt
Elevation: 3,805 ft / 1,159 m
Max Stay: 14 / Tent Camping: Yes

Blackwell Flats Campground

Army Corps Of Engineers
FR 228
Libby, MT 59923
406-293-7751
Official Website:
https://www.nws.usace.army.mil/Missions/C
ivil-Works/Locks-and-Dams/Libby-
Dam/Recreation/
GPS: 48.3686, -115.3226
Number of Sites:7/Elevation: 2,132 ft / 649 m
Max Stay: 14 /Tent Camping: Yes

McGinnis Creek Dispersed Camping

Flathead National Forest
FS 803
Columbia Falls, MT 59912
406-758-5208
Official Website:
https://www.fs.usda.gov/flathead
GPS: 48.5148, -114.1477
Number of Sites: 3
Pad Type: dirt
Open Seasonally: Yes
Elevation: 3,772 ft / 1,149 m
Max Stay: 16 / Tent Camping: Yes

Billings Village RV Park

325 S Billings Blvd
Billings, MT 59101
(406) 248-8685
Location: 45.76357, -108.53542
Daily/Weekly/Monthly **Rates: From 56 to 62 dollars**
Official website: https://bvrvmt.com/
Spaces Available: 79
Max Length: 60

Amenities and services

Emergency Phone
Folding Tent Campers Allowed
Pets Welcome
No Tents
79 Sites with WiFi
Restroom and Showers
Laundry
Onsite RV Service
Cable
Self-Service RV Wash
Playground
Outdoor Games

West Glacier RV

350 River Bend Drive
West Glacier, MT 59936
(844) 868-7474
Location: 48.49660, -113.98389
Daily/Weekly/Monthly **Rates: From 90 to 150 dollars**
Official website:
https://www.glacierparkcollection.com/lod ging/west-glacier-rv-park/
Spaces Available: 102
Max Length: 80

Amenities and services

Partial Handicap Access
Emergency Phone
Folding Tent Campers Allowed
Pets Welcome

No Tents
Cabin/Cottage Rentals (20)
WiFi at Park Supports Streaming
102 Sites with WiFi
Restroom and Showers
Laundry
RV Supplies
Metered LP Gas
Firewood
Ice
Groceries
Escort to Site
Restaurant
Guest Services
Onsite Rentals (20)
Pet Supplies

Activities/Sports

- ✓ Playground
- ✓ Outdoor Games
- ✓ Nature Trails
- ✓ Mini Golf

Ruby Valley Campground & RV Park

2280 MT Hwy 287
Alder, MT 59710
(406) 842-5677
Location: 45.32113, -112.09963
Daily/Weekly/Monthly Rates: From 38 to 53 dollars
Official website:
https://www.rubyvalleycampground.com/
Spaces Available: 37
Max Length: 85

Amenities and services

Dump Station
Emergency Phone
Limited Facilities – Winter
Folding Tent Campers Allowed
Pets Welcome
Tent Camping Allowed
Cabin/Cottage Rentals (5)
Overflow Area
Dedicated Tenting Area
WiFi at Park Supports Streaming
37 Sites with WiFi
Restroom and Showers

Laundry
RV Supplies
Metered LP Gas
Firewood
Ice
Groceries
Escort to Site
Onsite RV Service
Fishing Supplies
Onsite Rentals (5)
Pond

Activities/Sports

- ✓ Fishing
- ✓ Horseshoes
- ✓ Playground
- ✓ Outdoor Games
- ✓ Nature Trails

Fairmont RV Resort

1700 Fairmont Rd
Anaconda, MT 59711
(406) 797-3505
Location: 46.04197, -112.80511
Daily/Weekly/Monthly **Rates: From 60 to 71 dollars**
Official website:
https://www.fairmontrvresort.com
Spaces Available: 39
Max Length: 75

Amenities and services

Dump Station
Emergency Phone
Folding Tent Campers Allowed
Pets Welcome
No Tents
93 Sites with WiFi
Restroom and Showers
Laundry
RV Supplies
Ice
Groceries
Onsite RV Service
Fishing Guides
Fishing Supplies
Pet Supplies
Horseshoes

Activities/Sports
- ✓ Playground
- ✓ Outdoor Games
- ✓ Nature Trails
- ✓ Pickle Ball

Copper Court RV Park

300 North Polk Street
Anaconda, MT 59711
(406) 417-1050
Location: 46.13008, -112.92804
Daily/Weekly/Monthly **Rates: 66 dollars**
Official website:
https://coppercourtrvpark.com
Spaces Available: 103
Max Length: 70

Amenities and services

Dump Station
Partial Handicap Access
Emergency Phone
Folding Tent Campers Allowed
Pets Welcome
Tent Camping Allowed
Cabin/Cottage Rentals (4)
Overflow Area
Dedicated Tenting Area
WiFi at Park Supports Streaming
On-Site WiFi Tech Support
103 Sites with WiFi
Restroom and Showers
Laundry
RV Supplies
Firewood
Ice
Onsite RV Service
Guest Services
Onsite Rentals (4)
Horseshoes
Outdoor Games
Nature Trails

NEVADA

Free Rv Camping

Pahranagat National Wildlife Refuge

Dept. Fish & Wildlife
Great Basin Highway 93
Alamo, NV 89001 / 775-725-3417
Official Website:
https://www.fws.gov/refuge/pahranagat
GPS: 37.2999, -115.1221
Number of Sites: 15
Pad Type: dirt
Open Seasonally: Yes
Elevation: 3,346 ft / 1,019 m
Tent Camping: Yes

Government Wash Dispersed Camping

Lake Mead National Recreation Area
Government Wash Rd.
Boulder City, NV 89005 / 702-293-8990
Official Website:
https://www.nps.gov/lake/planyourvisit/bac
kcountry.htm
GPS: 36.1309, -114.8369
Pad Type: dirt
Elevation: 1,213 ft / 369 m
Max Stay: 15
Tent Camping: Yes

Sacramento Pass Recreation Area

US-50 / Ely, NV 89301 / 775-289-1800
Official Website:
https://www.blm.gov/visit/sacramento-pass-
rec-area
GPS: 39.1215, -114.3049
Number of Sites: 10
Pad Type: dirt
Elevation: 6,692 ft / 2,039 m
Max Stay: 14 / Tent Camping: Yes

Not Free Rv Camping

Lake Mead RV Village at Boulder Beach

268 Lakeshore Drive
Boulder City, NV 89005
(702) 293-2540
Location: 36.03496, -114.80093
Daily/Weekly/**Monthly Rates: From 50 to 70 dollars**
Official website:
https://lakemeadmohaveadventures.com/lake-mead-rv-village/
Spaces Available: 97
Max Length: 100

Amenities and services:

Dump Station
Partial Handicap Access
Emergency Phone
Pets Welcome
No Tents
97 Sites with WiFi
Restroom and Showers
Laundry
RV Supplies
Metered LP Gas
Firewood
Ice
Snack Bar
Groceries
Escort to Site
Sells Fishing License
Lake

Activities/Sports

- ✓ Swimming
- ✓ Fishing
- ✓ Body Of Water (Lake Mead)
- ✓ Horseshoes
- ✓ Rec Hall
- ✓ Planned Activities
- ✓ Nature Trails
- ✓ Rec Open to the Public
- ✓ Kayaking/Canoeing
- ✓ Watersports

Canyon Trail RV Park

1200 Industrial Rd
Boulder City, NV 89005
(702) 293-1200
Location: 35.97750, -114.85030
Daily/Weekly/Monthly **Rates: From 52 to 68 dollars**
Official website:
https://www.canyontrailrvpark.com/
Spaces Available: 106
Max Length: 50

Amenities and services

Dump Station
Partial Handicap Access; Emergency Phone;
Pets Welcome;
Tent Camping Allowed; Dedicated Tenting
Area
WiFi at Park Supports Streaming;
106 Sites with WiFi
Restroom and Showers
Laundry
RV Supplies
Ice
Self-Service RV Wash
Enclosed Dog Run

Activities/Sports

- ✓ Swimming
- ✓ Pool;
- ✓ Hot Tub;
- ✓ Swimming;
- ✓ Horseshoes;
- ✓ Outdoor Games
- ✓ Pavilion
- ✓ Nature Trails

Duck Creek RV Park

6635 Boulder Highway
Las Vegas, NV 89122
(866) 371-9712
Location: 36.08047, -115.02583
Daily/Weekly/Monthly **Rates: From 38 to 65 dollars**
Official website:
https://duckcreekrvparklv.com/
Spaces Available: 10
Max Length: 35

Amenities and services

Partial Handicap Access
Emergency Phone
Pets Welcome
No Tents
10 Sites with WiFi
Restroom and Showers
Laundry
RV Supplies
Metered LP Gas
Ice
Groceries
Near NASCAR® Track (15 mi to Las Vegas
Motor Speedway)
Dog Park

Activities/Sports

- ✓ Heated Pool
- ✓ Hot Tub
- ✓ Swimming
- ✓ Rec Hall
- ✓ Playground

Hitchin' Post RV Park

3640 Las Vegas Blvd North
Las Vegas, NV 89115
(888) 433-8402
Location: 36.22266, -115.08447
Daily/Weekly/Monthly Rates: From 49 to 77
dollars
Official website: https://www.hprvp.com
Spaces Available: 98
Max Length: 70

Amenities and services

Dump Station
Partial Handicap Access
Emergency Phone
Pets Welcome
No Tents
Lodge Room Rentals (13)
98 Sites with WiFi
Restroom and Showers
Laundry
Control Access Gate
ATM Machine
RV Supplies
Ice

Restaurant
Onsite RV Service
Cable
Cocktail Lounge
Self-Service RV Wash
Near NASCAR® Track (7 mi to Las Vegas
Motor Speedway)
Onsite Rentals (13)
Enclosed Dog Run
Dog Washing Station

<u>Activities/Sports</u>
- ✓ Heated Pool
- ✓ Swimming
- ✓ Driving Range
- ✓ Exercise Room
- ✓ Putting Green
- ✓ Casino

Groceries
Restaurant
Cable
Cocktail Lounge
Guest Services
Onsite Rentals (223)
Enclosed Dog Run

<u>Activities/Sports</u>
- ✓ Heated Pool
- ✓ Hot Tub
- ✓ Swimming
- ✓ Rec Hall
- ✓ Exercise Room
- ✓ Nature Trails
- ✓ Casino

Carson Valley RV Resort & Casino

1627 Hwy 395 N
Minden, NV 89423
(800) 321-6983
Location: 38.95660, -119.76958
Daily/Weekly/Monthly **Rates: From 45 to 75 dollars**
Official website:
https://carsonvalleyinn.com/accommodations
Spaces Available: 59
Max Length: 54

<u>Amenities and services:</u>

Dump Station; Partial Handicap Access
Emergency Phone
RV Age Restrictions
Pets Welcome
Day Max Stay (28)
No Tents
Lodge Room Rentals (223)
56 Sites with WiFi
Restroom and Showers
Laundry
ATM Machine
RV Supplies
Ice
Snack Bar

NEW MEXICO

Free Rv Camping

Chosa Primitive Campground

Dillahunty Rd.
Carlsbad, NM 88220
575-234-5972
Official Website:
https://www.nps.gov/places/gumo_chosa_c
ampground_blm.htm
GPS: 32.0885, -104.4321
Pad Type: gravel
Elevation: 3,707 ft / 1,129 m
Max Stay: 14
Tent Camping: Yes

Lake Holloman Dispersed Camping

US-70
Holloman Air Force Base, NM 88330
575-525-4300
Official Website: https://www.blm.gov/new-mexico
GPS: 32.8078, -106.1224
Pad Type: dirt
Elevation: 4,002 ft / 1,219 m
Max Stay: 14
Tent Camping: Yes

Sunset Reef Campground

Washington Ranch Rd.
Carlsbad, NM 88220
575-234-5972
Official Website:
https://www.nps.gov/places/gumo_sunsetre
efcampground_blm.htm
GPS: 32.1095, -104.4253
Number of Sites: 11
Pad Type: gravel
Elevation: 3,608 ft / 1,099 m
Max Stay: 5 /Tent Camping: Yes

Route 66 RV Resort

I40 Exit 140
Albuquerque, NM 87121
(505) 352-8000
Location: 35.02693, -106.95236
Daily/Weekly/Monthly **Rates: From 55 to 65 dollars**
Official website:
https://www.rt66rvresort.com/
Spaces Available: 100
Max Length: 85

Amenities and services:

Partial Handicap Access
Emergency Phone
RV Age Restrictions
Pets Welcome
Day Max Stay (28)
No Tents
WiFi at Park Supports Streaming
100 Sites with WiFi
Restroom and Showers
Laundry
Control Access Gate
ATM Machine
RV Supplies
Metered LP Gas
Firewood / Ice
Restaurant
Cocktail Lounge
Guest Services
Enclosed Dog Run
Dog Park / Dog Washing Station
Heated Pool
Hot Tub

Activities/Sports

- ✓ Swimming
- ✓ Horseshoes
- ✓ Game Room
- ✓ Planned Activities
- ✓ Pavilion
- ✓ Exercise Room
- ✓ Pickle Ball

- ✓ Putting
- ✓ GreenCasino

Isleta Lakes & RV Park

4051 Hwy 47 SE
Albuquerque, NM 87105
(505) 244-8102
Location: 34.94548, -106.67424
Daily/Weekly/Monthly **Rates: From 37 to 53 dollars**
Official website:
https://www.isleta.com/lakes-rv-park/
Spaces Available: 50
Max Length: 60

Amenities and services:

Dump Station
Partial Handicap Access
Folding Tent Campers Allowed
Pets Welcome
No Tents
No Reservations
50 Sites with WiFi;
Restroom and Showers
Laundry
Control Access Gate
ATM Machine
RV Supplies
Ice
Groceries / Restaurant
Cocktail Lounge
Guest Services
Fishing Supplies
Swimming Pool
Pool Extra Fee
Lake

Activities/Sports

- ✓ Swimming
- ✓ Fishing
- ✓ Body Of Water (Isleta Lake)
- ✓ Playground
- ✓ Golf
- ✓ Driving Range
- ✓ Pavilion
- ✓ Sauna
- ✓ Nature Trails
- ✓ Putting Green
- ✓ Casino

Bud's Place RV Park & Cabins

900 Standpipe Rd
Carlsbad, NM 88220
(575) 200-1865
Location: 32.41170, -104.25501
Daily/Weekly/Monthly **Rates: From 42 to 61 dollars**
Official website:
https://clearskiesrvparks.com/location/buds-place/
Spaces Available: 46
Max Length: 70

Amenities and services

Pets Welcome
No Tents
Cabin/Cottage Rentals (12)
WiFi at Park Supports Streaming
46 Sites with WiFi
Restroom and Showers
Laundry / Firewood / Ice
Onsite Rentals (12;)
Dog Park
Pond
Fishing
Horseshoes
Playground

Little Vineyard RV Resort

2901 E Pine St
Deming, NM 88030
(575) 546-3560
Location: 32.26908, -107.72642
Daily/Weekly/Monthly **Rates: 41 dollars**
Official website: https://littlevineyard.com
Spaces Available: 100
Max Length: 70

Amenities and services

Dump Station
Folding Tent Campers Allowed
Pets Welcome
No Tents;
100 Sites with WiFi
Restroom and Showers

Laundry
RV Supplies
Metered LP Gas
Ice
Cable
Enclosed Dog Run

Activities/Sports

- ✓ Heated Pool
- ✓ Hot Tub
- ✓ Rec Hall
- ✓ Game Room
- ✓ Planned Activities
- ✓ Playground

Desert View RV Park

661 Warm Springs Blvd
Elephant Butte, NM 87935
(575) 744-4472
Location: 33.18337, -107.22432
Daily/Weekly/Monthly **Rates: From 40 to 45 dollars**
Official website:
https://www.desertviewrvpark.com
Spaces Available: 71
Max Length: 75

Amenities and services

Folding Tent Campers Allowed
Pets Welcome
No Tents
WiFi at Park Supports Streaming
71 Sites with WiFi
Restroom and Showers
Laundry
RV Supplies
Rec Hall

Activities/Sports

- ✓ Game Room
- ✓ Planned Activities
- ✓ Exercise Room
- ✓ Pickle Ball

O
R
E
G
O
N

Camp Hart Mountain Campground

Hart Mountain Rd
Plush, OR 97637
541-947-3315
541-947-2177
Official Website:
https://onda.org/recommendations/visitors-guide-greater-hart-sheldon-region/
GPS: 42.5428, -119.7734
Number of Sites:9
Pad Type: gravel
Elevation: 4,560 ft / 1,389 m
Max Stay: 14

Lake Abert Pull Out South

US 395
Lakeview, OR 97630
541-947-2177
Official Website:
https://www.blm.gov/oregon-washington
GPS: 42.5298, -120.2329
Pad Type: gravel
Elevation: 4,265 ft / 1,299 m

Annie Creek Sno-Park

Fremont-Winema National Forest
Annie Creek Road
Fort Klamath, OR 97626
541-885-3400
541-947-2151
Official Website:
https://www.fs.usda.gov/recarea/fremont-winema/recarea/?recid=59833
GPS: 42.7612, -122.0588
Open Seasonally: Yes
Elevation: 4,330 ft / 1,319 m
Max Stay: 14
Tent Camping: Yes

Mt View RV on the Oregon Trail

2845 Hughes Ln
Baker City, OR 97814
(541) 523-4824
Location: 44.79564, -117.84140
Daily/Weekly/Monthly **Rates: From 50 to 55 dollars**
Official website: http://www.mtviewrv.com/
Spaces Available: 77
Max length: 70

Amenities and services

Dump Station
Partial Handicap Access
Emergency Phone
Limited Facilities – Winter
Folding Tent Campers Allowed
Pets Welcome
Tent Camping Allowed
Dedicated Tenting Area
Cooking Counters
WiFi at Overnite Sites
77 Sites with WiFi
Restroom and Showers
Laundry
RV Supplies
Metered LP Gas
Ice
Groceries
Cable
Enclosed Dog Run

Activities/Sports
- ✓ Heated Pool
- ✓ Hot Tub
- ✓ Swimming
- ✓ Rec Hall
- ✓ Playground
- ✓ Pavilion

Bend/Sisters Garden RV Resort

67667 Hwy 20
Bend, OR 97703
(541) 516-3036
Location: 44.25039, -121.48825
Daily/Weekly/Monthly **Rates: From 44 to 71 dollars**
Official website:
http://www.bendsistersgardenrv.com/
Spaces Available: 96
Max Length: 70

Amenities and services:

Partial Handicap Access
Emergency Phone
Folding Tent Campers Allowed
Pets Welcome
No Tents
RV Park Model Rentals (3)
Cabin/Cottage Rentals (3)
WiFi at Overnite Sites
96 Sites with WiFi
Restroom and Showers
Laundry
RV Supplies
Metered LP Gas
Firewood / Ice
Groceries
Escort to Site
CableFishing Supplies
Onsite Rentals (6)
Enclosed Dog Run
Heated Pool
Hot Tub
Lake

Activities/Sports
- ✓ Swimming
- ✓ Fishing
- ✓ Body Of Water (Branch Water Lake)
- ✓ Horseshoes
- ✓ Playground
- ✓ Outdoor Games
- ✓ Nature Trails
- ✓ Mini Golf

Boardman Marina & RV Park

1 W Marine Dr

Boardman, OR 97818
(541) 481-7217
Location: 45.84338, -119.70760
Daily/Weekly/Monthly **Rates: 45 dollars**
Official website:
https://boardmanparkandrec.com
Spaces Available: 63
Max Length: 80

(541) 839-3599
Location: 42.94232, -123.29254
Daily/Weekly/Monthly **Rates: From 80 to 81 dollars**
Official website:
https://www.sevenfeathersrvresort.com
Spaces Available: 191
Max Length: 60

Amenities and services

Dump Station
Partial Handicap Access
Limited Facilities – Winter
Folding Tent Campers Allowed
Pets Welcome
Day Max Stay (14)
Tent Camping Allowed
Dedicated Tenting Area
Cooking Counters
Covered Area w/Picnic Table
63 Sites with WiFi
Restroom and Showers
Laundry
Firewood
Ice
Escort to Site
Self-Service RV Wash
River

Amenities and services

Dump Station
Partial Handicap Access
Emergency Phone
Folding Tent Campers Allowed
Pets Welcome
Day Max Stay (28)
No Tents
Teepee/Yurt Rentals (3)
Cabin/Cottage Rentals (6)
191 Sites with WiFi
Restroom and Showers
Laundry
ATM Machine
Metered LP Gas
Ice
Groceries
Escort to Site
Restaurant
Cocktail Lounge
Guest Services
Onsite Rentals (9)
Enclosed Dog Run

Activities/Sports

- ✓ Boating
- ✓ Swimming
- ✓ Fishing
- ✓ Dock
- ✓ Ramp
- ✓ Boat Marina
- ✓ Body Of Water (Columbia River)
- ✓ Horseshoes
- ✓ Playground
- ✓ Pavilion
- ✓ Nature Trails
- ✓ Frisbee Golf
- ✓ Rec Open to the Public
- ✓ Kayaking/Canoeing
- ✓ Watersports

Activities/Sports

- ✓ Heated Pool
- ✓ Hot Tub
- ✓ Stream
- ✓ Body Of Water (Jordan Creek)
- ✓ Horseshoes
- ✓ Planned Activities
- ✓ Playground
- ✓ Pavilion
- ✓ Exercise Room
- ✓ Nature Trails
- ✓ Bike Rentals
- ✓ Rec Open to the Public
- ✓ Casino

Seven Feathers RV Resort

325 Quintioosa Blvd
Canyonville, OR 97417

Logan Road RV Park

4800 NE Logan Rd
Lincoln City, OR 97367
(877) 564-2678
Location: 45.00083, -124.00428
Daily/Weekly/Monthly **Rates: 65 dollars**
Official website:
https://loganroadrvpark.com
Spaces Available: 36
Max Length: 40

Amenities and services

Folding Tent Campers Allowed
Pets Welcome
Day Max Stay (28)
No Tents
WiFi at Park Supports Mobile Devices
36 Sites with WiFi
Restroom and Showers
Laundry
Metered LP Gas
Restaurant
Cable
Cocktail Lounge

Activities/Sports

- ✓ Heated Pool
- ✓ Hot Tub
- ✓ Swimming
- ✓ Game Room
- ✓ Planned Activities
- ✓ Golf
- ✓ Sauna
- ✓ Exercise Room
- ✓ Casino

UTHA

Free Rv Camping

Fillmore WMA Dispersed Campin

Dept. Fish & Wildlife
I-15 Frontage Rd.
Holden, UT 84636
435-865-6100
Official Website:
https://wildlife.utah.gov/wmas.html
GPS: 39.1659, -112.2156
Open Seasonally: May - November
Elevation: 5,479 ft / 1,669 m
Max Stay: 14
Tent Camping: Yes

Dalton Wash Road Dispersed Camping

Dalton Wash Rd.
Virgin, UT 84779
435-688-3200
GPS: 37.2272, -113.115
Pad Type: dirt
Elevation: 4,429 ft / 1,349 m

Smithsonian Butte Dispersed Camping

South Bench Road
Rockville, UT 84763
435-688-3200
Official Website:
https://www.blm.gov/documents/utah/public-room/map/smithsonian-butte-backcountry-byway-map
GPS: 37.1297, -113.0757
Pad Type: dirt
Elevation: 4,527 ft / 1,379 m
Max Stay: 14
Tent Camping: Yes

Not Free Rv Camping

Bryce Canyon Pines Country Store & Campground

Hwy 12 MP 10
Bryce, UT 84764
(435) 834-5441
Location: 37.71169, -112.21724
Daily/Weekly/Monthly **Rates: From 62 to 87 dollars**
Official website: https://bcpines.com/bryce-campgrounds/
Spaces Available: 30
Max Length: 40

Amenities and services:

Emergency Phone
Folding Tent Campers Allowed
Pets Welcome
Tent Camping Allowed
Cabin/Cottage Rentals (4)
Lodge Room Rentals (38)
Overflow Area
Dedicated Tenting Area
WiFi Hotspots (1)
Restroom and Showers
Laundry
RV Supplies
LP Bottles Only
Firewood; Ice
Snack Bar and Groceries
Onsite Rentals (42)
Horseback Riding
Nature Trails

WillowWind RV Park

80 S 1150 W
Hurricane, UT 84737
(435) 635-4154
Location: 37.17520, -113.30953
Daily/Weekly/Monthly **Rates: From 65 to 85 dollars**

Official website:
https://www.willowwindrvpark.com/
Spaces Available: 136
Max Length: 66

Amenities and services

Partial Handicap Access
Emergency Phone
Folding Tent Campers Allowed
Pets Welcome
No Tents
121 Sites with WiFi
Restroom and Showers
Laundry
Metered LP Gas
Ice
Escort to Site
Cable
Guest Services
Enclosed Dog Run
Dog Washing Station
Horseshoes
Rec Hall

Activities/Sports
- ✓ Planned Activities
- ✓ Outdoor Games
- ✓ Exercise Room

Portal RV Resort

1261 N Hwy 191
Moab, UT 84532
(435) 259-6108
Location: 38.59299, -109.56546
Daily/Weekly/Monthly **Rates: From 79 to 147 dollars**
Official website:
https://www.robertsresorts.com/resorts/portal-rv-resort/
Spaces Available: 93
Max Length: 75

Amenities and services

Dump Station
Emergency Phone
Age Restrictions May Apply
RV Age Restrictions
Pets Welcome

No Tents
Cabin/Cottage Rentals (6)
WiFi at Park Supports Streaming
94 Sites with WiFi
Restroom and Showers
Laundry
RV Supplies
Ice
Escort to Site
Cable
Onsite Rentals (6)
Enclosed Dog Run

Park City RV Resort

2200 Rasmussen Rd
Park City, UT 84098
(435) 649-2535
Location: 40.73693, -111.55416
Daily/Weekly/Monthly **Rates: From 65 to 89 dollars**
Official website:
https://www.robertsresorts.com/
Spaces Available: 51
Max Length: 73

Amenities and services

Dump Station
Pets Welcome
No Tents
51 Sites with WiFi
Restroom and Showers
Laundry
Enclosed Dog Run

Activities/Sports
- ✓ Swimming Pool
- ✓ Hot Tub
- ✓ Exercise Room
- ✓ Nature Trails

Lakeside RV Campground

4000 West Center St
Provo, UT 84601
(801) 373-5267
Location: 40.23561, -111.72813
Daily/Weekly/Monthly **Rates: From 59 to 63 dollars**

Official website:
https://lakesidervcampground.com
Spaces Available: 100
Max Length: 65

Amenities and services

Dump Station
Emergency Phone
Folding Tent Campers Allowed
Pets Welcome
Tent Camping Allowed
Dedicated Tenting Area
100 Sites with WiFi
Restroom and Showers
Laundry
RV Supplies
Metered LP Gas
Firewood
Ice
Groceries
Cable
Fishing Supplies
Enclosed Dog Run

Activities/Sports

- ✓ Heated Pool
- ✓ River
- ✓ Fishing
- ✓ Body Of Water (Provo River)
- ✓ Horseshoes
- ✓ Game Room
- ✓ Playground
- ✓ Outdoor Games
- ✓ Pavilion

RV Camping in the Midwest

ILLINOIS

Free Rv Camping

Cracker Barrel

502 Brock Dr
Bloomington, IL 61701
309-829-3155
Official Website:
GPS: 40.4836, -89.0255
Number of Sites: 7
Pad Type: asphalt
Elevation: 754 ft / 229 m
Max Stay: 1
Max Length: 50

Turkey Bayou Campground

Shawnee National Forest
1 Oakwood Bottom Rd.
Pomona, IL 62975
618-833-8576
618-253-7114
Official Website:
https://www.fs.usda.gov/recarea/shawnee/recreation/hunting/recarea/?recid=10676&actid=56
GPS: 37.6848, -89.4109
Number of Sites: 16
Open Seasonally: Yes
Elevation: 328 ft / 99 m
Tent Camping: Yes

Fort Defiance State Park

Illinois State Park
 Write a Review
Fort Defiance Road
Cairo, IL 62914
618-776-5689
Official Website:
https://dnr.illinois.gov/parks/park.fortdefiance.html
GPS: 36.9867, -89.1472
Number of Sites: 16
Pad Type: gravel / Elevation: 295 ft / 89 m

Not Free Rv Camping

Cahokia RV Parque

4060 Mississippi Ave
Cahokia, IL 62206
(618) 332-7700
Location: 38.57372, -90.18798
Daily/Weekly/Monthly **Rates: From 60 to 65 dollars**
Official website:
https://www.cahokiarvparque.com/
Spaces Available: 52
Max Length: 60

Amenities and services

Dump Station
Partial Handicap Access
Folding Tent Campers Allowed
Pets Welcome
No Tents
WiFi Hotspots (1)
52 Sites with WiFi
Restroom and Showers
Laundry
RV Supplies
Metered LP Gas
Firewood
Ice
Restaurant
Onsite RV Service
Self-Service RV Wash

Activities/Sports

- ✓ Swimming Pool
- ✓ Swimming
- ✓ Horseshoes
- ✓ Playground
- ✓ Outdoor Games
- ✓ Pavilion

DraftKings at Casino Queen RV Park

200 South Front St
East St Louis, IL 62201
(800) 777-0777

Location: 38.62620, -90.16856
Daily/Weekly/Monthly **Rates: From 55 to 65 dollars**
Official website:
https://draftkingsatcasinoqueen.com/stay/rv-park/
Spaces Available: 140
Max Length: 70

Overflow Area
Dedicated Tenting Area
310 Sites with WiFi
Restroom and Showers
Laundry
Control Access Gate
ATM Machine
RV Supplies
LP Bottles Only
Firewood
Ice
Snack Bar
Groceries
Escort to Site
Onsite RV Service
Fishing Supplies
Golf Carts
Onsite Rentals (42)

Amenities and services:

Dump Station
Partial Handicap Access
Emergency Phone
Limited Facilities – Winter
Folding Tent Campers Allowed
Pets Welcome
No Tents
140 Sites with WiFi
Showers
Laundry
ATM Machine
Snack Bar
Restaurant
Onsite RV Service
Cocktail Lounge

Activities/Sports

✓ Heated Pool
✓ Hot Tub
✓ Water Slide
✓ Lake
✓ Boating
✓ Swimming
✓ Wading Pool
✓ Fishing
✓ Boat Rental
✓ Paddle Boats
✓ Body Of Water (Paddleboard Lake)
✓ Horseshoes
✓ Rec Hall
✓ Game Room
✓ Planned Activities
✓ Playground
✓ Pavilion
✓ Nature Trails
✓ Mini Golf
✓ Kayaking/Canoeing

O'Connell's RV Campground

970 Green Wing Rd
Amboy, IL 61310
(888) 563-7040
Location: 41.72345, -89.26542
Daily/Weekly/Monthly **Rates: From 59 to 115 dollars**
Official website:
https://www.rvonthego.com/illinois/oconnells-rv-campground/
Spaces Available: 322 / Max Length: 65

Amenities and services

Dump Station
Partial Handicap Access
Emergency Phone
Folding Tent Campers Allowed
Pets Welcome
Tent Camping Allowed
RV Park Model Rentals (30)
Cabin/Cottage Rentals (12)

Thousand Trails Pine Country

5710 Shattuck Rd
Belvidere, IL 61008
(815) 547-5517
Location: 42.23864, -88.77847
Daily Rates: From 52 to 84 dollars

Spaces Available: 95
Max Length: 80

Amenities and services

Dump Station
Mobile Sewer Service
Partial Handicap Access
Emergency Phone
Folding Tent Campers Allowed
Pets Welcome
Tent Camping Allowed
RV Park Model Rentals
Dedicated Tenting Area
30 Sites with WiFi
Restroom and Showers
Laundry
Control Access Gate
Metered LP Gas
Firewood
Ice
Groceries
Onsite RV Service
Onsite Rentals
Pet Supplies
Heated Pool
Pond

Activities/Sports

- ✓ Swimming
- ✓ Wading Pool
- ✓ Fishing
- ✓ Horseshoes
- ✓ Rec Hall
- ✓ Game Room
- ✓ Planned Activities
- ✓ Playground
- ✓ Outdoor Games
- ✓ Pavilion
- ✓ Shuffleboard
- ✓ Nature Trails
- ✓ Bounce Pillow
- ✓ Lawn Bowling

Kamp Komfort RV Park & Campground

21408 N 600 East Rd
Carlock, IL 61725
(309) 376-4411
Location: 40.59546, -89.15647
Daily Rates: From 40 to 45 dollars
Official website:
https://kampkomfortcampground.com
Spaces Available: 68
Max Length: 70

Amenities and services

Dump Station
Partial Handicap Access
Emergency Phone
Pets Welcome
No Tents
68 Sites with WiFi
Restroom and Showers
Laundry
RV Supplies
Firewood
Ice
Snack Bar
Escort to Site
Onsite RV Service

Activities/Sports

- ✓ Swimming Pool
- ✓ Horseshoes
- ✓ Playground
- ✓ Outdoor Games
- ✓ Pavilion

INDIANA

Blackwell Horsecamp

Hoosier National Forest
Tower Ridge Road
Heltonville, IN 47436
812-275-5987
866-302-4173
Official Website:
https://www.fs.usda.gov/recarea/hoosier/recreation/horseriding-camping/recarea/?recid=41516&actid=30
GPS: 39.0175, -86.3899
Pad Type: gravel
Elevation: 787 ft / 239 m
Max Stay: 14 / Tent Camping: Yes

Indiana Dunes National Park Visitor Center

1215 IN-49
Porter, IN 46304
219-926-2255
219-395-1882
Official Website:
https://www.nps.gov/indu/index.htm
GPS: 41.6342, -87.0544
Number of Sites: 20
Pad Type: asphalt
Elevation: 656 ft / 199 m / Max Stay: 1

RV Hall of Fame & Musuem

21565 Executive Parkway
Elkhart, IN 46514
800-378-8694
574-293-2344
Official Website:
GPS: 41.7292, -85.8812
Pad Type: asphalt
Open Seasonally: April-October
Elevation: 754 ft / 229 m / Max Stay: 2

lkhart Campground

25608 CR 4 E
Elkhart, IN 46514
(574) 264-2914
Location: 41.73844, -85.95911
Daily Rates: From 30 to 70 dollars
Official website:
https://elkhartcampground.com/
Spaces Available: 314
Max Length: 70

Amenities and services

Dump Station
Partial Handicap Access
Emergency Phone
Folding Tent Campers Allowed
Pets Welcome
No Tents
Cabin/Cottage Rentals (9)

WiFi at Park Supports Streaming
238 Sites with WiFi
Restroom and Showers
Laundry
RV Supplies
Metered LP Gas
Firewood
Ice
Worship Services
Groceries
Onsite RV Service
Cable
Staffed RV Wash
Onsite Rentals (9)
Enclosed Dog Run
Dog Park
Pet Supplies

Activities/Sports
- ✓ Heated Pool
- ✓ Swimming
- ✓ Horseshoes
- ✓ Rec Hall
- ✓ Playground
- ✓ Outdoor Games
- ✓ Pavilion
- ✓ Exercise Room
- ✓ Nature Trails
- ✓ Pickle Ball
- ✓ Mini Golf

Caboose Lake Campground

3657 West US Hwy 24
Remington, IN 47977
(219) 261-3828
Location: 40.76555, -87.11518
Daily Rates: From 59 to 74 dollars
Official website:
https://www.cabooselake.com/
Spaces Available: 105
Max Length: 75

Amenities and services

Dump Station
Partial Handicap Access
Limited Facilities – Winter
Folding Tent Campers Allowed
Pets Welcome
No Tents
Teepee/Yurt Rentals (3)
Cabin/Cottage Rentals (8)
105 Sites with WiFi
Restroom and Showers
Laundry
Control Access Gate
RV Supplies
Metered LP Gas; Firewood; Ice
Snack Bar
Escort to Site
Onsite RV Service
Fishing Supplies
Golf Carts
Onsite Rentals (11)
Pet Supplies

Hidden Paradise Campground

802 East Jefferson St
St Paul, IN 47272
(765) 525-6582

Location: 39.42318, -85.62453
Daily Rates: From 50 to 65 dollars
Official website:
https://hiddenparadisecampground.com/
Spaces Available: 113
Max Length: 70

Amenities and services

Dump Station; Mobile Sewer Service
Partial Handicap Access
Emergency Phone
Limited Facilities – Winter
Folding Tent Campers Allowed
Pets Welcome
Tent Camping Allowed
Cabin/Cottage Rentals (6)
Overflow Area Dedicated Tenting
Area;Covered Area w/Picnic Table;
WiFi Hotspots (3); 105 Sites with WiFi
Restroom and Showers
Laundry
RV Supplies; Firewood; Ice; Snack Bar
Groceries; Onsite RV Service
Fishing Supplies
Golf Carts
Onsite Rentals (6)
Water Slide
Lake

Activities/Sports

- ✓ Swimming
- ✓ Fishing
- ✓ Paddle Boats
- ✓ Body Of Water (Dream Lake)
- ✓ Horseshoes
- ✓ Planned Activities
- ✓ Playground
- ✓ Outdoor Games
- ✓ Pavilion
- ✓ Nature Trails
- ✓ Watersports

Rising Star Casino Resort & RV Park

777 Rising Star Drive
Rising Sun, IN 47040
(800) 472-6311
Location: 38.95291, -84.84679

Daily/Weekly/Monthly **Rates: From 39 to 54 dollars**
Official website:
https://www.risingstarcasino.com
Spaces Available: 56
Max Length: 50

Amenities and services

Partial Handicap Access
Pets Welcome
Day Max Stay (10)
No Tents
Lodge Room Rentals (294)
56; Sites with WiFi;
Restroom and Showers
Laundry
Control Access Gate
ATM Machine; Ice; Snack Bar;
Restaurant; Escort to Site;
Onsite RV Service; Cable; Cocktail
Lounge; Complimentary Breakfast;
Guest Services;
Onsite Rentals (294)
Enclosed Dog Run

Activities/Sports

- ✓ Heated Pool
- ✓ River; Swimming
- ✓ Body Of Water (Ohio River)
- ✓ Golf;
- ✓ Pavilion
- ✓ Sauna
- ✓ Shuffleboard
- ✓ Exercise Room
- ✓ Rec Open to the Public
- ✓ Casino

Follow the River RV Resort

12273 Markland Town Rd
Florence, IN 47020
(812) 427-3330
Location: 38.78279, -84.98149
Daily/Weekly/Monthly **Rates: From 53 to 63 dollars**
Official website:
http://www.followtherivervresort.com

Spaces Available: 136
Max Length: 85

<u>Amenities and services</u>
Partial Handicap Access;
Limited Facilities – Winter;
Pets Welcome;
No Tents; Cabin/Cottage Rentals (6);
130; Sites with WiFi;
Restroom and Showers;
Laundry; RV Supplies;
Metered LP Gas; Firewood; Ice; Groceries;
Onsite RV Service; Self-Service RV Wash;
Fishing Supplies;
Near NASCAR® Track (6 mi to Kentucky Speedway)
Onsite Rentals (6)
Enclosed Dog Run

<u>Activities/Sports</u>
- ✓ Heated Pool
- ✓ Pond
- ✓ Swimming
- ✓ Fishing
- ✓ Horseshoes
- ✓ Rec Hall
- ✓ Game Room
- ✓ Planned Activities
- ✓ Playground
- ✓ Pavilion
- ✓ Nature Trails
- ✓ Bounce Pillow

I O W A

Free Rv Camping

Jones Creek Pond

Loess Hills State Forest
32023 County Hwy E60
Moorhead, IA 51558
712-456-2924
Official Website
GPS: 41.8715, -95.9257
Number of Sites: 5
Pad Type: gravel
Open Seasonally: Yes
Elevation: 1,115 ft / 339 m

David Bates Memorial Park

33155 305th St.
Union, IA 50258
641-648-9878
641-648-4361
Official Website:
https://www.mycountyparks.com/county/hardin/Park/David-Bates-Memorial-Park.aspx
GPS: 42.2618, -93.0579
Pad Type: grass
Elevation: 918 ft / 279 m

Eagle Lake State Game Management Area

Dept. Fish & Wildlife
260th Street
Britt, IA 50423
515-725-8200
Official Website: https://www.iowadnr.gov/
GPS: 43.1377, -93.7294

Not Free Rv Camping

Interstate RV Park

8448 N. Fairmount St
Davenport, IA 52806
(563) 386-7292
Location: 41.60589, -90.63126
Daily/Weekly/Monthly **Rates: From 40 to 50 dollars**
Official website: https://iowarvpark.com/
Spaces Available: 56
Max Length: 75

Amenities and services

Dump Station
Emergency Phone
Pets Welcome
No Tents
56 Sites with WiFi
Restroom and Showers
Laundry
RV Supplies
Groceries
Escort to Site
Guest Services
Self-Service RV Wash

Activities/Sports

- ✓ Swimming Pool
- ✓ Swimming
- ✓ Horseshoes
- ✓ Rec Hall
- ✓ Game Room
- ✓ Playground

Crossroads RV Park

708 S Iris St.
Mount Pleasant, IA 52641
(319) 385-9737
Location: 40.95789, -91.52507
Daily/Weekly/Monthly **Rates: 40 dollars**
Official website: https://xrdsrv.com/
Spaces Available: 34
Max Length: 90

Amenities and services

Dump Station
Partial Handicap Access
Emergency Phone
Folding Tent Campers Allowed
Pets Welcome
No Tents
WiFi at Park Supports Streaming
34 Sites with WiFi
Restroom and Showers
Laundry
RV Supplies
Metered LP Gas
Rec Hall

Activities/Sports

- ✓ Game Room
- ✓ Playground
- ✓ Outdoor Games
- ✓ Pavilion
- ✓ Nature Trails

R Campground

1910 Clark St
Charles City, IA 50616
(641) 257-0549
Location: 43.05873, -92.66175
Daily/Weekly/Monthly **Rates: From 26 to 34 dollars**
Official website: https://rcampground.com/
Spaces Available: 62
Max Length: 92

Amenities and services:

Dump Station
Folding Tent Campers Allowed
Pets Welcome
Tent Camping Allowed
Dedicated Tenting Area
62 Sites with WiFi
Restroom and Showers
Laundry
Metered LP Gas
Firewood
Escort to Site
Self-Service RV Wash
River

Activities/Sports

- ✓ Fishing
- ✓ Body Of Water (Cedar River)
- ✓ Horseshoes

- ✓ Playground
- ✓ Pavilion
- ✓ Nature Trails
- ✓ Kayaking/Canoeing

Amana RV Park & Event Center

3850 C St
Amana, IA 52203
(319) 622-7616
Location: 41.81396, -91.87819
Daily/Weekly/Monthly **Rates: From 38 to 40 dollars**
Official website:
https://amanarvpark.com/?utm_source=GoodSam
Spaces Available: 425
Max Length: 75

Amenities and services

Dump Station
Partial Handicap Access
Emergency Phone
Folding Tent Campers Allowed
Pets Welcome
Tent Camping Allowed
Overflow Area
Dedicated Tenting Area
400 Sites with WiFi
Restroom and Showers
Laundry
RV Supplies
Metered LP Gas
Firewood
Ice
Escort to Site
Guest Services
Horseshoes
Rec Hall
Playground
Outdoor Games
Pavilion
Nature Trails

Shady Brook Camping & RV Adventures

36026 Jewel Court
Earlham, IA 50072
(515) 238-1998
Location: 41.49157, -94.12298
Daily/Weekly/Monthly **Rates: From 42 to 65 dollars**
Official website:
https://www.shadybrookcampinghunting.com
Spaces Available: 23
Max Length: 47

Amenities and services

Dump Station
Mobile Sewer Service
Partial Handicap Access
Emergency Phone
Limited Facilities – Winter
Folding Tent Campers Allowed
Pets Welcome
Tent Camping Allowed
Teepee/Yurt Rentals (1)
RV Park Model Rentals (2)
Cabin/Cottage Rentals (2)
Dedicated Tenting Area
Privacy Barrier
Covered Area w/Picnic Table
WiFi Hotspots (1)
23 Sites with WiFi
Restroom and Showers
Control Access Gate
LP Bottles Only
FirewoodIce
Onsite RV Service
Onsite Rentals (5)
Dog Park
Stream

Activities/Sports

- Fishing
- Body Of Water (Bear Creek)
- Game Room
- Playground
- Outdoor Games
- Nature Trails

A R K A N S A S

176

| Free Rv Camping | Not Free Rv Camping |

Leavenworth State Fishing Lake

Dept. Fish & Wildlife
248 St
Tonganoxie, KS 66086
785-887-6882
Official Website:
https://ksoutdoors.com/KDWP-Info/Locations/State-Fishing-Lakes/Northeast-Region/Leavenworth
GPS: 39.1255, -95.1548
Elevation: 984 ft / 299 m
Max Stay: 14
Tent Camping: Yes

Chase State Fishing Lake

Dept. Fish & Wildlife
1130 Lake Road
Cottonwood Falls, KS 66846
620-767-5900
Official Website:
https://www.heartoftheflinthills.com/
GPS: 38.3669, -96.592
Pad Type: gravel
Elevation: 1,246 ft / 379 m
Tent Camping: Yes

Davis Park Campground

City Park
600 E. Kansas Avenue
Greensburg, KS 67054
620-723-1110
Official Website:
https://www.greensburgks.org/residents/parks-recreation
GPS: 37.6073, -99.2831
Number of Sites: 10
Pad Type: grass
Elevation: 2,198 ft / 669 m

Deer Creek Valley RV Park

3140 SE 21st Street
Topeka, KS 66607
(785) 357-8555
Location: 39.03068, -95.63377
Daily/Weekly/Monthly **Rates: 48 dollars**
Official website:
http://www.deercreekvalleyrvpark.com/?utm_source=GoodSam
Spaces Available: 59
Max Length: 59

Amenities and services
Dump Station
Partial Handicap Access
Emergency Phone
Pets Welcome
No Tents
59 Sites with WiFi
Restroom and Showers
Laundry
Control Access Gate
Metered LP Gas
Ice
Escort to Site
Onsite RV Service
Cable
Dog Park

Activities/Sports
- Heated Pool
- Swimming
- Horseshoes
- Rec Hall
- Playground
- Outdoor Games

Air Capital RV Park

609 E 47th St South
Wichita, KS 67216
(316) 201-1250
Location: 37.60778, -97.33006
Daily/Weekly/Monthly **Rates: From 52 to 63 dollars**

Official website: https://www.aircapital-rvpark.com/?utm_source=GoodSam
Spaces Available: 90
Max Length: 70

Partial Handicap Access
Emergency Phone
RV Age Restrictions
Pets Welcome
No Tents
90 Sites with WiFi
Restroom and Showers
Laundry
Escort to Site
Onsite RV Service
Cable
Guest Services
Self-Service RV Wash
Rec Hall
Playground

All Seasons RV Park

15520 W Maple Street
Goddard, KS 67052
(316) 722-1154
Location: 37.67903, -97.52080
Daily/Weekly/Monthly **Rates: From 42 to 45 dollars**
Official website:
https://www.allseasonsrvcampground.com/
Spaces Available: 30
Max Length: 65

Amenities and services

Dump Station
Emergency Phone
Folding Tent Campers Allowed
Pets Welcome
Tent Camping Allowed
Dedicated Tenting Area
WiFi at Park Supports Streaming
30 Sites with WiFi
Restroom and Showers
Laundry
RV Supplies
Metered LP Gas

Ice
Groceries
Onsite RV Service
Cable
Dog Park
Horseshoes
Rec Hall

Activities/Sports

- Playground
- Outdoor Games
- Nature Trails

Covered Wagon RV Resort

803 S Buckeye
Abilene, KS 67410
(785) 263-2343
Location: 38.90743, -97.21406
Daily/Weekly/Monthly **Rates: 42 dollars**
Official website:
https://coveredwagonrvks.com
Spaces Available: 45
Max Length: 70

Amenities and services

Dump Station
Folding Tent Campers Allowed
Pets Welcome
No Tents
WiFi at Park Supports Streaming
45 Sites with WiFi
Restroom and Showers
Laundry
RV Supplies
LP Bottles Only
Escort to Site

Activities/Sports

- Swimming Pool
- Swimming
- Horseshoes
- Playground
- Outdoor Games
- Pavilion

Flatland RV Park

2200 N Buckeye Ave
Abilene, KS 67410

(785) 263-1684
Location: 38.93866, -97.21496
Daily/Weekly/Monthly **Rates: 40 dollars**
Official website: https://24-7stores.com/flatland-rv-park
Spaces Available: 21
Max Length: 90

Amenities and services

Partial Handicap Access
Emergency Phone
WiFi at Park Supports Streaming
WiFi Hotspots (1)
21 Sites with WiFi
Restroom and Showers
Laundry
Control Access Gate
RV Supplies
Metered LP Gas
Ice
Groceries
Restaurant
Dog Park

MICHIGAN

Free Rv Camping

Green Road Dispersed Camping

Nordhouse Dunes Wilderness
Green Rd.
Free Soil, MI 49411
231-577-8902
Official Website:
https://www.fs.usda.gov/recarea/hmnf/recarea/?recid=18770
GPS: 44.1037, -86.4011
Pad Type: dirt
Elevation: 623 ft / 189 m
Tent Camping: Yes

Cooper Creek Road

Nordhouse Dunes Wilderness
Cooper Creek Rd.
Free Soil, MI 49411
231-723-2211
231-775-2421
Official Website:
https://www.fs.usda.gov/recarea/hmnf/recarea/?recid=18770
GPS: 44.1126, -86.3686
Pad Type: dirt
Elevation: 656 ft / 199 m
Max Stay: 14 / Tent Camping: Yes

French Farm Lake Campground

Dept. Natural Resources
French Farm Lake Road
Mackinaw City, MI 49701
Official Website:
http://www.michigandnr.com/publications/pdfs/huntingwildlifehabitat/sga/French_Farm_Lake_Flooding_SWMA_map.pdf
GPS: 45.764, -84.7684
Number of Sites: 6 / Elevation: 590 ft / 179 m

Not Free Rv Camping

Chain O'Lakes Campground

7231 S M 88
Bellaire, MI 49615
(231) 533-8432
Location: 44.92464, -85.18591
Daily/Weekly/Monthly **Rates: From 42 to 44 dollars**
Official website:
https://www.chainolakescamp.com/
Spaces Available: 37
Max Length: 100

Amenities and services

Dump Station
Emergency Phone
Folding Tent Campers Allowed
Pets Welcome
Tent Camping Allowed
Cabin/Cottage Rentals (10)
Dedicated Tenting Area
37 Sites with WiFi
Restroom and Showers
Laundry
RV Supplies
Firewood
Ice
Groceries
Onsite RV Service
Self-Service RV Wash
Onsite Rentals (10)

Activities/Sports

- Heated Pool
- Horseshoes
- Planned Activities
- Playground
- Outdoor Games
- Pavilion
- Nature Trails

Wayne County Fairgrounds RV Park

10871 Quirk Rd
Belleville, MI 48111
(734) 697-7002
Location: 42.22324, -83.49414
Daily/Weekly/Monthly **Rates: From 23 to 44 dollars**
Official website:
https://www.waynecountyfairgrounds.net/
Spaces Available: 107
Max Length: 68

Amenities and services

Dump Station
Mobile Sewer Service
Emergency Phone
Folding Tent Campers Allowed
Pets Welcome / Dog Park
No Tents
WiFi at Park Supports Streaming
107 Sites with WiFi
Restroom and Showers
Laundry
Metered LP Gas
Firewood / Ice
Escort to Site
Enclosed Dog Run
Horseshoes
Pavilion
Rec Open to the Public

Thousand Trails Bear Cave

4085 Bear Cave Rd
Buchanan, MI 49107
(888) 563-7040
Location: 41.88121, -86.36321
Daily/Weekly/Monthly **Rates: 78 dollars**
Official website: https://thousandtrails.com/
Spaces Available: 88
Max Length: 40

Amenities and services

Dump Station
Mobile Sewer Service
Partial Handicap Access

Emergency Phone
Folding Tent Campers Allowed
Pets Welcome
No Tents
RV Park Model Rentals (3)
WiFi at Park Supports Streaming
87 Sites with WiFi
Restroom and Showers
Laundry
Control Access Gate
Firewood / Ice
Self-Service RV Wash
Fishing Supplies
Golf Carts
Onsite Rentals (3)

Activities/Sports

- ✓ Heated Pool
- ✓ River
- ✓ Boating
- ✓ Swimming
- ✓ Fishing
- ✓ Dock
- ✓ Ramp
- ✓ Boat Rental
- ✓ Body Of Water (St Joseph River)
- ✓ Rec Hall
- ✓ Game Room
- ✓ Planned Activities
- ✓ Playground
- ✓ Outdoor Games
- ✓ Pavilion
- ✓ Shuffleboard
- ✓ Nature Trails
- ✓ Kayaking/Canoeing

Waffle Farm Campgrounds

790 N Union City Rd
Coldwater, MI 49036
(517) 278-4315
Location: 41.99736, -85.02510
Daily/Weekly/Monthly Rates: From 35 to 60 dollars
Official website: https://wafflefarm.com
Spaces Available: 110
Max Length: 75

Dump Station
Partial Handicap Access
Emergency Phone
Folding Tent Campers Allowed
Pets Welcome
Tent Camping Allowed
Cabin/Cottage Rentals (2)
Overflow Area
Dedicated Tenting Area
WiFi at Park Supports Streaming
On-Site WiFi Tech Support
110 Sites with WiFi
Restroom and Showers
RV Supplies
Metered LP Gas
Firewood / Ice
Groceries
Onsite RV Service
Cable; Self-Service RV Wash
Fishing Supplies
Golf Carts
Onsite Rentals (2)
Lake

Activities/Sports

- ✓ Boating
- ✓ Swimming
- ✓ Fishing
- ✓ Ramp
- ✓ Boat Rental
- ✓ Paddle Boats
- ✓ Body Of Water (Craig-Morrison Chain of 7 Lakes)
- ✓ Horseshoes
- ✓ Game Room
- ✓ Planned Activities
- ✓ Playground
- ✓ Outdoor Games
- ✓ Pavilion
- ✓ Nature Trails
- ✓ Pedal Carts
- ✓ Bounce Pillow
- ✓ Mini Golf
- ✓ Kayaking/Canoeing; Watersports

Hungry Horse Family Campground

2016 142nd Avenue
Dorr, MI 49323
(616) 681-9836
Location: 42.72209, -85.74385
Daily/Weekly/Monthly **Rates: From 44 to 58 dollars**
Official website:
https://hungryhorsecampground.com/?utm_source=GoodSam
Spaces Available: 73
Max Length: 70

Amenities and services

Dump Station
Mobile Sewer Service
Partial Handicap Access
Emergency Phone
Folding Tent Campers Allowed
Pets Welcome
Tent Camping Allowed
Cabin/Cottage Rentals (4)
Overflow Area
WiFi at Park Supports Streaming
71 Sites with WiFi
Restroom and Showers
Laundry
RV Supplies
Firewood
Ice
Worship Services
Groceries
Self-Service RV Wash
Onsite Rentals (4)

Activities/Sports

- Heated Pool
- Swimming
- Wading Pool
- Horseshoes
- Game Room
- Planned Activities
- Playground
- Pavilion
- Shuffleboard
- Nature Trails
- Bounce Pillow

MINNESOTA

Six Mile Campground

Chippewa National Forest
6 Mile Lake Road Northeast
Bena, MN 56626
218-335-8600
Official Website:
https://www.fs.usda.gov/activity/chippewa/recreation/camping-cabins/?recid=26620&actid=34
GPS: 47.3094, -94.1231
Pad Type: grass
Elevation: 1,279 ft / 389 m
Max Stay: 14
Tent Camping: Yes

Franklin Landing Campground

City Park
Sioux Trail
Franklin, MN 55333
507-557-2259
Official Website:
https://franklinmn.us/activities.html
GPS: 44.5192, -94.8844
Elevation: 853 ft / 259 m
Max Stay: 7
Tent Camping: Yes

Saint Croix Welcome Center & Rest Area

Rest Area
14100 I-94
Lakeland, MN 55082
651-296-0733
Official Website:
https://www.exploreminnesota.com/profile/st-croix-welcome-center/2077
GPS: 44.9502, -92.8191
Pad Type: concrete - Elevation: 885 ft / 269 m

Not Free Rv Camping

Old Barn Resort

24461 Heron Road
Preston, MN 55965
(507) 467-2512
Location: 43.71067, -92.03295
Daily/Weekly/Monthly **Rates: From 45 to 61 dollars**
Official website:
https://www.barnresort.com/
Spaces Available: 125
Max Length:60

Amenities and services

Dump Station
Partial Handicap Access
Folding Tent Campers Allowed
Pets Welcome
Tent Camping Allowed
Lodge Room Rentals (4)
WiFi Hotspots (1)
1 Sites with WiFi
Restroom and Showers
Restroom/Showers ($)
Laundry
ATM Machine
RV Supplies
Firewood
Ice
Snack Bar
Groceries
Restaurant
Cocktail Lounge
Golf Carts
Onsite Rentals (4)

Activities/Sports

- ✓ Heated Pool
- ✓ River
- ✓ Swimming
- ✓ Fishing
- ✓ Body Of Water (Root River)
- • Horseshoes
- • Playground
- • Outdoor Games

Grand Hinckley RV Resort

1326 Fire Monument Rd
Hinckley, MN 55037
(800) 472-6321
Location: 46.00981, -92.91177
Daily/Weekly/Monthly Rates: **From 39 to 99 dollars**
Official website:
https://grandcasinomn.com/lodging/rv-resort/
Spaces Available: 191
Max Length: 65

Amenities and services:

Partial Handicap Access
Emergency Phone
Pets Welcome
No Tents
Cabin/Cottage Rentals (50)
191 Sites with WiFi
Restroom and Showers
Laundry
Control Access Gate
ATM Machine
RV Supplies
Firewood
Ice
Snack Bar
Groceries
Restaurant
Cable
Cocktail Lounge
Guest Services
Self-Service RV Wash
Onsite Rentals (50)

Activities/Sports

- ✓ Heated Pool
- ✓ Swimming
- ✓ Horseshoes
- ✓ Playground
- ✓ Outdoor Games
- ✓ Golf

- ✓ Driving Range
- ✓ Pavilion
- ✓ Sauna
- ✓ Shuffleboard
- ✓ Exercise Room
- ✓ Casino

Royal Oaks RV Park

2874 Fenske Farm Lane SE
Bemidji, MN 56601
(218) 751-8357
Location: 47.43380, -94.86197
Daily/Weekly/Monthly **Rates: From 50 to 60 dollars**
Official website:
https://royaloaksrvpark.com/
Spaces Available: 84
Max Length: 80

Amenities and services:

Pets Welcome
No Tents
84 Sites with WiFi
Restroom and Showers
Laundry
RV Supplies
Firewood
Ice
Escort to Site
Cable
Guest Services
Dog Park
Horseshoes
Rec Hall

Activities/Sports

- ✓ Game Room
- ✓ Planned Activities
- ✓ Playground
- ✓ Outdoor Games
- ✓ Pavilion
- ✓ Nature Trails
- ✓ Bike Rentals

Ringler Family Campground

3064 Hwy 23
Brook Park, MN 55007

(320) 293-7075
Location: 45.92897, -93.13796
Daily/Weekly/Monthly **Rates: 35 dollars**
Spaces Available: 17
Max Length: 70

Amenities and services:

Dump Station
Pets Welcome
Tent Camping Allowed
Cabin/Cottage Rentals (3)
Dedicated Tenting Area
Restroom and Showers
Onsite Rentals (3)
Pond

Activities/Sports

- ✓ Swimming
- ✓ Horseshoes
- ✓ Playground
- ✓ Frisbee Golf
- ✓ Kayaking/Canoeing

Stony Point Resort RV Park & Campground

1326 Fire Monument Rd
5510 US 2 NW
Cass Lake, MN 56633
(218) 335-6311
Location: 47.37891, -94.57393
Daily/Weekly/Monthly **Rates: From to dollars**
Official website:
https://www.stonyptresortcasslake.com
Spaces Available: 60
Max Length: 85

Amenities and services:

Dump Station
Mobile Sewer Service
Partial Handicap Access
Folding Tent Campers Allowed
Pets Welcome
Tent Camping Allowed
Cabin/Cottage Rentals (11)
Overflow Area
Dedicated Tenting Area
Covered Area w/Picnic Table

60 Sites with WiFi
Restroom and Showers
Laundry
ATM Machine
RV Supplies
Metered LP Gas
Firewood
Ice
Groceries
Restaurant
Cocktail Lounge
Self-Service RV Wash
Fishing Guides
Fishing Supplies
Onsite Rentals (11)
Sells Fishing Licenses

Activities/Sports

- ✓ Heated Pool
- ✓ Hot Tub
- ✓ Splash Pad
- ✓ Lake
- ✓ Boating
- ✓ Swimming
- ✓ Wading Pool
- ✓ Fishing
- ✓ Dock
- ✓ Ramp
- ✓ Boat Rental
- ✓ Boat Marina
- ✓ Paddle Boats
- ✓ Body Of Water (Cass Lake)
- ✓ Game Room
- ✓ Planned Activities
- ✓ Playground
- ✓ Outdoor Games
- ✓ Pavilion
- ✓ Sauna
- ✓ Nature Trails
- ✓ Bike Rentals
- ✓ Kayaking/Canoeing
- ✓ Watersports

MISSOURI

Free Rv Camping

Whetstone Camping Area

Whetstone Creek Conservation Area
CR-1003
Williamsburg, MO 63388
573-254-3330
Official Website:
https://mdc.mo.gov/discover-
nature/places/whetstone-creek-ca
GPS: 38.9665, -91.7302
Pad Type: gravel
Elevation: 787 ft / 239 m
Max Stay: 14
Tent Camping: Yes

Pinewoods Lake Campground

Mark Twain National Forest
Ellsinore, MO 63937
573-785-1475
573-364-4621
Official Website:
https://www.fs.usda.gov/recarea/mtnf/recar
ea/?recid=21828
GPS: 36.9219, -90.7736
Number of Sites: 16
Pad Type: asphalt
Elevation: 787 ft / 239 m
Max Stay: 14
Tent Camping: Yes

Lamar City Park

Maple Street
Lamar, MO 64759
417-682-5422
417-682-5851
Official Website:
GPS: 37.4857, -94.2826
Pad Type: grass
Elevation: 918 ft / 279 m
Max Stay: 7

Not Free Rv Camping

Bull Creek RV Park

150 Haney Rd
Branson, MO 65616
(417) 605-2038
Location: 36.71259, -93.19984
Daily/Weekly/Monthly **Rates: From 59 to 110 dollars**
Official website:
https://www.bullcreekrv.com/
Spaces Available: 39
Max Length: 60

Amenities and services

RV Age Restrictions
Pets Welcome
No Tents
RV Park Model Rentals (4)
WiFi at Park Supports Streaming
39 Sites with WiFi
Control Access Gate
Firewood
Onsite Rentals (4)
Enclosed Dog Run
Stream

Activities/Sports

✓ Fishing
✓ Body Of Water (Bull Creek)
✓ Horseshoes
✓ Playground
✓ Outdoor Games
✓ Rec Open to the Public

America's Best Campground

499 Buena Vista Rd
Branson, MO 65616
417 3364399
Location: 36.68314, -93.25802
Daily/Weekly/Monthly Rates: From 59 to 64
dollars
Official website:
https://americasbestcampground.com/
Spaces Available: 149

Max Length: 70

Dump Station
Partial Handicap Access
Folding Tent Campers Allowed
Pets Welcome
No Tents
Cabin/Cottage Rentals (12)
WiFi at Park Supports Streaming
155 Sites with WiFi
Restroom and Showers
Laundry
RV Supplies
Metered LP Gas
Firewood
Ice
Groceries
Escort to Site
Cable
Guest Services
Self-Service RV Wash
Golf Carts
Onsite Rentals (12)
Dog Park

Activities/Sports

- ✓ Swimming Pool
- ✓ Hot Tub
- ✓ Swimming
- ✓ Horseshoes
- ✓ Game Room
- ✓ Planned Activities
- ✓ Playground
- ✓ Outdoor Games
- ✓ Pavilion

Musicland Kampground

116 Gretna Rd
Branson, MO 65616
(417) 334-0848
Location: 36.64064, -93.28022
Daily/Weekly/Monthly **Rates: From 43 to 59 dollars**
Official website:
https://www.musiclandkampground.com/
Spaces Available: 101
Max Length: 60

Amenities and services:

Dump Station
Emergency Phone
No Tents
RV Park Model Rentals (2)
Cabin/Cottage Rentals (5)
WiFi at Park Supports Streaming
101 Sites with WiFi
Restroom and Showers
Laundry
Control Access Gate
RV Supplies
Metered LP Gas
Firewood
Ice
Escort to Site
Onsite RV Service
Guest Services
Onsite Rentals (7)
Enclosed Dog Run

Activities/Sports

- ✓ Swimming Pool
- ✓ Swimming
- ✓ Rec Hall
- ✓ Playground
- ✓ Outdoor Games

Cooper Creek Resort & Campground

471 Cooper Creek Road
Branson, MO 65616
(417) 334-4871
Location: 36.61832, -93.24798
Daily/Weekly/Monthly **Rates: From 42 to 55 dollars**
Official website:
https://coopercreekresort.com
Spaces Available: 74
Max Length: 70

Amenities and services

Emergency Phone
Limited Facilities - Winter
Folding Tent Campers Allowed
Pets Welcome
No Tents
RV Park Model Rentals (3)
Cabin/Cottage Rentals (22)

WiFi at Park Supports Streaming
74 Sites with WiFi
Restroom and Showers
Laundry
RV Supplies
LP Bottles Only
Firewood
Ice
Groceries
Onsite RV Service
Cable
Fishing Guides
Fishing Supplies
Onsite Rentals (25)
Sells Fishing Licenses

Partial Handicap Access
Limited Facilities - Winter
Folding Tent Campers Allowed
Pets Welcome
Tent Camping Allowed
Overflow Area
Dedicated Tenting Area
Covered Area w/Picnic Table
25 Sites with WiFi
Restroom and Showers
Laundry
RV Supplies
Metered LP Gas
Firewood
Snack Bar
Escort to Site
Dog Park
Horseshoes

Activities/Sports

- ✓ Swimming Pool
- ✓ Lake
- ✓ Boating
- ✓ Swimming
- ✓ Fishing
- ✓ Dock
- ✓ Boat Rental
- ✓ Boat Marina
- ✓ Body Of Water (Lake Taneycomo)
- ✓ Horseshoes
- ✓ Game Room
- ✓ Playground
- ✓ Outdoor Games
- ✓ Pavilion
- ✓ Nature Trails
- ✓ Kayaking/Canoeing

Activities/Sports

- ✓ Outdoor Games
- ✓ Pavilion
- ✓ Mini Golf
- ✓ Rec Open to the Public

Cozy C RV Campground

16733 US-54
Bowling Green, MO 63334
(573) 324-3055
Location: 39.37291, -91.16341
Daily/Weekly/Monthly **Rates: From 40 to 80 dollars**
Official website:
http://www.cozyccampground.com
Spaces Available: 45
Max Length: 60

Amenities and services

Dump Station

189

NEBRASKA

Streeter Park Campground

Streeter Park
1201 Q Street
Aurora, NE 68818
402-694-6992
Official Website:
http://cityofaurora.org/departments/parks-and-recreation/streeter-park/
GPS: 40.8732, -98.0027
Number of Sites: 18
Pad Type: gravel
Elevation: 1,738 ft / 529 m
Max Stay: 4 (Tent Camping: Yes

Bayard City Campground

E. 11th St.
Bayard, NE 69334
308-586-1121
Official Website:
https://www.cityofbayard.net/vnews/display.v/SEC/Departments%7CParks%20and%20Recreation%3E%3ECamping
GPS: 41.7622, -103.322
Number of Sites: 3
Pad Type: gravel
Elevation: 3,805 ft / 1,159 m /Max Stay: 14

Oliver Reservoir State Recreation Area

Dept. Natural Resources
Lincoln Highway
Kimball, NE 69145
308-254-2377
Official Website:
https://www.spnrd.org/oliverreservoir
GPS: 41.2313, -103.8241
Number of Sites: 48
Open Seasonally: March - October
Elevation: 4,822 ft / 1,469 m
Max Stay: 14 / Tent Camping: Yes

Not Free Rv Camping

Pine Grove RV Park

23403 Mynard Rd
Greenwood, NE 68366
(402) 944-3550
Location: 40.97150, -96.39558
Daily/Weekly/Monthly **Rates: From 32 to 63 dollars**
Official website:
https://pinegrovervpark.com/
Spaces Available: 100
Max Length: 80

Amenities and services:

Dump Station
Folding Tent Campers Allowed
Pets Welcome
Tent Camping Allowed
Cabin/Cottage Rentals (1)
Overflow Area
Dedicated Tenting Area
Covered Area w/Picnic Table
100 Sites with WiFi
Restroom and Showers
Laundry
RV Supplies
Firewood / Ice
Snack Bar
Groceries
Cocktail Lounge
Onsite Rentals (1)
Enclosed Dog Run
Pet Supplies

Activities/Sports

- Swimming Pool
- Wading Pool
- Horseshoes
- Rec Hall
- Planned Activities
- Playground
- Outdoor Games
- Tennis
- Bounce Pillow
- Pickle Ball

Robidoux RV Park

585 Five Rocks Rd
Gering, NE 69341
(308) 436-2046
Location: 41.81134, -103.67503
Daily/Weekly/Monthly Rates: **From 37 to 46 dollars**
Official website: https://www.gering.org/
Spaces Available: 42
Max Length: 65

Amenities and services

Dump Station
Folding Tent Campers Allowed
Pets Welcome
Tent Camping Allowed
Overflow Area
Dedicated Tenting Area
42 Sites with WiFi
Restroom and Showers
Laundry
Enclosed Dog Run
Rec HallPlayground

Camp A Way RV Park

200 Campers Circle
Lincoln, NE 68521
(402) 476-2282
Location: 40.85753, -96.71765
Daily/Weekly/Monthly Rates: **From 45 to 99 dollars**
Official website: https://campaway.com/
Spaces Available: 96
Max Length: 70

Amenities and services:

Dump Station
Folding Tent Campers Allowed
Pets Welcome Dog Park Pet Supplies
Tent Camping Allowed
Cabin/Cottage Rentals (2)
Overflow Area
Dedicated Tenting Area
92 Sites with WiFi
Restroom and Showers
Laundry

RV Supplies
Firewood / Ice
Groceries
Escort to Site
Cable
Guest Services
Self-Service RV Wash
Onsite Rentals (2)
Enclosed Dog Run

Activities/Sports

- ✓ Heated Pool
- ✓ Hot Tub
- ✓ Water Slide
- ✓ Horseshoes
- ✓ Game Room
- ✓ Planned Activities
- ✓ Playground
- ✓ Outdoor Games
- ✓ Pedal Carts
- ✓ Bike Rentals
- ✓ Bounce Pillow
- ✓ Frisbee Golf

Holiday RV Park & Campground

601 E. Halligan Dr
North Platte, NE 69101
(308) 534-2265
Location: 41.11124, -100.75597
Daily/Weekly/Monthly **Rates: From 52 to 72 dollars**
Official website: https://holidayrvparkne.com
Spaces Available: 92
Max Length: 70

Amenities and services

Dump Station
Emergency Phone
Limited Facilities - Winter
Folding Tent Campers Allowed
Pets Welcome Dog Park
Tent Camping Allowed
Overflow Area
Dedicated Tenting Area
WiFi Hotspots (6)
92 Sites with WiFi
Restroom and Showers

Laundry
RV Supplies
Ice / Groceries
Cable
Guest Services
Staffed RV Wash
Self-Service RV Wash

Activities/Sports

- ✓ Heated Pool
- ✓ Swimming
- ✓ Horseshoes
- ✓ Playground
- ✓ Outdoor Games
- ✓ Pavilion
- ✓ Exercise Room
- ✓ Mini Golf

Ashland RV Campground

1301 Ash Street
Ashland, NE 68003
(402) 401-4231
Location: 41.04569, -96.36242
Daily/Weekly/Monthly Rates: **From 45 to 55 dollars**
Official website:
https://ashlandrvcampground.com
Spaces Available: 30
Max Length: 90

Amenities and services

Dump Station
Folding Tent Campers Allowed
Pets Welcome
Day Max Stay (14)
No Tents
WiFi at Park Supports Streaming
30 Sites with WiFi
Restroom and Showers
Laundry / Firewood
Playground
Nature Trails / Frisbee Golf

NORTH DAKOTA

Scoria Pit Dispersed Camping

Little Missouri National Grassland
West River Rd.
Medora, ND 58645
701-227-7800
Official Website:
https://www.fs.usda.gov/recarea/dpg/recarea/?recid=79469
GPS: 46.9454, -103.5886
Pad Type: dirt / Open Seasonally: Yes
Elevation: 2,591 ft / 789 m
Max Stay: 14 / Tent Camping: Yes

Painted Canyon Visitor Center Parking Lot

Theodore Roosevelt National Park
I-94 Exit 32
Belfield, ND 58622
Official Website:
https://www.nps.gov/thro/planyourvisit/visitorcenters.htm
GPS: 46.8952, -103.381
Number of Sites: 30
Pad Type: asphalt
Elevation: 2,755 ft / 839 m

Michigan City Park

rd Street
Michigan, ND 58259
701-351-8113
701-259-2553
Official Website:
https://michigannd.com/?SEC=12097A82-0F78-4CE5-9C66-2F4940D89E01
GPS: 48.0263, -98.1276
Number of Sites: 4
Pad Type: grass / Elevation: 1,509 ft / 459 m
Tent Camping: Yes

Not Free Rv Camping

Red Trail Campground

Red Trail Street
Medora, ND 58645
(800) 621-4317
Location: 46.90896, -103.52471
Daily/Weekly/Monthly Rates: **From 40 to 57 dollars**
Official website:
https://redtrailcampground.com/
Spaces Available: 120
Max Length: 60

Amenities and services

Dump Station
Partial Handicap Access
Emergency Phone
Folding Tent Campers Allowed
Pets Welcome
Tent Camping Allowed
Overflow Area
Dedicated Tenting Area
120 Sites with WiFi
Restroom and Showers
Laundry
RV Supplies
Ice
Groceries
Escort to Site
Cable
Guest Services
Self-Service RV Wash
Pet Supplies
Playground
Outdoor Games
Pavilion

Jamestown Campground

3605 80th Ave SE
Jamestown, ND 58401
(701) 252-6262
Location: 46.89122, -98.77707
Daily/Weekly/**Monthly Rates: From 30 to 40 dollars**

Official website:
https://jamestowncampground.com/
Spaces Available: 38
Max Length: 75

Amenities and services:

Dump Station
Emergency Phone
Folding Tent Campers Allowed
Pets Welcome
Tent Camping Allowed
Cabin/Cottage Rentals (2)
Overflow Area
Dedicated Tenting Area
38 Sites with WiFi
Restroom and Showers
Laundry
RV Supplies
Firewood
Ice
Guest Services
Onsite Rentals (2)
Dog Park
Horseshoes

Activities/Sports

- ✓ Playground
- ✓ Outdoor Games
- ✓ Pavilion
- ✓ Nature Trails

Governors' RV Park Campground

2050 Governors' Dr
Casselton, ND 58012
(888) 847-4524
Location: 46.87633, -97.21260
Daily/Weekly/Monthly **Rates: From 49 to 64 dollars**
Official website:
https://governorsinnnd.com/
Spaces Available: 65
Max Length: 70

Amenities and services

Dump Station
Partial Handicap Access
Folding Tent Campers Allowed

Pets Welcome
Pet Restriction on Quantity
Tent Camping Allowed
Lodge Room Rentals (55)
44 Sites with WiFi
Restroom and Showers
Laundry
ATM Machine
Ice
Restaurant
Cocktail Lounge
Guest Services
Onsite Rentals (55)

Activities/Sports

- ✓ Heated Pool
- ✓ Pool Extra Fee ($)
- ✓ Hot Tub
- ✓ Water Slide
- ✓ Wading Pool
- ✓ Game Room
- ✓ Exercise Room
- ✓ Rec Open to the Public

North Park RV Campground

2320 Buckskin Dr
Dickinson, ND 58601
(701) 227-8498
Location: 46.90662, -102.77717
Daily/Weekly/Monthly **Rates: 47 dollars**
Official website:
https://www.campnorthpark.com
Spaces Available: 70
Max Length: 110

Amenities and services

Dump Station
Partial Handicap Access
Emergency Phone
Folding Tent Campers Allowed
Pets Welcome
Tent Camping Allowed
Dedicated Tenting Area
70 Sites with WiFi
Restroom and Showers
Laundry
Escort to Site

Guest Services
Self-Service RV Wash
Outdoor Games
Bike Rentals

A Prairie Breeze RV Park

2810 158th St NE
Menoken, ND 58558
(701) 224-8215
Location: 46.83446, -100.54261
Daily/Weekly/Monthly Rates: **From 35 to 40 dollars**
Official website:
Spaces Available: 42
Max Length: 80

Amenities and services

Dump Station
Partial Handicap Access
Folding Tent Campers Allowed
Pets Welcome
Tent Camping Allowed
Dedicated Tenting Area
WiFi at Park Supports Streaming
42 Sites with WiFi
Restroom and Showers
Laundry
Horseshoes

OHIO

Hidden Hollow Campground

Fernwood State Forest
11 Township Road 181
Bloomingdale, OH 43910
740-266-6021 / 877-247-8733
Official Website: https://ohiodnr.gov/go-and-do/plan-a-visit/find-a-property/fernwood-state-forest
GPS: 40.3344, -80.7642
Number of Sites: 22 / Pad Type: asphalt
Elevation: 1,148 ft / 349 m
Max Stay: 14 / Tent Camping: Yes

Hook Lake Campground

Jesse Owens State Park & Wildlife Area
9160 N. St. Rt. 83
McConnelsville, OH 43756
740-962-1205
Official Website: https://ohiodnr.gov/go-and-do/plan-a-visit/find-a-property/jesse-owens-state-park-campground
GPS: 39.7279, -81.7079
Pad Type: mixed
Open Seasonally: April 1 to mid of December
Elevation: 853 ft / 259 m
Max Stay: 14 / Tent Camping: Yes

Sand Hollow Campground

Jesse Owens State Park & Wildlife Area
9290 State Route 284
McConnelsville, OH 43756
740-439-3521
Official Website: https://ohiodnr.gov/go-and-do/plan-a-visit/find-a-property/jesse-owens-state-park-campground
GPS: 39.7349, -81.7317
Pad Type_ mixed / Tent Camping: Yes
Open Seasonally: April 1 to mid of December
Elevation: 853 ft / 259 m / Max Stay: 14

Not Free Rv Camping

Sun Valley Campground

10105 CR-550
Chillicothe, OH 45601
(740) 775-3490
Location: 39.38219, -83.08528
Daily/Weekly/Monthly **Rates: From 45 to 60 dollars**
Spaces Available: 32
Max Amps: 50
Max Length: 100

Amenities and services

Dump Station
Limited Facilities - Winter
Folding Tent Campers Allowed
Pets Welcome
Tent Camping Allowed
Overflow Area
Dedicated Tenting Area
Covered Area w/Picnic Table
32 Sites with WiFi
estroom and Showers
Firewood
Escort to Site
Onsite RV Service
Pond
Fishing
Game Room
Playground
Outdoor Games
Pavilion

Camp Cedar

5158 Kings Island Drive
Mason, OH 45040
(513) 701-9635
Location: 39.35849, -84.2581
Daily/Weekly/Monthly **Rates: From 49 to 142 dollars**
Official website: https://visitcampcedar.com
Spaces Available: 164
Max Amps: 50
Max Length: 56

Amenities and services

Partial Handicap Access
Pets Welcome
No Tents
Cabin/Cottage Rentals (73)
On-Site WiFi Tech Support
164 Sites with WiFi
Restroom and Showers
Laundry
Control Access Gate
ATM Machine
RV Supplies
LP Bottles Only
Firewood
Ice
Snack Bar
Groceries
Restaurant
Cocktail Lounge
Guest Services
Golf Carts
Onsite Rentals (73)

Activities/Sports

- ✓ Heated Pool
- ✓ Water Slide
- ✓ Water Umbrella
- ✓ Swimming
- ✓ Wading Pool
- ✓ Playground
- ✓ Outdoor Games
- ✓ Exercise Room
- ✓ Nature Trails
- ✓ Lawn Bowling
- ✓ Pickle Ball

Countryside Campground

2687 State Route 43
Mogadore, OH 44260
(330) 628-1212
Location: 41.06194, -81.34738
Daily/Weekly/Monthly **Rates: From 51 to 56 dollars**
Official website:
https://countrysidecampgrounds.com/
Spaces Available: 30
Max Length: 74

Amenities and services

Dump Station
Mobile Sewer Service
Emergency Phone
Folding Tent Campers Allowed
Pets Welcome
Tent Camping Allowed
RV Park Model Rentals (3)
Cabin/Cottage Rentals (3)
WiFi at Overnite Sites $
30 Sites with WiFi
Restroom and Showers
Laundry
Control Access Gate
RV Supplies
Metered LP Gas
Firewood
Ice
Snack Bar
Groceries
Onsite RV Service
Fishing Supplies
Golf Carts
Onsite Rentals (6)
Enclosed Dog Run
Dog Park
Sells Fishing Licenses

Activities/Sports

Heated Pool
Lake
Swimming
Fishing
Electric Motors Only
Body Of Water (Mogadore Reservoir)
Game Room
Planned Activities
Playground
Outdoor Games
Nature Trails
Mini Golf
Kayaking/Canoeing

Cherokee Park Campground

3064 State Route 43
Mogadore, OH 44260
(330) 673-1964

Location: 41.07184, -81.33937
Daily/Weekly/Monthly **Rates: From to dollars**
Official website:
https://cherokeeparkcampground.com
Spaces Available: 30
Max Length: 50

Amenities and services

Dump Station
Partial Handicap Access
Emergency Phone
Folding Tent Campers Allowed
Pets Welcome
Tent Camping Allowed
30 Sites with WiFi
Restroom and Showers
Laundry
Metered LP Gas
Firewood
Ice
Escort to Site
Onsite RV Service
Self-Service RV Wash
Pond

Activities/Sports

✓ Fishing
✓ Paddle Boats
✓ Horseshoes
✓ Rec Hall
✓ Game Room
✓ Planned Activities
✓ Playground
✓ Outdoor Games
✓ Pavilion
✓ Shuffleboard
✓ Pedal Carts
✓ Bike Rentals
✓ Frisbee Golf

Sauder Village Campground

22611 SR 2
Archbold, OH 43502
(800) 590-9755
Location: 41.54320, -84.30272

Daily/Weekly/Monthly **Rates: From 32 to 56 dollars**
Official website: https://saudervillage.org
Spaces Available: 77
Max Length: 75

Amenities and services

Dump Station
Partial Handicap Access
Emergency Phone
Folding Tent Campers Allowed
Pets Welcome
Tent Camping Allowed
Lodge Room Rentals (98)
Overflow Area
Dedicated Tenting Area
77 Sites with WiFi
Restroom and Showers
Laundry
Firewood / Ice
Groceries
Restaurant
Onsite RV Service
Guest Services
Onsite Rentals (98)

Activities/Sports

- ✓ Heated Pool
- ✓ Hot Tub
- ✓ Splash Pad
- ✓ Pond
- ✓ Swimming
- ✓ Fishing
- ✓ Horseshoes
- ✓ Game Room
- ✓ Planned Activities
- ✓ Playground
- ✓ Outdoor Games
- ✓ Pavilion
- ✓ Sauna
- ✓ Shuffleboard
- ✓ Nature Trails

SOUTH DAKOTA

Free Rv Camping

Nomad View Dispersed Camping

Buffalo Gap National Grassland
Hwy 240
Wall, SD 57790
605-279-2126 / 308-432-0300
GPS: 43.8931, -102.2385
Pad Type: grass
Open Seasonally: Yes
Elevation: 2,985 ft / 909 m
Max Stay: 14 / Tent Camping: Yes

Steer Pasture Overlook Dispersed Camping

Buffalo Gap National Grassland
Hwy 240
Wall, SD 57790
605-279-2125 / 308-432-0300
Official Website:
https://www.ioverlander.com/places/135551-steer-pasture-overlook-dispersed-camping
GPS: 43.919, -102.2384
Pad Type: grass / Open Seasonally: Yes
Elevation: 2,887 ft / 879 m
Max Stay: 14 / Tent Camping: Yes

Dude Ranch Lakeside Use Area

Dept. Fish & Wildlife
County Highway 6
Chamberlain, SD 57325
605-223-7660
Official Website: https://gfp.sd.gov/lakeside-use-areas/
GPS: 43.7813, -99.4253
Pad Type: gravel / Open Seasonally: Yes
Elevation: 1,345 ft / 409 m
Max Stay: 7
Tent Camping: Yes

Not Free Rv Camping

Oasis Campground

605 East SD Hwy16
Oacoma, SD 57365
(800) 675-6959
Location: 43.80205, -99.38755
Daily/Weekly/Monthly **Rates: From 60 to 70 dollars**
Official website: https://oasiscampsd.com
Spaces Available: 75
Max Length: 65

Amenities and services

Dump Station
Partial Handicap Access
Folding Tent Campers Allowed
Pets Welcome
Tent Camping Allowed
Cabin/Cottage Rentals (8)
Dedicated Tenting Area
75 Sites with WiFi
Restroom and Showers
Laundry
RV Supplies
Firewood
Ice
Guest Services
Onsite Rentals (8)

Activities/Sports

Heated Pool
River
Swimming
Body Of Water (Missouri)
Playground
Outdoor Games
Pavilion

Beaver Lake Campground

12005 US Hwy 16
Custer, SD 57730
(605) 673-2464
Location: 43.73967, -103.65685
Daily/Weekly/Monthly **Rates: From 55 to 89 dollars**

Official website:
https://beaverlakecampground.net
Spaces Available: 89
Max Length: 60

Amenities and services

Dump Station
Mobile Sewer Service
Folding Tent Campers Allowed
Pets Welcome
Tent Camping Allowed
Cabin/Cottage Rentals (9)
Overflow Area
Dedicated Tenting Area
WiFi Hotspots (2)
88 Sites with WiFi
Restroom and Showers
Laundry
RV Supplies
Metered LP Gas
Firewood
Ice
Groceries
Escort to Site
Onsite RV Service
Cable
Guest Services
Onsitc Rentals (9)
Dog Park

Activities/Sports

- ✓ Heated Pool
- ✓ Swimming
- ✓ Horseshoes
- ✓ Rec Hall
- ✓ Playground
- ✓ Outdoor Games
- ✓ Pavilion

Rafter J Bar Ranch Camping Resort

12325 Rafter J Rd.
Hill City, SD 57745
(605) 574-2527
Location: 43.89461, -103.59104
Daily/Weekly/Monthly **Rates: From 63 to 103 dollars**
Official website: https://www.rafterj.com

Spaces Available: 180
Max Amps: 50
Max Length: 80

Amenities and services

Dump Station
Emergency Phone
Folding Tent Campers Allowed
Pets Welcome
No Tents
Cabin/Cottage Rentals (27)
On-Site WiFi Tech Support
45 Sites with WiFi
Restroom and Showers
Laundry
ATM Machine
RV Supplies
Metered LP Gas
Firewood
Ice
Snack Bar
Groceries
Escort to Site
Onsite RV Service
Guest Services
Fishing Supplies
Onsite Rentals (27)

Activities/Sports

- ✓ Heated Pool
- ✓ Hot Tub
- ✓ Stream
- ✓ Swimming
- ✓ Fishing
- ✓ Body Of Water (Spring Creek)
- ✓ Planned Activities
- ✓ Playground
- ✓ Outdoor Games
- ✓ Pavilion
- ✓ Nature Trails

Rafter J Bar Ranch Camping Resort

4110 S Hwy 16 / Mt Rushmore Rd
Rapid City, SD 57701
(605) 342-2751
Location: 44.04317, -103.24416

Daily/Weekly/Monthly **Rates: From 45 to 67 dollars**
Official website: https://rcrvpark.com
Spaces Available: 72
Max Length: 60

Amenities and services

Emergency Phone
Folding Tent Campers Allowed
Pets Welcome
Tent Camping Allowed
Cabin/Cottage Rentals (6)
Lodge Room Rentals (3)
Overflow Area
Dedicated Tenting Area
WiFi at Park Supports Streaming
On-Site WiFi Tech Support
72 Sites with WiFi
Restroom and Showers
Laundry
Control Access Gate
RV Supplies
Firewood
Groceries
Escort to Site
Guest Services
Onsite Rentals (9)
Pet Supplies

Activities/Sports

Swimming Pool
Lake
Body Of Water (Canyon Lake)
Planned Activities
Playground

Heartland RV Park & Cabins

24743 Hwy 79
Hermosa, SD 57744
(605) 255-5460
Location: 43.81876, -103.20265
Daily/Weekly/Monthly **Rates: From 29 to 79 dollars**
Official website: https://heartlandrvpark.com
Spaces Available: 231
Max Length: 80

Amenities and services

Dump Station
Folding Tent Campers Allowed
Pets Welcome
Tent Camping Allowed
Cabin/Cottage Rentals (16)
231 Sites with WiFi
Restroom and Showers
Laundry
RV Supplies
Metered LP Gas
Firewood
Ice
Snack Bar
Cable
Guest Services
Onsite Rentals (16)
Enclosed Dog Run
Dog Park

Activities/Sports

Heated Pool
Hot Tub
Rec Hall
Planned Activities
Playground
Exercise Room
Pickle Ball

W I S C O N S I N

Potawatomi Carter Casino Hotel

618 State Hwy 32
Wabeno, WI 54566
715-473-2021
Official Website:
GPS: 45.3982, -88.6264
Number of Sites: 20
Elevation: 1,541 ft / 469 m

Cabela's

1350 Cabela Dr.
Sun Prairie, WI 53590
608-478-4100
Official Website:
https://stores.cabelas.com/us/wi/sun-prairie/1350-cabela-drive.html
GPS: 43.165, -89.2728
Number of Sites: 10
Pad Type: asphalt
Elevation: 951 ft / 289 m
Max Stay: 1

Not Free Rv Camping

Mont du Lac Resort

3125 South Mont du Lac Rd.
Superior, WI 54880
(218) 626-3797
Location: 46.65214, -92.28444
Daily/Weekly/Monthly **Rates: From 57 to 129 dollars**
Official website: https://mdlresort.com
Spaces Available: 37
Max Length: 60

Amenities and services

Dump Station
Limited Facilities - Winter
Pets Welcome
Day Max Stay (14)
Tent Camping Allowed
Cabin/Cottage Rentals (18)
Dedicated Tenting Area
WiFi at Park Supports Streaming
On-Site WiFi Tech Support
37 Sites with WiFi
Restroom and Showers
Laundry
ATM Machine
RV Supplies
Firewood
Ice
Snack Bar
Restaurant
Cable
Guest Services
Fishing Guides
Fishing Supplies
Golf Carts
Onsite Rentals (18)
Dog Park

Activities/Sports

- ✓ Swimming Pool
- ✓ Water Slide
- ✓ Water Umbrella
- ✓ River
- ✓ Boating
- ✓ Fishing
- ✓ Dock
- ✓ Ramp
- ✓ Boat Rental
- ✓ Body Of Water (St. Louis River)
- ✓ Horseshoes
- ✓ Rec Hall
- ✓ Game Room
- ✓ Playground
- ✓ Outdoor Games
- ✓ Shuffleboard
- ✓ Nature Trails
- ✓ Frisbee Golf
- ✓ Rec Open to the Public
- ✓ Archery Range
- ✓ Kayaking/Canoeing
- ✓ Watersports

Sherwood Forest Camping & RV Park

2852 Wisconsin Dells Parkway
Wisconsin Dells, WI 53965
(877) 474-3796
Location: 43.63178, -89.78841
Daily/Weekly/Monthly **Rates: From 40 to 65 dollars**
Official website:
https://www.sherwoodforestcamping.com
Spaces Available: 165
Max Length: 60

Amenities and services

Dump Station
Partial Handicap Access
Emergency Phone
Folding Tent Campers Allowed
Pets Welcome
Tent Camping Allowed
RV Park Model Rentals (3)
Cabin/Cottage Rentals (13)
Cooking Counters
130 Sites with WiFi
Restroom and Showers
Laundry
ATM Machine
RV Supplies
LP Bottles Only

Firewood / Ice
Snack Bar
Groceries
Onsite Rentals (16)

Activities/Sports
- ✓ Heated Pool
- ✓ Splash Pad
- ✓ Swimming
- ✓ Horseshoes
- ✓ Game Room
- ✓ Playground
- ✓ Outdoor Games
- ✓ Pavilion
- ✓ Bounce Pillow

HTR Door County

8164 State Hwy 42
Egg Harbor, WI 54209
(920) 868-3278
Location: 45.06682, -87.26379
Daily/Weekly/Monthly **Rates: From 53 to 73 dollars**
Official website:
https://www.htrresorts.com/destinations/door-county
Spaces Available: 100
Max Length: 90

Amenities and services
Dump Station
Mobile Sewer Service
Pets Welcome
Tent Camping Allowed
Cabin/Cottage Rentals (8)
Dedicated Tenting Area
100 Sites with WiFi
Restroom and Showers
Laundry
RV Supplies
Firewood / Ice
Groceries
Escort to Site
Onsite Rentals (8)

Activities/Sports
- ✓ Heated Pool
- ✓ Swimming
- ✓ Horseshoes

- ✓ Game Room
- ✓ Playground
- ✓ Pavilion
- ✓ Rec Open to the Public

Hiawatha Trailer Resort

1077 Old Hwy 51S
Woodruff, WI 54568
(715) 356-6111
Location: 45.90269, -89.68811
Daily/Weekly/Monthly **Rates: From 42 to 47 dollars**
Official website:
https://www.hiawathatrailerresort.com
Spaces Available: 20
Max Length: 65

Amenities and services
Partial Handicap Access
Emergency Phone
Folding Tent Campers Allowed
Pets Welcome
No Tents
20 Sites with WiFi
Restroom and Showers
Laundry
RV Supplies
Firewood / Ice
Escort to Site / Lake

Activities/Sports
- ✓ Boating
- ✓ Swimming
- ✓ Fishing
- ✓ Dock
- ✓ Ramp
- ✓ Boat Rental
- ✓ Body Of Water (Lake Arrowhead)
- ✓ Horseshoes
- ✓ Rec Hall
- ✓ Planned Activities
- ✓ Playground
- ✓ Outdoor Games

Fremont RV Campground

E6506 Hwy 110
Fremont, WI 54940
(888) 563-7040

Location: 44.26551, -88.90183
Daily/Weekly/Monthly **Rates: From 59 to 79 dollars**
Official website:
https://thousandtrails.com/wisconsin/fremont-rv-campground &pc=GoodSamweb
Spaces Available: 125
Max Length: 65

- ✓ Playground
- ✓ Pavilion
- ✓ Shuffleboard
- ✓ Nature Trails
- ✓ Pedal Carts
- ✓ Bounce Pillow
- ✓ Mini Golf

Amenities and services

Dump Station
Mobile Sewer Service
Partial Handicap Access
Folding Tent Campers Allowed
Pets Welcome
Tent Camping Allowed
Cabin/Cottage Rentals (46)
Dedicated Tenting Area
Privacy Barrier
125 Sites with WiFi
Restroom and Showers
Laundry
ATM Machine
RV Supplies
Metered LP Gas
Firewood
Ice
Snack Bar
Groceries
Fishing Supplies
Golf Carts
Onsite Rentals (46)
Heated Pool
Water Slide
Lake

Activities/Sports

- ✓ Boating
- ✓ Swimming
- ✓ Wading Pool
- ✓ Fishing
- ✓ Dock
- ✓ Ramp
- ✓ Boat Rental
- ✓ Paddle Boats
- ✓ Body Of Water (Partridge Lake)
- ✓ Horseshoes
- ✓ Game Room
- ✓ Planned Activities

SOUTH
ALABAMA

Eagle Landing RV Park

1900 Lee Road 137
Auburn, AL 36832
334-821-8805
Official Website: http://eagleslandingrv.com/
GPS: 32.5825, -85.5194
Number of Sites: 60
Elevation: 590 ft / 179 m

Tuskegee Primitive Camp #10

Tuskegee National Forest
NF-908
Tuskegee, AL 36083
334-439-0244
Official Website:
https://www.fs.usda.gov/recarea/alabama/re
creation/camping-
cabins/recarea/?recid=30193&actid=29
GPS: 32.4864, -85.5883
Number of Sites: 1
Pad Type: dirt
Elevation: 426 ft / 129 m
Max Stay: 14
Tent Camping: Yes

McDougle Hunt Camp

William B. Bankhead National Forest
Moulton, AL 35650
205-489-5111
Official Website:
https://www.fs.usda.gov/recarea/alabama/re
carea/?recid=30099
GPS: 34.338, -87.346
Elevation: 951 ft / 289 m
Tent Camping: Yes

Not Free Rv Camping

Ahoy RV Resort

13000 Springsteen Ln
Foley, AL 36535
(251) 233-7250
Location: 30.41414, -87.65023
Daily/Weekly/Monthly **Rates: From 55 to 89 dollars**
Official website:
https://www.ahoyrvresort.com
Spaces Available: 75
Max Length: 100

Amenities and services

Partial Handicap Access
Folding Tent Campers Allowed
Pets Welcome
No Tents
75 Sites with WiFi
Restroom and Showers
Laundry
ATM Machine
RV Supplies
Metered LP Gas
Firewood
Ice
Escort to Site
Onsite RV Service
Cable
Self-Service RV Wash

Activities/Sports

- ✓ Fishing Supplies
- ✓ Enclosed Dog Run
- ✓ Dog Park
- ✓ Pet Supplies
- ✓ Swimming Pool
- ✓ Splash Pad
- ✓ Water Slide / Water Umbrella
- ✓ Gulf
- ✓ Swimming
- ✓ Wading Pool
- ✓ Fishing
- ✓ Paddle Boats
- ✓ Body Of Water (Lake Rougaroux)
- ✓ Horseshoes
- ✓ Rec Hall
- ✓ Planned Activities
- ✓ Outdoor Games
- ✓ Shuffleboard
- ✓ Exercise Room
- ✓ Frisbee Golf
- ✓ Pickle Ball
- ✓ Kayaking/Canoeing

Dothan RV Park

4100 S Oates (Hwy 231 S)
Dothan, AL 36301
(334) 792-3313
Location: 31.16722, -85.40249
Daily/Weekly/Monthly **Rates: 56 dollars**
Official website:
http://www.cherryblossomrv.com
Spaces Available: 47
Max Length: 70

Amenities and services

Partial Handicap Access
RV Age Restrictions
Pets Welcome
No Tents
Cabin/Cottage Rentals (8)
WiFi at Park Supports Streaming
47 Sites with WiFi
Restroom and Showers
Laundry
Cable
Self-Service RV Wash
Onsite Rentals (8)
Dog Park

Activities/Sports

- ✓ Swimming Pool
- ✓ Horseshoes
- ✓ Playground
- ✓ Outdoor Games
- ✓ Pavilion
- ✓ Shuffleboard
- ✓ Nature Trails
- ✓ Pickle Ball
- ✓ Putting Green

Noccalula Falls Campground

1600 Noccalula Rd
Gadsden, AL 35904
(256) 549-4663
Location: 34.04219, -86.02062
Daily/Weekly/Monthly **Rates: 48 dollars**
Official website:
https://www.noccalulafallspark.com
Spaces Available: 127
Max Length: 70

Amenities and services

Dump Station
Partial Handicap Access
Folding Tent Campers Allowed
Pets Welcome
Day Max Stay (28)
Tent Camping Allowed
Cabin/Cottage Rentals (2)
Overflow Area
95 Sites with WiFi
Restroom and Showers
Laundry
Control Access Gate
RV Supplies
Firewood
Ice
Cable
Onsite Rentals (2)

Activities/Sports

- ✓ Swimming Pool
- ✓ River
- ✓ Fishing
- ✓ Body Of Water (Noccalula Falls)
- ✓ Rec Hall
- ✓ Playground
- ✓ Pavilion

Quail Creek RV Resort

233 Quail Creek Drive
Hartselle, AL 35640
(256) 784-5033
Location: 34.39167, -86.86355
Daily/Weekly/Monthly **Rates: 40 dollars**
Official website: https://www.qcresort.com

Spaces Available: 28
Max Length: 95

Amenities and services

Emergency Phone
Folding Tent Campers Allowed
Pets Welcome
Tent Camping Allowed
Lodge Room Rentals (14)
WiFi at Park Supports Streaming
28 Sites with WiFi
Restroom and Showers
Laundry
Firewood
Ice
Worship Services
Snack Bar
Self-Service RV Wash

Activities/Sports

- ✓ Golf Carts
- ✓ Onsite Rentals (14)
- ✓ Swimming Pool
- ✓ Pond
- ✓ Fishing
- ✓ Rec Hall
- ✓ Game Room
- ✓ Playground
- ✓ Golf
- ✓ Driving Range
- ✓ Pavilion
- ✓ Exercise Room
- ✓ Nature Trails
- ✓ Frisbee Golf
- ✓ Putting Green
- ✓ Rec Open to the Public

Windemere Cove RV

10174 County Rd 67
Langston, AL 35755
(256) 228-3010
Location: 34.53499, -86.08907
Daily/Weekly/Monthly **Rates: From 47 to 59 dollars**
Official website:
https://www.windemerecove.com
Spaces Available: 106
Max Length: 80

Amenities and services

Partial Handicap Access
Emergency Phone
RV Age Restrictions
Pets Welcome
No Tents
WiFi at Park Supports Streaming
106 Sites with WiFi
Restroom and Showers
Laundry
Control Access Gate
Staffed RV Wash
Self-Service RV Wash

Activities/Sports

✓ Fishing Guides
✓ Swimming Pool
✓ Lake
✓ Boating
✓ Fishing
✓ Dock
✓ Ramp
✓ Body Of Water (Lake Guntersville)
✓ Horseshoes
✓ Rec Hall
✓ Planned Activities
✓ Outdoor Games
✓ Pavilion
✓ Exercise Room
✓ Kayaking/Canoeing
✓ Watersports

ARKANSAS

Free Rv Camping

County Road 122 Dispersed Camping

Mike Freeze Wattensaw WMA
County Rd. 122
Hazen, AR 72064
877-734-4581
Official Website: https://www.agfc.com/en/
GPS: 34.8361, -91.5489
Elevation: 196 ft / 59 m
Tent Camping: Yes

Sam's Throne Recreation Area

Ozark National Forest
AR-123
Mount Judea, AR 72655
479-284-3150
Official Website:
https://www.fs.usda.gov/recarea/osfnf/recre
ation/natureviewing/recarea/?recid=43483&
actid=64
GPS: 35.879, -93.0451
Number of Sites: 15
Pad Type: dirt
Elevation: 2,001 ft / 609 m
Max Stay: 14 / Tent Camping: Yes

Crystal Campground

Ouachita National Forest
Collier Springs Road
Norman, AR 71960
870-867-2101 / 501-321-5202
Official Website:
https://www.fs.usda.gov/recarea/ouachita/re
carea/?recid=10719
GPS: 34.4796, -93.6389
Number of Sites: 9
Elevation: 951 ft / 289 m
Max Stay: 14 / Tent Camping: Yes

Not Free Rv Camping

Denton Ferry RV Park & Cabin Rental

740 Denton Ferry Rd.
Cotter, AR 72626
(870) 435-7275
Location: 36.29259, -92.52139
Daily/Weekly/Monthly **Rates: From 40 to 55 dollars**
Official website: https://dentonrv.com
Spaces Available: 40
Max Length: 65

Amenities and services

Partial Handicap Access
Emergency Phone
Pets Welcome
No Tents
40 Sites with WiFi
Restroom and Showers
Laundry
RV Supplies
Metered LP Gas
Firewood
Ice
Escort to Site
Onsite RV Service
Guest Services
Fishing Guides
Onsite Rentals (1)
Enclosed Dog Run
Sells Fishing Licenses
River

Activities/Sports

✓ Fishing
✓ Body Of Water (White River)
✓ Horseshoes
✓ Rec Hall
✓ Game Room
✓ Outdoor Games
✓ Nature Trails
✓ Bike Rentals
✓ Kayaking/Canoeing

Wanderlust RV Park

468 Passion Play Road
Eureka Springs, AR 72632
(479) 253-7385
Location: 36.39771, -93.71383
Daily/Weekly/Monthly Rates: **From 37 to 60 dollars**
Official website:
https://wanderlustrvpark.com
Spaces Available: 83
Max Amps: 50
Max Length: 84

Amenities and services

Dump Station
Emergency Phone
Folding Tent Campers Allowed
Pets Welcome
No Tents
Cabin/Cottage Rentals (2)
WiFi at Park Supports Streaming
81 Sites with WiFi
Restroom and Showers
Laundry
RV Supplies
Firewood
Escort to Site
Onsite RV Service
Guest Services
Onsite Rentals (2)
Pet Supplies
Swimming Pool
Swimming
Rec Hall
Pavilion

Tom Sawyer's RV Park

1286 S 8th St
West Memphis, AR 72301
(870) 735-9770
Location: 35.12999, -90.16714
Daily/Weekly/Monthly **Rates: From 28 to 59 dollars**
Official website:
https://tomsawyersrvpark.com
Spaces Available: 110
Max Length: 130

Amenities and services

Emergency Phone
Folding Tent Campers Allowed
Pets Welcome
Tent Camping Allowed
Overflow Area
Dedicated Tenting Area
110 Sites with WiFi
Restroom and Showers
Laundry
Control Access Gate
Firewood
Ice / Escort to Site
Self-Service RV Wash

Activities/Sports

- ✓ River
- ✓ Boating
- ✓ Fishing
- ✓ Ramp
- ✓ Body Of Water (Mississippi River)
- ✓ Outdoor Games
- ✓ Nature Trails
- ✓ Kayaking/Canoeing

Blowing Springs RV Park

700 Blowing Spring Rd
Bella Vista, AR 72715
(479) 855-8075
Location: 36.44115, -94.22869
Daily/Weekly/Monthly **Rates: 35 dollars**
Official website: https://bellavistapoa.com
Spaces Available: 60
Max Length: 50

Amenities and services

Dump Station
Folding Tent Campers Allowed
Pets Welcome
Day Max Stay (14)
Tent Camping Allowed
Dedicated Tenting Area
60 Sites with WiFi
Restroom and Showers
Laundry
Control Access Gate
Firewood

Stream
Body Of Water (Blowing Springs)
Pavilion
Nature Trails

J & J RV Park

2000 E Grand Ave
Hot Springs, AR 71901
(501) 321-9852
Location: 34.50833, -93.01000
Daily/Weekly/Monthly **Rates: 45 dollars**
Official website: http://www.jjrvpark.com
Spaces Available: 46
Max Length: 70

menities and services

Partial Handicap Access
Folding Tent Campers Allowed
Pets Welcome
No Tents
46 Sites with WiFi
Restroom and Showers
Laundry
Ice
Escort to Site
Cable
Stream
Body Of Water (Gulpha Creek)
Horseshoes
Pavilion

D
E
L
A
W
A
R
E

Free Rv Camping	Not Free Rv Camping

Smyrna Rest Area

5500 Dupont Pkwy
Smyrna, DE 19977
302-653-8910
Official Website: https://www.deldot.gov/
GPS: 39.3227, -75.6177
Pad Type: asphalt
Elevation: 32 ft / 9 m
Max Stay: 1

Harrington Raceway & Casino

18500 S Dupont Hwy.
Harrington, DE 19952
302-398-4920
888-887-5687
Official Website:
https://casino.harringtonraceway.com/
GPS: 38.911, -75.5748

Yogi Bear's Jellystone Park At Delaware Beaches

8295 Brick Granary Rd
Lincoln, DE 19960
(302) 491-6614
Location: 38.87449, -75.36021
Daily/Weekly/Monthly **Rates: From 65 to 199 dollars**
Official website:
https://www.delawarejellystone.com
Spaces Available: 229
Max Length: 65

Amenities and services

Dump Station
Partial Handicap Access
Emergency Phone
Pets Welcome
Tent Camping Allowed
Cabin/Cottage Rentals (49)
229 Sites with WiFi
Restroom and Showers
Laundry
Control Access Gate
RV Supplies
Firewood
Ice
Worship Services
Snack Bar
Groceries
Escort to Site
Cable
Guest Services
Golf Carts
Onsite Rentals (49)
Enclosed Dog Run

Activities/Sports

✓ Swimming Pool
✓ Splash Pad
✓ Water Slide
✓ Horseshoes
✓ Rec Hall
✓ Game Room

- ✓ Planned Activities
- ✓ Playground
- ✓ Outdoor Games
- ✓ Pavilion
- ✓ Pedal Carts
- ✓ Bounce Pillow

Sun Outdoors Rehoboth Bay

20628 Long Beach Drive
Millsboro, DE 19966
(302) 947-2600
Location: 38.62534, -75.10381
Daily/Weekly/Monthly **Rates: From 61 to 139 dollars**
Official website:
https://www.sunoutdoors.com/delaware
Spaces Available: 254
Max Length: 90

Amenities and services:

Partial Handicap Access
Folding Tent Campers Allowed
Pets Welcome
Tent Rentals (10)
Cabin/Cottage Rentals (63)
254 Sites with WiFi
Restroom and Showers
Laundry
Control Access Gate
ATM Machine
RV Supplies
LP Bottles Only
Firewood
Ice
Snack Bar
Groceries
Escort to Site
Restaurant
Onsite RV Service
Cable
Cocktail Lounge
Guest Services
Fishing Supplies
Golf Carts
Near NASCAR® Track (40 mi to Dover International Speedway)

Onsite Rentals (73)
Enclosed Dog Run
Pet Supplies

Activities/Sports

- ✓ Heated Pool
- ✓ Water Slide
- ✓ Lake
- ✓ Boating
- ✓ Fishing
- ✓ Dock
- ✓ Ramp
- ✓ Boat Rental
- ✓ Paddle Boats
- ✓ Body Of Water (Roman Pond)
- ✓ Game Room
- ✓ Planned Activities
- ✓ Playground
- ✓ Pavilion
- ✓ Bike Rentals
- ✓ Kayaking/Canoeing

Big Oaks Family Campground

35567 Big Oaks Lane
Rehoboth Beach, DE 19971
(302) 645-6838
Location: 38.73765, -75.12912
Daily/Weekly/Monthly **Rates: From 65 to 110 dollars**
Official website: https://bigoakscamping.com
Spaces Available: 45
Max Length: 50

Amenities and services

Dump Station
Folding Tent Campers Allowed
Tent Camping Allowed
RV Park Model Rentals (5)
Cabin/Cottage Rentals (20)
Dedicated Tenting Area
Covered Area w/Picnic Table
WiFi at Park Supports Streaming
45 Sites with WiFi
Restroom and Showers
Laundry
RV Supplies
Firewood

Ice
Groceries
Onsite RV Service
Cable
Near NASCAR® Track (43 mi to Dover International Speedway)
Onsite Rentals (25)
Pet Supplies

Activities/Sports

- ✓ Swimming Pool
- ✓ Rec Hall
- ✓ Game Room
- ✓ Planned Activities
- ✓ Playground
- ✓ Outdoor Games
- ✓ Pavilion
- ✓ Shuffleboard

Killens Pond

5025 Killens Pond Rd
Felton, DE 19943
(302) 284-4526
Daily/Weekly/Monthly **Rates: From 20 to 37 dollars**
Spaces Available: 59
Max Length: 38

Amenities and services

Partial Handicap Access
Pets Welcome
Day Max Stay (14)
Tent Camping Allowed
Road Condition (Good)
Road Type (Paved/Gravel)
Restroom and Showers
Laundry

Activities/Sports

- ✓ Swimming Pool
- ✓ Boating
- ✓ Pond
- ✓ Wading Pool
- ✓ Fishing
- ✓ Ramp
- ✓ Boat Rental
- ✓ Horseshoes
- ✓ Playground
- ✓ Shuffleboard

- ✓ Kayaking/Canoeing

Treasure Beach RV Park

37291 Lighthouse Rd
Selbyville, DE 19975
(302) 436-8001
Daily/Weekly/Monthly **Rates: From 95 to 170 dollars**
Spaces Available: 326
Max Length: 80

Amenities and services

Partial Handicap Access
Pets Welcome
Tent Camping Allowed
WiFi Hotspots (4)
326 Sites with WiFi
Restroom and Showers
Laundry
ATM Machine
Guest Services
Self-Service RV Wash
Dog Park

Activities/Sports

- ✓ Swimming Pool
- ✓ Ocean
- ✓ Swimming
- ✓ Fishing
- ✓ Ramp
- ✓ Body Of Water (Little Assawoman Bay)
- ✓ Horseshoes
- ✓ Rec Hall
- ✓ Game Room
- ✓ Playground

F L O R I D A

DuPuis Campground

Water Management District
SW Kanner Hwy.
Indiantown, FL 34956 / 561-924-5310
Official Website:
https://www.sfwmd.gov/recreation-site/dupuis-management-area
GPS: 27.0062, -80.5605
Number of Sites: 23
Pad Type: grass
Elevation: 0 ft / 0 m / Max Stay: 8
Tent Camping: Yes

Lake Panasoffkee Wildlife Management Area

Southwest Florida Water Management District
7519 NW 18th Way
Wildwood, FL 34785
352-796-7211 / 800-423-1476
https://www.swfwmd.state.fl.us/recreation/lake-panasoffkee
GPS: 28.8653, -82.1327
Pad Type: grass / Reservations: yes
Elevation: 32 ft / 9 m
Max Stay: 7 / Tent Camping: Yes

Hickory Hammock Equestrian Campground

Water Management District
McArthur Rd. / Lorida, FL 33857
866-433-6312
https://www.sfwmd.gov/recreation-site/boney-marsh-and-bluff-hammock-management-units-and-hickory-hammock-wildlife-1
GPS: 27.4478, -81.1771 / Reservations: yes
Elevation: 0 ft / 0 m
Max Stay: 8
Tent Camping: Yes

Not Free Rv Camping

Bonita Terra

25581 Trost Blvd
Bonita Springs, FL 34135
(239) 992-3030
Location: 26.37078, -81.75093
Daily/Weekly/Monthly **Rates: From 40 to 85 dollars**
Official website: https://bonitaterra.com
Spaces Available: 160
Max Length: 60

Amenities and services:
Dump Station
Partial Handicap Access
Folding Tent Campers Allowed
Pets Welcome
No Tents
WiFi at Overnite Sites $
172 Sites with WiFi
Restroom and Showers
Laundry
Metered LP Gas
Worship Services
Escort to Site
Cable
Self-Service RV Wash
Enclosed Dog Run

Activities/Sports
- ✓ Heated Pool
- ✓ Horseshoes
- ✓ Rec Hall
- ✓ Game Room
- ✓ Planned Activities
- ✓ Driving Range
- ✓ Pavilion
- ✓ Shuffleboard
- ✓ Nature Trails
- ✓ Pickle Ball

Belle Parc RV Resort

11050 Elliots Way
Brooksville, FL 34601
(352) 593-5852
Location: 28.58613, -82.37573
Daily/Weekly/Monthly **Rates: From 80 to 110 dollars**
Official website:
https://belleparcrvresorts.com
Spaces Available: 200
Max Length: 60

Amenities and services
Partial Handicap Access
RV Age Restrictions
Pets Welcome
No Tents
WiFi Hotspots (1)
200 Sites with WiFi
Restroom and Showers
Laundry
Control Access Gate
Worship Services
Snack Bar
Escort to Site
Cable
Guest Services
Enclosed Dog Run

Activities/Sports
- ✓ Heated Pool
- ✓ Hot Tub
- ✓ Pond
- ✓ Swimming
- ✓ Fishing
- ✓ Rec Hall
- ✓ Planned Activities
- ✓ Outdoor Games
- ✓ Pavilion
- ✓ Shuffleboard
- ✓ Exercise Room
- ✓ Pickle Ball

Orange Lake RV Resort

18365 NW 45th Ave. Rd
Citra, FL 32113
(352) 878-4855
Location: 29.41605, -82.20012
Daily/Weekly/Monthly **Rates: 95 dollars**
Official website:
https://www.orangelakervresort.com
Spaces Available: 489
Max Length: 90

Pets Welcome
No Tents
489 Sites with WiFi
Laundry
Metered LP Gas
Escort to Site
Cable
Dog Park
Rec Hall
Nature Trails

Sonrise Palms RV Park

660 Tucker Ln
Cocoa, FL 32926
(321) 633-4335
Location: 28.35061, -80.79176
Daily/Weekly/Monthly Rates: 72 dollars
Official website:
http://www.sonrisepalmsrv.com
Spaces Available: 96
Max Length: 60

Amenities and services

Dump Station
Partial Handicap Access
Pets Welcome
No Tents
RV Park Model Rentals (10)
WiFi at Park Supports Streaming
96 Sites with WiFi
Restroom and Showers
Laundry
Metered LP Gas
Escort to Site
Cable
Self-Service RV Wash
Onsite Rentals (10)
Enclosed Dog Run

Activities/Sports

- ✓ Heated Pool
- ✓ Pond
- ✓ Swimming
- ✓ Fishing
- ✓ Rec Hall
- ✓ Game Room
- ✓ Exercise Room

GEORGIA

Free Rv Camping	Not Free Rv Camping

Barrington County Park

Barrington Road
Townsend, GA 31331
912-437-6657
Official Website:
http://www.mcintoshcountyga.com/
GPS: 31.4717, -81.6068
Elevation: 0 ft / 0 m
Max Stay: 7
Tent Camping: Yes

Southern Retreat RV Park

7445 Blythe Island Hwy
Brunswick, GA 31523
(912) 261-1025
Location: 31.14542, -81.57653
Daily/Weekly/Monthly **Rates: From 55 to 65 dollars**
Official website:
https://southernretreatrvpark.com
Spaces Available: 126
Max Length: 80

Amenities and services

Partial Handicap Access
Emergency Phone
Folding Tent Campers Allowed
Pets Welcome
Tent Camping Allowed
Cabin/Cottage Rentals (2)
Dedicated Tenting Area
122 Sites with WiFi
Restroom and Showers
Laundry
RV Supplies
Metered LP Gas
Firewood
Ice
Restaurant
Onsite RV Service
Cable
Cocktail Lounge
Staffed RV Wash
Self-Service RV Wash
Onsite Rentals (2)
Enclosed Dog Run

Activities/Sports

- ✓ Swiming Pool
- ✓ Horseshoes
- ✓ Rec Hall
- ✓ Planned Activities
- ✓ Playground
- ✓ Outdoor Games
- ✓ Pavilion
- ✓ Exercise Room

Iron Mountain Resort

116 Iron Mountain Parkway
Dahlonega, GA 30533
(706) 216-7275
Location: 34.54760, -84.13800
Daily/Weekly/Monthly **Rates: 65 dollars**
Official website:
https://ironmountainresort.com
Spaces Available: 82
Max Length: 80

Amenities and services

Dump Station
Folding Tent Campers Allowed
Pets Welcome
Tent Camping Allowed
Cabin/Cottage Rentals (26)
Dedicated Tenting Area
WiFi Hotspots (1)
Restroom and Showers
Control Access Gate
RV Supplies
Ice
Snack Bar
Groceries
Restaurant
Cocktail Lounge
Golf Carts
Onsite Rentals (26)
Dog Park
Rec Hall
Playground
Outdoor Games
Pavilion
Nature Trails
Rec Open to the Public

Stone Mountain Park Campground

4003 Stonewall Jackson Dr.
Stone Mountain, GA 30083
(770) 498-5710
Location: 33.81979, -84.13347
Daily/Weekly/Monthly **Rates: From 44 to 77 dollars**

Official website:
https://stonemountainpark.com
Spaces Available: 335
Max Length: 55

Amenities and services

Dump Station
Partial Handicap Access
Emergency Phone
Folding Tent Campers Allowed
Pets Welcome
Tent Camping Allowed
Tent Rentals (1)
Teepee/Yurt Rentals (20)
RV Park Model Rentals (6)
Overflow Area
Dedicated Tenting Area
335 Sites with WiFi
Restroom and Showers
Laundry
Control Access Gate
ATM Machine
RV Supplies
Metered LP Gas
Firewood
Ice
Snack Bar
Groceries
Restaurant
Cable
Fishing Supplies
Onsite Rentals (27)

Activities/Sports

- ✓ Swimming Pool
- ✓ Lake
- ✓ Boating
- ✓ Fishing
- ✓ Dock
- ✓ Ramp
- ✓ Body Of Water (Stone Mountain Lake)
- ✓ Horseshoes
- ✓ Playground
- ✓ Golf
- ✓ Driving Range
- ✓ Pavilion
- ✓ Nature Trails
- ✓ Bike Rentals
- ✓ Mini Golf
- ✓ Rec Open to the Public

✓ Kayaking/Canoeing

Southern Trails RV Resort

2690 Arena Rd
Unadilla, GA 31091
(478) 627-3254
Location: 32.24037, -83.73928
Daily/Weekly/**Monthly Rates: 45 dollars**
Official website:
https://southerntrailsrvresort.com/?utm_source=GoodSam
Spaces Available: 161
Max Length: 50

Amenities and services

Dump Station
Folding Tent Campers Allowed
Pets Welcome
Tent Camping Allowed
161 Sites with WiFi
Restroom and Showers
Laundry
Onsite RV Service

Activities/Sports

✓ Swimming Pool
✓ Pond
✓ Fishing
✓ Horseshoes
✓ Playground
✓ Mini Golf

Coastal Georgia RV Resort

287 South Port Parkway
Brunswick, GA 31523
(912) 264-3869
Location: 31.13385, -81.58251
Daily/Weekly/Monthly **Rates: 60 dollars**
Official website:
https://www.coastalgarvresort.com/?utm_source=GoodSam
Spaces Available: 117
Max Length: 75

Amenities and services

Pets Welcome
No Tents
WiFi Hotspots (3)

117 Sites with WiFi
Restroom and Showers
Laundry
RV Supplies
Metered LP Gas
Firewood
Ice
Cable
Self-Service RV Wash
Enclosed Dog Run

Activities/Sports

✓ Swimming Pool
✓ Lake
✓ Fishing
✓ Body Of Water (Lake Earl)
✓ Horseshoes
✓ Rec Hall
✓ Game Room
✓ Pavilion

K E N T U K Y

Turkey Foot Campground

Daniel Boone National Forest
Elsam Fork Road
McKee, KY 40447
606-864-4163 / 859-745-3100
Official Website:
https://www.fs.usda.gov/recarea/dbnf/recarea/?recid=39574
GPS: 37.468, -83.917
Number of Sites: 15 /Pad Type: gravel
Elevation: 853 ft / 259 m
Max Stay: 14 /Tent Camping: Yes

Swain Ridge Road Dispersed Camping

Beaver Creek Wilderness
Swain Ridge Road
Parkers Lake, KY 42634
606-376-5323
Official Website:
https://www.fs.usda.gov/recarea/dbnf/recarea/?recid=70793
GPS: 36.9038, -84.4214
Pad Type: grass
Elevation: 1,148 ft / 349 m
Max Stay: 14 / Tent Camping: Yes

Wilson Creek Recreation Area Campground

Green River Lake Army Corps of Engineers
FD-1005
Elk Horn, KY 42733
270-465-4463
https://www.lrl.usace.army.mil/Missions/Civil-Works/Recreation/
GPS: 37.2857, -85.2556
Number of Sites: 5 / Pad Type: gravel
Elevation: 688 ft / 209 m / Tent Camping:
Yes

Cave Country RV Campground

216 Gaunce Dr
Cave City, KY 42127
(270) 773-4678
Location: 37.13496, -85.96861
Daily/Weekly/Monthly **Rates: 52 dollars**
Official website: https://cavecountryrv.com
Spaces Available: 51
Max Length: 65

Amenities and services

Dump Station
Partial Handicap Access
Emergency Phone
Folding Tent Campers Allowed
Pets Welcome
No Tents
On-Site WiFi Tech Support
51 Sites with WiFi
Restroom and Showers
Laundry
RV Supplies
Metered LP Gas
Firewood
Ice
Escort to Site
Cable
Staffed RV Wash
Self-Service RV Wash
Enclosed Dog Run
Dog Park

Activities/Sports

✓ Heated Pool
✓ Swimming
✓ Rec Hall
✓ Game Room
✓ Pavilion
✓ Exercise Room

Laurel Lake Camping Resort

80 Robert A Blair Memorial Hwy
Corbin, KY 40701
(606) 526-7876
Location: 36.92074, -84.25977
Daily/Weekly/Monthly **Rates: From 54 to 64 dollars**
Official website:
https://laurellakecamping.com
Spaces Available: 120
Max Length: 80

Amenities and services

Partial Handicap Access
Emergency Phone
Folding Tent Campers Allowed
Pets Welcome
Tent Camping Allowed
Cabin/Cottage Rentals (21)
Overflow Area
120 Sites with WiFi
Restroom and Showers
Laundry
Control Access Gate
ATM Machine
RV Supplies
LP Bottles Only
Firewood
Ice
Groceries
Escort to Site
Restaurant
Cable
Fishing Supplies
Golf Carts
Onsite Rentals (21)
Pet Supplies
Sells Fishing Licenses
Pond

Activities/Sports

✓ Swimming
✓ Fishing
✓ No Motors
✓ Paddle Boats
✓ Horseshoes
✓ Game Room

- ✓ Planned Activities
- ✓ Playground
- ✓ Outdoor Games
- ✓ Nature Trails
- ✓ Pedal Carts
- ✓ Bike Rentals
- ✓ Frisbee Golf
- ✓ Mini Golf
- ✓ Putting Green
- ✓ Kayaking/Canoeing

Northern KY RV Park

3315 Dixie Highway
Dry Ridge, KY 41035
(859) 428-2000
Location: 38.74925, -84.60307
Daily/Weekly/Monthly **Rates: From 55 to 110 dollars**
Official website:
https://www.northernkyrv.com
Spaces Available: 55
Max Length: 65

Amenities and services

Dump Station
Emergency Phone
Folding Tent Campers Allowed
Pets Welcome
No Tents
WiFi Hotspots (2)
55 Sites with WiFi
Restroom and Showers
Laundry
RV Supplies
Metered LP Gas
Ice
Escort to Site
Guest Services
Near NASCAR® Track (25 mi to Kentucky Speedway)
Dog Park
Pet Supplies
Pond

Activities/Sports
- ✓ Fishing
- ✓ Horseshoes
- ✓ Playground

- ✓ Outdoor Games

Elkhorn Creek RV Park

165 N Scruggs Ln
Frankfort, KY 40601
(502) 695-9154
Location: 38.21000, -84.80050
Daily/Weekly/Monthly **Rates: From 50 to 70 dollars**
Official website:
https://www.elkhorncreekrvpark.com
Spaces Available: 130
Max Length: 80

Amenities and services

Dump Station
Partial Handicap Access
Emergency Phone
Folding Tent Campers Allowed
Pets Welcome
No Tents
130 Sites with WiFi
Restroom and Showers
Laundry
RV Supplies
Metered LP Gas
Firewood
Ice
Snack Bar
Groceries
Cable
Fishing Supplies

Activities/Sports
- ✓ Swimming Pool
- ✓ Stream
- ✓ Fishing
- ✓ Body Of Water (Elkhorn Creek)
- ✓ Horseshoes
- ✓ Rec Hall
- ✓ Game Room
- ✓ Planned Activities
- ✓ Playground
- ✓ Outdoor Games
- ✓ Pavilion
- ✓ Mini Golf

Whispering Hills RV Park

257 Rogers Gap Rd
Georgetown, KY 40324
(502) 863-2552
Location: 38.30173, -84.55041
Daily/Weekly/Monthly **Rates: From to dollars**
Official website:
https://www.whisperinghillsrv.com
Spaces Available: 104
Max Length: 90

Amenities and services

Partial Handicap Access
Emergency Phone
Folding Tent Campers Allowed
Pets Welcome
No Tents
140 Sites with WiFi
Restroom and Showers
Laundry
RV Supplies
Metered LP Gas
Firewood
IceWorship Services
Escort to Sit
Fishing Supplies
Dog Park

Activities/Sports

✓ Swimming Pool
✓ Water Slide
✓ Pond
✓ Fishing
✓ Planned Activities
✓ Playground
✓ Outdoor Games
✓ Pavilion
✓ Bounce Pillow

LOUISIANA

Free Rv Camping	Not Free Rv Camping

Rutherford Beach Dispersed Camping

Dept. Fish & Wildlife
Parish Rd. 359
Creole, LA 70632
Official Website: https://rutherford-beach.business.site/
GPS: 29.7602, -93.1241

Bonnet Carre Spillway Campground

Army Corps Of Engineers
Lower Guide Levee Road
Norco, LA 70079
985-764-0126
985-764-7484
Official Website:
https://www.scpparksandrec.com/facilities/spillway-rental
GPS: 30.0213, -90.409
Number of Sites: 15
Pad Type: grass
Elevation: 0 ft / 0 m
Tent Camping: Yes

Custis Camp

Kisatchie National Forest
Par Road 341
Natchitoches, LA 71457
318-472-1840
318-471-7160
Official Website:
https://www.fs.usda.gov/recarea/kisatchie/recarea/?recid=34799
GPS: 31.542, -93.026
Pad Type: grass
Elevation: 295 ft / 89 m

Coushatta Luxury RV Resort at Red Shoes Park

711 Pow Wow Parkway
Kinder, LA 70648
(800) 584-7263
Location: 30.54197, -92.81937
Daily/Weekly/**Monthly Rates: From 25 to 65 dollars**
Official website:
https://www.coushattacasinoresort.com
Spaces Available: 107
Max Length: 70

Amenities and services

Dump Station
Partial Handicap Access
Emergency Phone
Pets Welcome
Day Max Stay (14)
No Tents
Cabin/Cottage Rentals (100)
107 Sites with WiFi
Restroom and Showers
Laundry
ATM Machine
Ice
Snack Bar
Restaurant
Cable
Self-Service RV Wash
Onsite Rentals (100)
Enclosed Dog Run
Dog Park

Activities/Sports

✓ Heated Pool
✓ Splash Pad
✓ Water Slide
✓ Water Umbrella
✓ Pond
✓ Fishing
✓ Horseshoes
✓ Rec Hall
✓ Golf

- ✓ Pavilion
- ✓ Exercise Room
- ✓ Casino

Pine Crest RV Park of New Orleans

2601 Old Spanish Trail
Slidell, LA 70461
(800) 879-5936
Location: 30.24194, -89.75796
Daily/Weekly/Monthly **Rates: From 49 to 55 dollars**
Official website: http://www.pinecrestrv.com
Spaces Available: 30
Max Length: 65

Amenities and services

Dump Station
Partial Handicap Access
Emergency Phone
Pets Welcome
No Tents
30 Sites with WiFi
Restroom and Showers
Laundry
Metered LP Gas
Ice
Onsite RV Service
Cable
Self-Service RV Wash

Activities/Sports

- ✓ Fishing Guides
- ✓ Pond
- ✓ Fishing
- ✓ Horseshoes
- ✓ Playground
- ✓ Outdoor Games
- ✓ Pavilion
- ✓ Shuffleboard
- ✓ Nature Trails
- ✓ Lawn Bowling
- ✓ Pickle Ball
- ✓ Casino
- ✓ Hiking
- ✓ Houseboating
- ✓ Kayaking/Canoeing
- ✓ Boating
- ✓ Marina

- ✓ Road Biking Trails
- ✓ Watersports

Beyonder Resort Cajun Moon

4631 Louisiana Highway 27
Sulphur, LA 70665
337 5832631
Location: 30.18130, -93.37601
Daily/Weekly/Monthly **Rates: From 45 to 50 dollars**
Official website:
https://beyondercamp.com/cajun-moon-sulphur-la
Spaces Available: 134
Max Length: 70

Amenities and services:

Partial Handicap Access
Pets Welcome
No Tents
20 Sites with WiFi
Restroom and Showers
Laundry
Metered LP Gas
Cable
Dog Park

Activities/Sports

- ✓ Swimming Pool
- ✓ Hot Tub
- ✓ Water Umbrella
- ✓ Pond
- ✓ Wading Pool
- ✓ Fishing
- ✓ Game Room
- ✓ Playground
- ✓ Outdoor Games
- ✓ Pavilion
- ✓ Sauna
- ✓ Shuffleboard
- ✓ Exercise Room

River View RV Park and Resort

800 Martin Luther King Ave
Vidalia, LA 71373

(318) 336-1400
Location: 31.55576, -91.43441
Daily/Weekly/Monthly **Rates: From 32 to 44 dollars**
Official website:
https://www.riverviewrvpark.com
Spaces Available: 135
Max Length: 60

Amenities and services:

Dump Station
Folding Tent Campers Allowed
Pets Welcome
Tent Camping Allowed
Cabin/Cottage Rentals (2)
Dedicated Tenting Area
135 Sites with WiFi
Restroom and Showers
Laundry
RV Supplies
Metered LP Gas
Firewood / Ice
Self-Service RV Wash
Onsite Rentals (2)
Dog Park

Activities/Sports

- Swimming Pool
- Hot Tub
- River
- Boating
- Fishing
- Ramp
- Body Of Water (Mississippi River)
- Rec Hall
- Playground
- Outdoor Games
- Pavilion
- Nature Trails
- Bike Rentals

Daily/Weekly/Monthly **Rates: From 28 to 50 dollars**
Official website:
https://www.paragoncasinoresort.com
Spaces Available: 205
Max Length: 80

Amenities and services:

Dump Station
Emergency Phone
Folding Tent Campers Allowed
Pets Welcome / Day Max Stay (14)
No Tents
Cabin/Cottage Rentals (30)
205 Sites with WiFi
Restroom and Showers
Laundry
ATM Machine
Ice
Restaurant / Cocktail Lounge
Cable
Guest Services
Self-Service RV Wash
Onsite Rentals (30)

Activities/Sports

- Swimming Pool
- Hot Tub
- Splash Pad
- Horseshoes
- Game Room
- Playground
- Golf
- Driving Range
- Pavilion
- Sauna
- Exercise Room
- Nature Trails
- Rec Open to the Public
- Casino

Paragon Casino RV Resort

124 Earl J Barbry Sr Blvd.
Marksville, LA 71351
(800) 946-1946
Location: 31.10556, -92.05825

MARYLAND

Furnace Town Parking Lot

3816 Old Furnace Rd.
Snow Hill, MD 21863
410-632-2032
Official Website:
http://www.furnacetown.org/
GPS: 38.2052, -75.4715

Hollofield Campground

Patapsco Valley State Park - Hollofield Area
8020 Baltimore National Pike
Ellicott City MD 21043
Official Website:
https://dnr.maryland.gov/publiclands/Pages
/central/PatapscoValley/Hollofield/Hollofiel
d-Area.aspx
GPS 39.295459 76.788858

Gambrill State Park

Gambrill State Park
8602 Gambrill Park Road
Frederick MD 21702
Official Website:
*https://dnr.maryland.gov/publiclands/Page
s/western/gambrill.aspx*
GPS: 39.4787125°N, -77.4913755°W

Ramblin' Pines Family Campground & RV Park

801 Hoods Mill Rd
Woodbine, MD 21797
(410) 795-5161
Location: 39.36728, -77.02505
Daily/Weekly/Monthly **Rates: 70 dollars**
Official website:
https://ramblinpinescampground.com
Spaces Available: 90
Max Length: 70

Amenities and services

Dump Station
Partial Handicap Access
Folding Tent Campers Allowed
Pets Welcome
Tent Camping Allowed
Cabin/Cottage Rentals (5)
Overflow Area
Dedicated Tenting Area
Covered Area w/Picnic Table
70 Sites with WiFi
Restroom and Showers
Laundry
Control Access Gate
ATM Machine
RV Supplies
Metered LP Gas
Firewood
Ice
Groceries
Escort to Site
Cable
Fishing Supplies
Onsite Rentals (5)
Enclosed Dog Run
Dog Park

Activities/Sports

- Heated Pool
- Water Umbrella
- Pond
- Fishing
- Horseshoes
- Rec Hall
- Game Room
- Planned Activities
- Playground
- Pavilion
- Shuffleboard
- Exercise Room
- Nature Trails
- Bounce Pillow
- Mini Golf

Cherry Hill Park

9800 Cherry Hill Rd
College Park, MD 20740
(301) 937-7116
Location: 39.02510, -76.94028
Daily/Weekly/Monthly **Rates: From 90 to 140 dollars**
Official website:
https://www.cherryhillpark.com
Spaces Available: 350
Max Length: 70

Amenities and services

Dump Station
Partial Handicap Access
Emergency Phone
Folding Tent Campers Allowed
Pets Welcome
Tent Camping Allowed
Teepee/Yurt Rentals (11)
Cabin/Cottage Rentals (15)
Dedicated Tenting Area
WiFi at Park Supports Streaming
On-Site WiFi Tech Support
350 Sites with WiFi
Restroom and Showers
Laundry
Control Access Gate
ATM Machine
RV Supplies
Metered LP Gas
Firewood
Ice
Snack Bar
Groceries

Cable
Guest Services
Self-Service RV Wash
Golf Carts
Onsite Rentals (26)
Enclosed Dog Run
Dog Park

Activities/Sports

- Heated Pool
- Hot Tub
- Splash Pad
- Water Umbrella
- Pond
- Fishing
- Rec Hall
- Game Room
- Planned Activities
- Playground
- Pavilion
- Sauna
- Exercise Room
- Nature Trails
- Mini Golf

Bar Harbor RV Park & Marina

4228 Birch Ave
Abingdon, MD 21009
(410) 679-0880
Location: 39.46031, -76.24424
Daily/Weekly/Monthly **Rates: From 81 to 91 dollars**
Official website:
https://www.barharborrvpark.com
Spaces Available: 73
Max Length: 50

Amenities and services

Dump Station
Emergency Phone
Limited Facilities - Winter
Pets Welcome
No Tents
73 Sites with WiFi
Restroom and Showers
Laundry

Control Access Gate
RV Supplies
Metered LP Gas
Firewood
Ice
Groceries
Onsite RV Service
Cable
Fishing Supplies
Enclosed Dog Run
Pet Supplies

Activities/Sports

- Swimming Pool
- River
- Boating
- Fishing
- Dock
- Ramp
- Boat Rental
- Body Of Water (Bush River)
- Rec Hall
- Game Room
- Playground
- Nature Trails

Sun Outdoors Ocean City Gateway

11224 Dale Road
Whaleyville, MD 21872
(888) 322-7717
Location: 38.38407, -75.31191
Daily/Weekly/Monthly **Rates: From 69 to 189 dollars**
Official website:
https://www.sunoutdoors.com/maryland/sun-outdoors-ocean-city-gateways
Spaces Available: 170
Max Length: 70

Amenities and services:

Dump Station
Mobile Sewer Service
Emergency Phone
Pets Welcome
Tent Camping Allowed
RV Park Model Rentals (24)

Cabin/Cottage Rentals (10)
Dedicated Tenting Area
On-Site WiFi Tech Support
150 Sites with WiFi
Restroom and Showers
Laundry
Control Access Gate
ATM Machine
RV Supplies
Metered LP Gas
Firewood
Ice
Snack Bar
Groceries
Cable
Fishing Supplies
Golf Carts
Onsite Rentals (34)
Enclosed Dog Run
Dog Park

Activities/Sports

- Heated Pool
- Boating
- Pond
- Fishing
- Boat Rental
- Paddle Boats
- Horseshoes
- Game Room
- Planned Activities
- Playground
- Outdoor Games
- Pavilion
- Tennis
- Shuffleboard
- Pedal Carts
- Bike Rentals
- Pickle Ball
- Mini Golf

Take-It-Easy Campground

45285 Take-It-Easy Ranch Rd
Callaway, MD 20620
(301) 994-0494
Daily/Weekly/Monthly **Rates: From 55 to 65 dollars**
Spaces Available: 160

Max Length: 55

Amenities and services:

Partial Handicap Access
Pets Welcome
No Tents
WiFi at Park Supports Streaming
160 Sites with WiFi
Restroom and Showers
Laundry

Activities/Sports

- Swimming Pool
- Pond
- Fishing
- Horseshoes
- Rec Hall
- Playground

M I S S I S S I P P I

Jeff Busby Campground

Natchez Trace Parkway
Natchez Trace Pkwy. (MP 193.1)
Ackerman, MS 39735
662-680-4025 / 800-305-7417
https://www.nps.gov/natr/planyourvisit/camping.htm
GPS: 33.4171, -89.2689
Number of Sites: 18 / Pad Type: asphalt
Elevation: 393 ft / 119 m
Max Stay: 14 / Max Length: 55 ft
Tent Camping: Yes

Rocky Springs Campground

Natchez Trace Parkway
Natchez Trace Pkwy.
Hermanville, MS 39086
662-680-4025 / 800-305-7417
https://www.nps.gov/natr/planyourvisit/camping.htm
GPS: 32.0868, -90.7994
Number of Sites: 22
Pad Type: asphalt
Elevation: 164 ft / 49 m / Tent Camping: Yes

Bynum Creek Campground

Army Corps Of Engineers
Cliff Finch Rd.
Water Valley, MS 38965
662-563-4571
https://www.mvk.usace.army.mil/Missions/Recreation/Enid-Lake/Enid-Lake-Recreation/
GPS: 34.1778, -89.7356
Number of Sites: 5
Elevation: 262 ft / 79 m
Tent Camping: Yes

Not Free Rv Camping

Cajun RV Park

1860 Beach Blvd.
Biloxi, MS 39531
(877) 225-8699
Location: 30.39380, -88.94910
Daily/Weekly/Monthly **Rates: From 59 to 89 dollars**
Official website: https://cajunrvpark.com
Spaces Available: 100
Max Length: 60

Amenities and services

Emergency Phone
Age Restrictions May Apply
Folding Tent Campers Allowed
RV Age Restrictions
Pets Welcome
No Tents
WiFi at Park Supports Streaming
100 Sites with WiFi
Restroom and Showers
Laundry
RV Supplies
Metered LP Gas
Ice
Cable
Complimentary Breakfast
Guest Services
Self-Service RV Wash
Enclosed Dog Run
Dog Park

Activities/Sports

- ✓ Swimming Pool
- ✓ Gulf
- ✓ Swimming
- ✓ Body Of Water (Gulf of Mexico)
- ✓ Horseshoes
- ✓ Rec Hall
- ✓ Planned Activities
- ✓ Playground
- ✓ Outdoor Games
- ✓ Pavilion

Indian Point RV Resort

1600 Indian Point Parkway
Gautier, MS 39553
(228) 497-1011
Location: 30.40631, -88.63450
Daily/Weekly/Monthly **Rates: 40 dollars**
Official website: https://indianpt.weebly.com
Spaces Available: 100
Max Length: 75

Amenities and services:

Dump Station
Partial Handicap Access
Emergency Phone
Pets Welcome
No Tents
RV Park Model Rentals (13)
Cabin/Cottage Rentals (23)
17 Sites with WiFi
Restroom and Showers
Laundry
Metered LP Gas
Ice
Restaurant
Cable
Self-Service RV Wash
Fishing Guides
Onsite Rentals (36)

Activities/Sports

- ✓ Swimming Pool
- ✓ River
- ✓ Boating
- ✓ Swimming
- ✓ Fishing
- ✓ Dock
- ✓ Ramp
- ✓ Body Of Water (Sioux Bayou)
- ✓ Horseshoes
- ✓ Playground
- ✓ Pavilion
- ✓ Mini Golf
- ✓ Kayaking/Canoeing

Sun Roamers RV Resort

41 Mississippi Pines Blvd
Picayune, MS 39466
(601) 798-5818

Location: 30.50998, -89.64984
Daily/Weekly/Monthly Rates: **From 40 to 43 dollars**
Official website:
http://www.sunroamers.com
Spaces Available: 118
Max Length: 60

Amenities and services:

Dump Station
Partial Handicap Access
Emergency Phone
Folding Tent Campers Allowed
Pets Welcome
Tent Camping Allowed
RV Park Model Rentals (7)
Cabin/Cottage Rentals (12)
Overflow Area
118 Sites with WiFi
Restroom and Showers
Laundry
Metered LP Gas
Ice
Worship Services
Snack Bar
Escort to Site
Guest Services
Self-Service RV Wash
Onsite Rentals (19)
Dog Park

Activities/Sports

✓ Swimming Pool
✓ Pond
✓ Fishing
✓ Horseshoes
✓ Rec Hall
✓ Playground
✓ Outdoor Games
✓ Driving Range
✓ Pavilion
✓ Exercise Room
✓ Nature Trails
✓ Mini Golf
✓ Rec Open to the Public

EZ Daze RV Park

536 W.E. Ross Pkwy
Southaven, MS 38671
(662) 342-7720
Location: 34.94186, -89.99883
Daily/Weekly/Monthly Rates: From 57 to 72 dollars
Official website:
http://www.ezdazervpark.com
Spaces Available: 50
Max Length: 75

Amenities and services

Partial Handicap Access
Emergency Phone
Pets Welcome
No Tents
50 Sites with WiFi
Restroom and Showers
Laundry
Metered LP Gas
Ice
Worship Services
Onsite RV Service
Cable
Guest Services
Staffed RV Wash
Enclosed Dog Run
Dog Park

Activities/Sports

✓ Swimming Pool
✓ Swimming
✓ Rec Hall
✓ Playground
✓ Pavilion
✓ Exercise Room

Hollywood Casino RV Park- Gulf Coast

711 Hollywood Blvd.
Bay St Louis, MS 39520
(228) 469-2100
Location: 30.33264, -89.35424
Daily/Weekly/Monthly **Rates: From 39 to 119 dollars**
Official website:
https://www.hollywoodgulfcoast.com

Spaces Available: 100
Max Length: 60

Amenities and services

Partial Handicap Access
Emergency Phone
Pets Welcome
No Tents
100 Sites with WiFi
Restroom and Showers
Laundry
ATM Machine
Metered LP Gas
Ice
Snack Bar
Restaurant
Onsite RV Service
Cable
Cocktail Lounge
Guest Services
Self-Service RV Wash

Activities/Sports

- ✓ Fishing Guides
- ✓ Golf Carts
- ✓ Swimming Pool
- ✓ Hot Tub
- ✓ River
- ✓ Boating
- ✓ Ramp
- ✓ Boat Marina
- ✓ Body Of Water (Jourdan River)
- ✓ Game Room
- ✓ Golf
- ✓ Driving Range
- ✓ Pavilion
- ✓ Exercise Room
- ✓ Putting Green
- ✓ Rec Open to the Public
- ✓ Casino

NORTH CAROLINA

Free Rv Camping	Not Free Rv Camping

Santeetlah Lake

Nantahala National Forest
Pine Ridge Road
Robbinsville, NC 28771
828-479-6431
Official Website:
https://www.fs.usda.gov/recarea/nfsnc/recre
ation/camping-
cabins/recarea/?recid=49694&actid=34
GPS: 35.3663, -83.8551
Number of Sites: 11 /Open Seasonally: Yes
Elevation: 1,935 ft / 589 m
Tent Camping: Yes

Blue Valley Designated Dispersed Campsites

Nantahala National Forest
Blue Valley Rd. (SR-1618)
Highlands, NC 28741
828-524-6441
828-257-4200
Official Website:
GPS: 35.0133, -83.2319
Number of Sites: 22
Elevation: 2,624 ft / 799 m
Max Stay: 14 / Tent Camping: Yes

Magazine Branch Lake Access

Nantahala National Forest
River Road
Tapoco, NC
828-479-6431
Official Website:
https://www.fs.usda.gov/recarea/nfsnc/recar
ea/?recid=48634
GPS: 35.453, -83.945
Number of Sites: 11
Pad Type: dirt / Tent Camping: Yes
Elevation: 1,148 ft / 349 m

Asheville Bear Creek RV Park

81 South Bear Creek Rd
Asheville, NC 28806
(828) 253-0798
Location: 35.55749, -82.60465
Daily/Weekly/Monthly **Rates: 60 dollars**
Official website:
https://ashevillebearcreek.com
Spaces Available: 94
Max Length: 60

Amenities and services

Partial Handicap Access
Emergency Phone
Folding Tent Campers Allowed
Pets Welcome
No Tents
94 Sites with WiFi
Restroom and Showers
Laundry
RV Supplies
Metered LP Gas
Ice
Cable
Staffed RV Wash

Activities/Sports

- ✓ Heated Pool
- ✓ Swimming
- ✓ Rec Hall
- ✓ Playground

Camping World Racing Resort

6600 Bruton Smith Blvd
Concord, NC 28027
(704) 455-4445
Location: 35.35896, -80.69059
Daily/Weekly/Monthly **Rates: From 40 to 45 dollars**
Official website:
https://www.charlottemotorspeedway.com

Spaces Available: 380
Max Length: 100

Amenities and services:
Dump Station
Partial Handicap Access
Folding Tent Campers Allowed
Pets Welcome
Tent Camping Allowed
Overflow Area
Dedicated Tenting Area
WiFi at Park Supports Streaming
380 Sites with WiFi
Restroom and Showers
Laundry
RV Supplies
LP Bottles Only
Firewood
Ice
Escort to Site
Near NASCAR® Track (0 mi to Charlotte Motor Speedway)
Enclosed Dog Run
Horseshoes
Playground
Outdoor Games
Pavilion

The Great Outdoors RV Resort

321 Thumpers Trail
Franklin, NC 28734
(828) 349-0412
Location: 35.23335, -83.34779
Daily/Weekly/Monthly **Rates: From 62 to 99 dollars**
Official website: https://gorvresort.com
Spaces Available: 63
Max Length: 60

Amenities and services
Partial Handicap Access
Emergency Phone
Pets Welcome
No Tents
Cabin/Cottage Rentals (3)
63 Sites with WiFi

Restroom and Showers
Laundry
RV Supplies
Metered LP Gas
Firewood
Ice
Escort to Site
Cable
Self-Service RV Wash
Onsite Rentals (3)
Enclosed Dog Run
Dog Washing Station
Pet Supplies

Activities/Sports
- ✓ Swimming Pool
- ✓ Swimming
- ✓ Horseshoes
- ✓ Rec Hall
- ✓ Outdoor Games
- ✓ Exercise Room

Broad River Campground

120 Broad River Campground Rd
Mooresboro, NC 28114
(828) 338-9598
Location: 35.19566, -81.66516
Daily/Weekly/Monthly **Rates: From 49 to 75 dollars**
Official website:
https://broadrivercampgroundnc.com
Spaces Available:200
Max Length:

Amenities and services:
Dump Station
Pets Welcome
No Tents
Teepee/Yurt Rentals (5)
Cabin/Cottage Rentals (10)
WiFi at Park Supports Streaming
16 Sites with WiFi
Restroom and Showers
Firewood
Escort to Site
Onsite Rentals (15)

Activities/Sports
- ✓ River

- ✓ Fishing
- ✓ Body Of Water (Broad River)
- ✓ Rec Hall
- ✓ Pavilion
- ✓ Kayaking/Canoeing

Mama Gertie's Hideaway Campground

15 Uphill Rd
Swannanoa, NC 28778
(828) 686-4258
Location: 35.58622, -82.40493
Daily/Weekly/Monthly **Rates: From 75 to 181 dollars**
Official website:
https://www.mamagerties.com
Spaces Available: 44
Max Length: 60

Amenities and services:
Dump Station
Partial Handicap Access
Emergency Phone
Limited Facilities - Winter
Folding Tent Campers Allowed
Pets Welcome / No Tents
Tent Rentals (4)
Teepee/Yurt Rentals (1)
Cabin/Cottage Rentals (4)
44 Sites with WiFi
Restroom and Showers
Laundry
RV Supplies
Metered LP Gas
Firewood / Ice
Escort to Site
Cable
Onsite Rentals (9)
Enclosed Dog Run
Horseshoes
Outdoor Games
Pavilion
Exercise Room

OKLAHOMA

Free Rv Camping

Black Kettle Campground

Black Kettle National Grassland
U.S. 283
Crawford, OK 73638
580-497-2143
Official Website:
https://www.fs.usda.gov/recarea/cibola/recreation/camping-cabins/recarea/?recid=64090&actid=29
GPS: 35.7453, -99.714
Number of Sites: 12 / Pad Type: asphalt
Elevation: 2,066 ft / 629 m
Tent Camping: Yes

Camping World of Tulsa

Parking Lot
 Write a Review
9005 E Skelly Dr.
Tulsa, OK 74129
844-468-0243
Official Website:
https://rv.campingworld.com/dealer/tulsa-oklahoma
GPS: 36.1285, -95.8766
Number of Sites: 5
Pad Type: asphalt / Elevation: 623 ft / 189 m

Skipout Campground

Black Kettle National Grassland
N1750 Road
Reydon, OK 73660
580-497-2143 / 505-346-3804
Official Website:
https://www.fs.usda.gov/recarea/cibola/recreation/recarea/?recid=64094&actid=29
GPS: 35.6351, -99.8797
Number of Sites: 12
Elevation: 2,263 ft / 689 m
Tent Camping: Yes

Not Free Rv Camping

Do Drop Inn RV Resort & Cabins

560 Platter Dike Rd
Calera, OK 74730
(580) 965-3600
Location: 33.90364, -96.54089
Daily/Weekly/Monthly **Rates: From 45 to 52 dollars**
Official website: https://www.dodropinn.com
Spaces Available: 111
Max Length: 60

Amenities and services

Dump Station
Partial Handicap Access
Emergency Phone
RV Age Restrictions
Pets Welcome
No Tents
RV Park Model Rentals (7)
Cabin/Cottage Rentals (5)
WiFi at Park Supports Streaming
WiFi Hotspots (12)
111 Sites with WiFi
Restroom and Showers
Laundry
RV Supplies
Metered LP Gas
Firewood
Ice
Worship Services
Snack Bar
Restaurant
Escort to Site
Cocktail Lounge
Guest Services
Onsite Rentals (12)
Dog Park

Activities/Sports

- ✓ Swimming Pool
- ✓ Hot Tub
- ✓ Boating
- ✓ Pond

- ✓ Fishing
- ✓ Boat Rental
- ✓ Rec Hall
- ✓ Outdoor Games
- ✓ Exercise Room
- ✓ Nature Trails

Council Road RV Park

8108 SW 8th St
Oklahoma City, OK 73128
(405) 789-2103
Location: 35.45394, -97.65515
Daily/Weekly/Monthly **Rates: 40 dollars**
Official website: https://councilrdrvpark.com
Spaces Available: 66
Max Length: 60

Amenities and services

Dump Station
Partial Handicap Access
Emergency Phone
Pets Welcome
No Tents
iFi at Overnite Sites
66 Sites with WiFi
Restroom and Showers
Laundry
Metered LP Gas
Ice
Snack Bar
Escort to Site
Onsite RV Service
Cable
Horseshoes
Pavilion

Rockwell RV Park

720 S Rockwell Ave
Oklahoma City, OK 73128
(405) 787-5992
Location: 35.45843, -97.63430
Daily/Weekly/Monthly **Rates: 53 dollars**
Official website:
http://www.rockwellrvpark.com
Spaces Available: 51
Max Length: 70

Amenities and services

Partial Handicap Access
Emergency Phone
Folding Tent Campers Allowed
RV Age Restrictions
Pets Welcome
No Tents
Cabin/Cottage Rentals (13)
WiFi at Park Supports Streaming
51 Sites with WiFi
Restroom and Showers
Laundry
LP Bottles Only
Ice
Worship Services
Cable
Complimentary Breakfast
Onsite Rentals (13)
Dog Park
Dog Washing Station

Activities/Sports

- ✓ Heated Pool
- ✓ Hot Tub
- ✓ Lake
- ✓ Fishing
- ✓ Body Of Water (Crystal Lake)
- ✓ Horseshoes
- ✓ Rec Hall
- ✓ Planned Activities
- ✓ Playground
- ✓ Outdoor Games
- ✓ Sauna
- ✓ Shuffleboard
- ✓ Exercise Room
- ✓ Nature Trails
- ✓ Kayaking/Canoeing

Fun Town RV Park at WinStar

21902 Merle Wolfe Rd
Thackerville, OK 73459
(580) 276-8900
Location: 33.75334, -97.12650
Daily/Weekly/Monthly **Rates: From 40 to 100 dollars**

Official website:
https://www.winstar.com/stay/accomodations/fun-town-rv-park-at-winstar
Spaces Available: 152
Max Length: 80

Amenities and services

Dump Station
Partial Handicap Access
Emergency Phone
Folding Tent Campers Allowed
Pets Welcome
No Tents
152 Sites with WiFi
Restroom and Showers
Laundry
ATM Machine
RV Supplies
Ice
Snack Bar
Guest Services

Activities/Sports
- ✓ Swimming Pool
- ✓ Hot Tub
- ✓ Horseshoes
- ✓ Playground
- ✓ Golf
- ✓ Driving Range
- ✓ Pavilion
- ✓ Putting Green
- ✓ Casino

Tent Camping Allowed
WiFi at Park Supports Streaming
72 Sites with WiFi
Restroom and Showers
Laundry
RV Supplies
Metered LP Gas
Firewood
Ice
Escort to Site
Cable
Dog Park

Activities/Sports
- ✓ Swimming Pool
- ✓ River
- ✓ Swimming
- ✓ Body Of Water (Caney River)
- ✓ Horseshoes
- ✓ Outdoor Games
- ✓ Pavilion
- ✓ Nature Trails

Riverside RV Park

1211 SE Adams Blvd.
Bartlesville, OK 74003
(918) 336-6431
Location: 36.74618, -95.96386
Daily/Weekly/Monthly **Rates: 39 dollars**
Official website: https://resortrv.com
Spaces Available: 72
Max Length: 60

Amenities and services

Dump Station
Emergency Phone
Folding Tent Campers Allowed
Pets Welcome

SOUTH CAROLINA

Santee Coastal Reserve Wildlife Management Area

Dept. Natural Resources
220 Santee Gun Club Rd.
McClellanville, SC 29458
843-546-8665
Official Website:
https://www2.dnr.sc.gov/ManagedLands/ManagedLand/ManagedLand/61
GPS: 33.1538, -79.3668
Number of Sites: 8
Pad Type: dirt
Max Stay: 4
Tent Camping: Yes

Elmwood Recreation Area

Francis Marion National Forest
Forest Service Road 211
McClellanville, SC 29458
843-336-2200 / 803-561-4000
Official Website:
https://www.fs.usda.gov/recarea/scnfs/recarea/?recid=47297
GPS: 33.199, -79.47
Max Stay: 14
Tent Camping: Yes

Grapevine Campground

Sumter National Forest
FS 764
Mountain Rest, SC 29664
864-638-9568
Official Website:
https://www.fs.usda.gov/recarea/scnfs/recarea/?recid=47097
GPS: 34.823, -83.1805
Number of Sites: 15
Pad Type: dirt
Elevation: 1,312 ft / 399 m
Tent Camping: Yes

Not Free Rv Camping

Savannah Lakes RV Resort

170 Savannah Lakes Drive
Hardeeville, SC 29927
(843) 628-2006
Location: 32.24474, -80.98380
Daily/Weekly/Monthly Rates: From 45 to 120 dollars
Official website:
https://savannahlakesrvresort.com
Spaces Available: 317
Max Length: 75

Amenities and services:

Age Restrictions May Apply
RV Age Restrictions
Pets Welcome
No Tents
Control Access Gate

Hilton Head Harbor RV Resort & Marina

43A Jenkins Island Rd
Hilton Head Island, SC 29926
(843) 681-3256
Location: 32.22328, -80.77140
Daily/Weekly/Monthly **Rates: From 99 to 199 dollars**
Official website:
https://www.hiltonheadharbor.com
Spaces Available: 200
Max Length: 65

Amenities and services

Pets Welcome
No Tents
WiFi at Park Supports Streaming
200 Sites with WiFi
Restroom and Showers
Laundry
Firewood / Ice
Restaurant
Onsite RV Service
Cable

Cocktail Lounge
Self-Service RV Wash
Fishing Guides

Activities/Sports

✓ Heated Pool
✓ Hot Tub
✓ River
✓ Boating
✓ Fishing
✓ Dock
✓ Ramp
✓ Boat Rental
✓ Boat Marina
✓ Body Of Water (Intracoastal Waterway)
✓ Playground
✓ Tennis
✓ Exercise Room
✓ Pickle Ball
✓ Kayaking/Canoeing
✓ Watersports

Apache Family Campground & Pier

9700 Kings Rd
Myrtle Beach, SC 29572
(800) 553-1749
Location: 33.76320, -78.78140
Daily/Weekly/Monthly **Rates: From 46 to 92 dollars**
Official website:
https://www.apachefamilycampground.com
Spaces Available: 227
Max Length: 60

Amenities and services:

Dump Station
Partial Handicap Access
Folding Tent Campers Allowed
Pets Welcome
Tent Camping Allowed
RV Park Model Rentals (23)
Covered Area w/Picnic Table
WiFi at Park Supports Streaming
227 Sites with WiFi
Restroom and Showers
Laundry

Control Access Gate
ATM Machine
RV Supplies
Metered LP Gas
Firewood / Ice
Worship Services
Groceries / Restaurant
Onsite RV Service
Cable
Cocktail Lounge
Guest Services
Self-Service RV Wash
Fishing Supplies
Golf Carts
Onsite Rentals (23)
Electric Vehicle Charging Station

Activities/Sports

- ✓ Swimming Pool
- ✓ Splash Pad
- ✓ Water Umbrella
- ✓ Ocean
- ✓ Wading Pool
- ✓ Fishing
- ✓ Body Of Water (Atlantic Ocean)
- ✓ Rec Hall
- ✓ Game Room
- ✓ Planned Activities
- ✓ Playground
- ✓ Outdoor Games
- ✓ Pavilion
- ✓ Kayaking/Canoeing

Oak Plantation Campground

3540 Savannah Hwy
Charleston, SC 29455
(843) 766-5936
Location: 32.80308, -80.10704
Daily/Weekly/Monthly **Rates: From 55 to 73 dollars**
Official website:
https://oakplantationcampground.com
Spaces Available: 220
Max Length: 80

Amenities and services

Dump Station
Folding Tent Campers Allowed
Pets Welcome
No Tents
On-Site WiFi Tech Support
220 Sites with WiFi
Restroom and Showers
Laundry
RV Supplies
Metered LP Gas
Firewood / Ice
Worship Services
Onsite RV Service
Cable
Self-Service RV Wash

Activities/Sports

- ✓ Swimming Pool
- ✓ Pond
- ✓ Fishing
- ✓ Horseshoes
- ✓ Playground
- ✓ Outdoor Games
- ✓ Pavilion
- ✓ Nature Trails
- ✓ Frisbee Golf
- ✓ Rec Open to the Public

Springwood RV Park

810 Donaldson Rd
Greenville, SC 29605
(864) 277-9789
Location: 34.76017, -82.38466
Daily/Weekly/Monthly **Rates: 50 dollars**
Official website:
https://springwoodrvpark.com
Spaces Available: 30
Max Length: 65

Amenities and services

Pets Welcome
No Tents
WiFi at Park Supports Streaming
30 Sites with WiFi
Restroom and Showers
Laundry
Escort to Site
Self-Service RV Wash

TENNESSEE

Meriwether Lewis Campground

Natchez Trace Parkway
Natchez Trace Pkwy. (MP 385.9)
Hohenwald, TN 38462
662-680-4025 / 800-305-7417
Official Website:
https://www.nps.gov/natr/planyourvisit/camping.htm
GPS: 35.5225, -87.4559
Number of Sites: 7 / Pad Type: asphalt
Elevation: 1,771 ft / 539 m

Rhea Springs Recreation Area Campground

County Park
Rhea Springs Road
Spring City, TN 37381
423-775-7801 / 423-775-5553
https://tennesseerivervalleygeotourism.org/entries/rhea-springs-recreation-area/ffe64ff2-4d3f-458a-aaaf-adc001774f32
GPS: 35.6832, -84.8262
Pad Type: mixed
Open Seasonally: April - November
Elevation: 754 ft / 229 m
Max Stay: 14 / Tent Camping: Yes

Citico Creek Designated Dispersed Campsites

Cherokee National Forest
Citico Rd.
Vonore, TN 37885 / 423-397-8455
https://www.fs.usda.gov/recarea/cherokee/recarea/?recid=35032
GPS: 35.4563, -84.1194
Pad Type: dirt
Elevation: 984 ft / 299 m
Max Stay: 14 / Tent Camping: Yes

Chattanooga Holiday Travel Park

1709 Mack Smith Rd
Chattanooga, TN 37412
(800) 693-2877
Location: 34.98624, -85.21101
Daily/Weekly/Monthly **Rates: 56 dollars**
Official website: https://chattacamp.com
Spaces Available: 60
Max Length: 60

Amenities and services

Dump Station
Folding Tent Campers Allowed
Pets Welcome / Dog Park
Tent Camping Allowed
Cabin/Cottage Rentals (5)
Overflow Area
Dedicated Tenting Area
60 Sites with WiFi
Restroom and Showers
Laundry
RV Supplies
Metered LP Gas
Firewood / Ice
Onsite RV Service
Cable
Onsite Rentals (5)

Activities/Sports

- ✓ Swimming Pool
- ✓ Horseshoes
- ✓ Rec Hall
- ✓ Playground
- ✓ Pavilion
- ✓ Shuffleboard

Twin Creek RV Resort

1202 E Parkway
Gatlinburg, TN 37738
(865) 436-7081
Location: 35.72597, -83.48291
Daily/Weekly/Monthly **Rates: From 94 to 98 dollars**
Official website:
https://twincreekrvresort.com
Spaces Available: 85
Max Length: 60

Amenities and services

Pets Welcome
No Tents
RV Park Model Rentals (2)
Cabin/Cottage Rentals (2)
85 Sites with WiFi
Restroom and Showers
Laundry
RV Supplies
Firewood / Ice
Worship Services
Groceries
Escort to Site
Onsite RV Service
Cable
Onsite Rentals (4)

Activities/Sports

- ✓ Heated Pool
- ✓ Hot Tub
- ✓ Stream
- ✓ Swimming
- ✓ Wading Pool
- ✓ Fishing
- ✓ Body Of Water (Dudley Creek)
- ✓ Playground

Two Rivers Campground

2616 Music Valley Drive
Nashville, TN 37214
(615) 883-8559
Location: 36.23431, -86.70369
Daily/Weekly/Monthly **Rates: From 56 to 66 dollars**
Official website:
https://www.tworiverscampground.com
Spaces Available: 104
Max Length: 54

Amenities and services

Dump Station
Pets Welcome / Enclosed Dog Run
No Tents
104 Sites with WiFi

Restroom and Showers
Laundry
ATM Machine
RV Supplies
Ice
Groceries
Onsite RV Service
Cable

Activities/Sports
- ✓ Swimming Pool
- ✓ Rec Hall
- ✓ Playground
- ✓ Outdoor Games
- ✓ Pavilion

Riveredge RV Park & Cabin Rentals

4220 Huskey St
Pigeon Forge, TN 37863
(866) 777-6127
Location: 35.77388, -83.53718
Daily/Weekly/Monthly **Rates: From 77 to 110** dollars
Official website:
https://www.stayriveredge.com
Spaces Available: 168
Max Length: 55

Amenities and services:
Partial Handicap Access
Emergency Phone
Pets Welcome
No Tents
Cabin/Cottage Rentals (34)
168 Sites with WiFi
Restroom and Showers
Laundry
RV Supplies
Firewood
Ice
Groceries
Onsite RV Service
Cable
Onsite Rentals (34)
Pet Supplies

Activities/Sports
- ✓ Heated Pool

- ✓ Hot Tub
- ✓ Splash Pad
- ✓ Swimming
- ✓ Wading Pool
- ✓ Game Room
- ✓ Playground

Pine Mountain RV Park by the Creek

411 Pine Mountain Rd
Pigeon Forge, TN 37863
(877) 753-9994
Location: 35.78999, -83.56639
Daily/Weekly/Monthly **Rates: From 55 to 101 dollars**
Official website:
https://pinemountainrvpark.com
Spaces Available: 61
Max Length: 60

Amenities and services
Pet Restriction on Size
No Tents
Cabin/Cottage Rentals (2)
WiFi at Park Supports Streaming
61 Sites with WiFi
Restroom and Showers
Laundry
RV Supplies
Firewood
Ice
Onsite RV Service
Cable
Onsite Rentals (2)

Activities/Sports
- ✓ Heated Pool
- ✓ Hot Tub
- ✓ Splash Pad
- ✓ Stream
- ✓ Fishing
- ✓ Body Of Water (Mill Creek)
- ✓ Exercise Room

TEXAS

Magnolia Beach Dispersed Camping

County Park
North Ocean Dr.
Port Lavaca, TX 77979
Official Website:
https://www.calhouncotx.org/Parks/index.html
GPS: 28.5599, -96.537
Max Stay: 14

Fort Lancaster Scenic Overlook Overnight Parking

Hwy 290
Sheffield, TX 79781
432-836-4391
Official Website:
https://www.thc.texas.gov/historic-sites/fort-lancaster-state-historic-site
GPS: 30.678, -101.6727
Pad Type: asphalt
Elevation: 2,624 ft / 799 m
Max Stay: 1

South Beach Dispersed Camping

Padre Island National Seashore
Park Road 22
Corpus Christi, TX 78418
361-949-8068
Official Website:
https://www.nps.gov/pais/planyourvisit/south_beach.htm
GPS: 27.4155, -97.3016
Max Stay: 14
Tent Camping: Yes

Not Free Rv Camping

Fort Amarillo RV Resort

10101 Business Interstate 40
Amarillo, TX 79124
(806) 331-1700
Location: 35.19122, -101.95817
Daily/Weekly/Monthly **Rates: 55 dollars**
Official website: http://fortrvparks.com
Spaces Available: 105
Max Length: 75

Amenities and services

Pets Welcome
No Tents
WiFi at Park Supports Streaming
70 Sites with WiFi
Restroom and Showers
Laundry
Ice
Self-Service RV Wash
Dog Park

Activities/Sports

- ✓ Heated Pool
- ✓ Pond
- ✓ Swimming
- ✓ Fishing
- ✓ Rec Hall
- ✓ Game Room
- ✓ Playground
- ✓ Outdoor Games
- ✓ Pavilion
- ✓ Tennis
- ✓ Exercise Room

Oasis RV Resort

2715 Arnot Rd
Amarillo, TX 79124
(888) 789-9697
Location: 35.18388, -102.00949
Daily/Weekly/Monthly Rates: From 67 to 73 dollars
Official website:
https://www.robertsresorts.com/resorts/oasis-amarillo

Spaces Available: 149
Max Length: 75

Amenities and services:

Dump Station
Partial Handicap Access
Emergency Phone
Folding Tent Campers Allowed
Pets Welcome
No Tents
Cabin/Cottage Rentals (10)
149 Sites with WiFi
Restroom and Showers
Laundry
RV Supplies
Metered LP Gas
Ice
Cable
Onsite Rentals (10)
Enclosed Dog Run

Activities/Sports

- ✓ Swimming Pool
- ✓ Hot Tub
- ✓ Horseshoes
- ✓ Rec Hall
- ✓ Game Room
- ✓ Playground
- ✓ Outdoor Games
- ✓ Pavilion
- ✓ Exercise Room

Southern Oaks RV Resort

1850 Hwy 35 Bypass
Aransas Pass, TX 78336
(361) 758-1249
Location: 27.92728, -97.15629
Daily/Weekly/Monthly **Rates: 70 dollars**
Official website: https://www.sorvresort.com
Spaces Available: 234
Max Length: 75

Amenities and services

Partial Handicap Access
Emergency Phone
RV Age Restrictions
Pets Welcome
Pet Restriction on Quantity

No Tents
WiFi Hotspots (1)
234 Sites with WiFi
Restroom and Showers
Laundry
Self-Service RV Wash
Enclosed Dog Run
Dog Park

- ✓ Heated Pool
- ✓ Pond
- ✓ Swimming
- ✓ Fishing
- ✓ Rec Hall
- ✓ Game Room
- ✓ Planned Activities
- ✓ Shuffleboard
- ✓ Exercise Room
- ✓ Nature Trails
- ✓ Pickle Ball

Shady Creek RV Park and Storage

1893 FM 1385
Aubrey, TX 76227
(972) 347-5384
Location: 33.23544, -96.89525
Daily/Weekly/Monthly Rates: 70 dollars
Official website:
https://www.shadycreekrvpark.com
Spaces Available: 133
Max Length: 65

Amenities and services

Partial Handicap Access
Emergency Phone
Pets Welcome
Pet Restrictions on Size
No Tents
WiFi at Overnite Sites
133 Sites with WiFi
Restroom and Showers
Laundry
Metered LP Gas
Escort to Site
Self-Service RV Wash
Dog Park

Activities/Sports

- ✓ Swimming Pool
- ✓ Pond
- ✓ Fishing
- ✓ Rec Hall
- ✓ Playground
- ✓ Outdoor Games

The Retreat at Shady Creek

15038 Fishtrap Rd
Aubrey, TX 76227
(972) 347-5384
Location: 33.23016, -96.89998
Daily/Weekly/Monthly **Rates: 80 dollars**
Official website:
https://www.theretreatatshadycreek.com
Spaces Available: 115
Max Length: 95

Amenities and services

Partial Handicap Access
Emergency Phone
Pets Welcome
No Tents
115 Sites with WiFi
Restroom and Showers
Laundry
Control Access Gate
Metered LP Gas
Escort to Site
Self-Service RV Wash
Enclosed Dog Run

Activities/Sports

- ✓ Swimming Pool
- ✓ Pond
- ✓ Fishing
- ✓ Rec Hall
- ✓ Outdoor Games
- ✓ Pavilion
- ✓ Exercise Room
- ✓ Nature Trails
- ✓ Putting Green

VIRGINIA

Oronoco Campground Dispersed Camping Area

George Washington & Jefferson National Forests
Pedlar River Rd.
Vesuvius, VA 24483
540-291-2188 / 540-265-5100
https://www.fs.usda.gov/main/gwj/
GPS: 37.7477, -79.2638
Pad Type: dirt
Elevation: 1,673 ft / 509 m
Max Stay: 21 / Tent Camping: Yes

Little Fort Campground

George Washington & Jefferson National Forests
SR0758 / Fort Valley, VA 22652
540-984-4101 / 540-265-5100
https://www.fs.usda.gov/recarea/gwj/recarea/?recid=73807
GPS: 38.8682, -78.4421
Number of Sites: 9
Pad Type: gravel
Elevation: 1,312 ft / 399 m
Max Stay: 14 / Tent Camping: Yes

Crisman Hollow Road Dispersed Camping

George Washington & Jefferson National Forests
Crisman Hollow Rd. (FR-724)
New Market, VA / 540-984-4101
https://www.fs.usda.gov/activity/gwj/recreation/camping-cabins/?recid=73539&actid=34
GPS: 38.6924, -78.5793
Number of Sites: 8 / Pad Type: dirt
Open Seasonally: Yes
Elevation: 1,902 ft / 579 m
Max Stay: 21
Tent Camping: Yes

Not Free Rv Camping

Lake Gaston Americamps

9 Lakeside Lane
Bracey, VA 23919
(434) 636-2668
Location: 36.56216, -78.07183
Daily/Weekly/Monthly **Rates: From 49 to 66 dollars**
Official website:
http://www.lakegastonamericamps.com
Spaces Available: 124
Max Length: 55

Amenities and services

Dump Station
Mobile Sewer Service
Limited Facilities - Winter
Folding Tent Campers Allowed
Pets Welcome
Tent Camping Allowed
Cabin/Cottage Rentals (8)
Covered Area w/Picnic Table
124 Sites with WiFi
Restroom and Showers
Laundry
Control Access Gate
RV Supplies
Metered LP Gas
Firewood
Ice
Worship Services
Snack Bar
Groceries
Escort to Site
Onsite RV Service
Self-Service RV Wash
Fishing Guides
Fishing Supplies
Golf Carts
Onsite Rentals (8)

Activities/Sports

- ✓ Swimming Pool
- ✓ Lake
- ✓ Boating
- ✓ Wading Pool
- ✓ Fishing
- ✓ Dock
- ✓ Ramp
- ✓ Boat Rental
- ✓ Body Of Water (Lake Gaston)
- ✓ Horseshoes
- ✓ Rec Hall
- ✓ Game Room
- ✓ Planned Activities
- ✓ Playground
- ✓ Outdoor Games
- ✓ Pavilion
- ✓ Mini Golf
- ✓ Watersports

Misty Mountain Camp Resort

56 Misty Mountain Rd
Greenwood, VA 22943
(888) 647-8900
Location: 38.03953, -78.73961
Daily/Weekly/Monthly **Rates: From 45 to 70 dollars**
Official website:
https://www.mistymountaincampresort.com
Spaces Available: 99
Max Length: 100

Amenities and services

Dump Station
Partial Handicap Access
Folding Tent Campers Allowed
Pet Restriction on Quantity
Tent Camping Allowed
Cabin/Cottage Rentals (16)
Overflow Area
WiFi at Park Supports Streaming
99 Sites with WiFi
Restroom and Showers
Laundry
RV Supplies
Metered LP Gas
Firewood
Ice
Snack Bar
Groceries
Onsite RV Service

Cable
Cocktail Lounge
Guest Services
Fishing Supplies
Golf Carts
Onsite Rentals (16)
Dog Park

Activities/Sports

- ✓ Swimming Pool
- ✓ Splash Pad
- ✓ Pond
- ✓ Fishing
- ✓ Body Of Water (Stockton Creek)
- ✓ Horseshoes
- ✓ Rec Hall
- ✓ Game Room
- ✓ Planned Activities
- ✓ Playground
- ✓ Outdoor Games
- ✓ Pavilion
- ✓ Horseback Riding
- ✓ Exercise Room
- ✓ Nature Trails
- ✓ Pedal Carts
- ✓ Bounce Pillow
- ✓ Rec Open to the Public

Picture Lake Campground

7818 Boydton Plank Rd
Dinwiddie, VA 23803
(804) 861-0174
Location: 37.16432, -77.51302
Daily/Weekly/Monthly **Rates: From 55 to 65 dollars**
Official website:
http://www.picturelakecampground.com/?utm_source=GoodSam
Spaces Available: 195
Max Length: 60

Amenities and services

Dump Station
Mobile Sewer Service
Folding Tent Campers Allowed
Pets Welcome
Tent Camping Allowed
Cabin/Cottage Rentals (12)
Overflow Area
Covered Area w/Picnic Table

195 Sites with WiFi
Restroom and Showers
Laundry
RV Supplies
Metered LP Gas
Firewood
Ice
Snack Bar
Groceries
Escort to Site
Self-Service RV Wash
Fishing Supplies
Near NASCAR® Track (30 mi to Richmond Raceway)
Onsite Rentals (12)

Activities/Sports

- ✓ Swimming Pool
- ✓ Lake
- ✓ Boating
- ✓ Fishing
- ✓ Boat Rental
- ✓ Body Of Water (Picture Lake)
- ✓ Horseshoes
- ✓ Playground
- ✓ Outdoor Games
- ✓ Pavilion
- ✓ Rec Open to the Public
- ✓ Kayaking/Canoeing

American Heritage RV Park

146 Maxton Lane
Williamsburg, VA 23188
(888) 530-2267
Location: 37.37708, -76.76866
Daily/Weekly/Monthly **Rates: From 64 to 109 dollars**
Official website:
http://americanheritagervpark.com
Spaces Available: 145
Max Length: 60

Amenities and services

Dump Station
Folding Tent Campers Allowed
Pets Welcome
No Tents

RV Park Model Rentals (1)
Cabin/Cottage Rentals (12)
145 Sites with WiFi
Restroom and Showers
Laundry
ATM Machine
RV Supplies
Metered LP Gas
Firewood
Ice
Groceries
Cable
Golf Carts
Onsite Rentals (13)
Enclosed Dog Run
Pet Supplies

RV Supplies
Metered LP Gas
Ice
Groceries
Cable
Fishing Supplies

Activities/Sports

- Heated Pool
- Game Room
- Playground
- Outdoor Games
- Pavilion

Activities/Sports

- Swimming Pool
- Horseshoes
- Rec Hall
- Game Room
- Playground
- Outdoor Games
- Nature Trails
- Pedal Carts
- Pickle Ball
- Mini Golf

Fort Chiswell RV Park

312 Ft. Chiswell Rd
Max Meadows, VA 24360
(276) 637-6868
Location: 36.94028, -80.94322
Daily/Weekly/Monthly **Rates: From 40 to 50 dollars**
Official website:
https://properties.camping.com/fort-chiswell-rv-campground
Spaces Available: 110
Max Length: 60

Amenities and services:

Folding Tent Campers Allowed
Pets Welcome
No Tents
110 Sites with WiFi
Restroom and Showers
Laundry

WEST VIRGINIA

St. Albans Roadside Park Campground

City Park
Write a Review
612-736 MacCorkle Ave SW
St. Albans, WV 25177
304-722-4625
Official Website:
https://www.saparkswv.com/places/roadside-park-port-of-st-albans/
GPS: 38.3884, -81.8249
Number of Sites: 3 / Pad Type: asphalt
Elevation: 557 ft / 169 m
Max Stay: 2

Army Camp Campground

New River Gorge National Park
174 Prince Army Camp Rd.
Prince, WV 25907
304-465-0508
Official Website:
https://www.nps.gov/neri/planyourvisit/army-camp-campground.htm
GPS: 37.8585, -81.0986
Number of Sites:11
Pad Type: asphalt
Elevation:1,115 ft / 339 m
Max Stay: 14 / Tent Camping: Yes

Squirrel Gap Dispersed Camping

George Washington & Jefferson National Forests
Wardensville, WV 26851
888-265-0019
GPS: 39.067, -78.6416
Pad Type: dirt
Elevation: 1,541 ft / 469 m
Max Stay: 21 / Tent Camping: Yes

Not Free Rv Camping

Rifrafters Campground

448 Laurel Creek Rd
Fayetteville, WV 25840
(304) 574-1065
Location: 38.04765, -81.12596
Daily/Weekly/Monthly **Rates: From 45 to 48 dollars**
Official website: https://www.rifrafters.com
Spaces Available: 25
Max Length: 50

Amenities and services

Dump Station
Partial Handicap Access
Emergency Phone
Limited Facilities - Winter
Folding Tent Campers Allowed
Pets Welcome
Tent Camping Allowed
Cabin/Cottage Rentals (8)
Overflow Area
Dedicated Tenting Area
On-Site WiFi Tech Support
16 Sites with WiFi
Restroom and Showers
Laundry
RV Supplies
Firewood
Ice
Escort to Site
Cable
Onsite Rentals (8)
Pond

Activities/Sports

- ✓ Fishing
- ✓ Playground
- ✓ Outdoor Games
- ✓ Pavilion
- ✓ Nature Trails

Robert Newlon RV Park

6090 Kyle Lane
Huntington, WV 25702
(304) 733-1240
Location: 38.46092, -82.31013
Daily/Weekly/Monthly **Rates: From 36 to 42 dollars**
Official website: https://robertnewlon.com
Spaces Available: 42
Max Length: 65

Amenities and services

Pets Welcome
No Tents
42 Sites with WiFi
Restroom and Showers
Laundry
ATM Machine
Metered LP Gas
Firewood
Ice
Restaurant
Onsite RV Service
Cocktail Lounge
Dog Park
River

- ✓ Boating
- ✓ Swimming
- ✓ Fishing
- ✓ Boat Rental
- ✓ Body Of Water (Ohio River)
- ✓ Pavilion
- ✓ Nature Trails
- ✓ Frisbee Golf
- ✓ Rec Open to the Public
- ✓ Kayaking/Canoeing

State Fair of West Virginia Campground

947 Maplewood Ave
Lewisburg, WV 24901
(304) 645-1090
Location: 37.77863, -80.46327
Daily/Weekly/Monthly **Rates: 45 dollars**
Official website:
https://statefairofwv.com/camping
Spaces Available: 742
Max Length: 90

Amenities and services

Folding Tent Campers Allowed
Pets Welcome
Tent Camping Allowed
Overflow Area
Dedicated Tenting Area
700 Sites with WiFi
Restroom and Showers
Onsite RV Service
Rec Open to the Public

Just Plane Adventures Lodging & Campground

59 Just Plane Adventures Lane
Medley, WV 26710
(304) 703-5898
Location: 39.17736, -79.05667
Daily/Weekly/Monthly **Rates: 42 dollars**
Official website:
https://justplaneadventures.com
Spaces Available: 24
Max Length: 80

Amenities and services

Folding Tent Campers Allowed
Pets Welcome
Tent Camping Allowed
RV Park Model Rentals (2)
Cabin/Cottage Rentals (3)
Lodge Room Rentals (2)
Overflow Area
Dedicated Tenting Area
24 Sites with WiFi
Restroom and Showers
Laundry
Firewood
Worship Services
Escort to Site
Onsite Rentals (7)
Pond

Activities/Sports

- ✓ Fishing
- ✓ Horseshoes
- ✓ Rec Hall
- ✓ Nature Trails

Brushcreek Falls RV Resort

5127 Eads Mill Rd
Princeton, WV 24739
(304) 431-1950
Location: 37.45133, -81.06224
Daily/Weekly/Monthly **Rates: From 48 to 68 dollars**
Official website:
https://www.brushcreekfalls.com
Spaces Available: 60
Max Length: 60

Amenities and services

Limited Facilities - Winter
Pets Welcome
No Tents
Cabin/Cottage Rentals (4)
Lodge Room Rentals (3)
60 Sites with WiFi
Restroom and Showers
Laundry
Control Access Gate
ATM Machine
RV Supplies
Metered LP Gas
Firewood
Ice
Snack Bar
Groceries
Guest Services
Fishing Supplies
Onsite Rentals (7)

Activities/Sports

- ✓ Swimming Pool
- ✓ Splash Pad
- ✓ Swimming
- ✓ Game Room
- ✓ Playground
- ✓ Outdoor Games
- ✓ Mini Golf

RV Camping in the North East

CONNECTICUT

Foxwoods Resort Casino

350 Trolley Line Blvd.
Mashantucket, CT 06338
800-369-9663
Official Website:
https://www.foxwoods.com/
GPS: 41.471, -71.9536
Number of Sites: 28
Pad Type: asphalt
Elevation: 164 ft / 49 m
Max Stay: 10

Not Free Rv Camping

Stateline Campresort & Cabins

1639 Hartford Pike
East Killingly, CT 06243
(860) 774-3016
Location: 41.84802, -71.79518
Daily/Weekly/Monthly **Rates: From 55 to 83 dollars**
Official website:
https://statelinecampresort.com/
Spaces Available: 50
Max Length: 43

Amenities and services

Dump Station
Mobile Sewer Service
Emergency Phone
olding Tent Campers Allowed
Pet Restriction on Quantity
No Tents
Cabin/Cottage Rentals (16)
50 Sites with WiFi
Restroom and Showers
Laundry
Control Access Gate
ATM Machine
RV Supplies
Metered LP Gas
Firewood
Ice
Snack Bar
Groceries
Escort to Site
Onsite RV Service
Cable
Guest Services
Fishing Supplies
Near NASCAR® Track (12 mi to Thompson Speedway Motorsports Park)
Onsite Rentals (16)
Enclosed Dog Run

Activities/Sports
- ✓ Swimming Pool
- ✓ Splash Pad
- ✓ Water Umbrella
- ✓ Boating
- ✓ Lake
- ✓ Fishing
- ✓ Dock
- ✓ Boat Rental
- ✓ Body Of Water (Campground Lake)
- ✓ Horseshoes
- ✓ Rec Hall
- ✓ Game Room
- ✓ Planned Activities
- ✓ Playground
- ✓ Outdoor Games
- ✓ Pavilion
- ✓ Nature Trails

Gentile's Campground

223 Mount Tobe Rd. (Rt 262)
Plymouth, CT 06782
(860) 283-8437
Location: 41.62941, -73.04841
Daily/Weekly/Monthly **Rates: 67 dollars**
Official website:
https://gentilescampground.com
Spaces Available: 140
Max Length: 80

Amenities and services

Dump Station
Emergency Phone
Limited Facilities - Winter
Pets Welcome
Tent Camping Allowed
Dedicated Tenting Area
WiFi at Park Supports Streaming
140 Sites with WiFi
Restroom and Showers
Restroom/Showers ($)
Control Access Gate
ATM Machine
Metered LP Gas
Firewood
Ice
Worship Services
Golf Carts
Dog Park

- ✓ Swimming Pool
- ✓ Horseshoes
- ✓ Rec Hall
- ✓ Game Room
- ✓ Planned Activities
- ✓ Playground
- ✓ Outdoor Games
- ✓ Pavilion
- ✓ Tennis
- ✓ Mini Golf

Hidden Acres Family Campground

47 River Rd
Preston, CT 06365
(860) 887-9633
Location: 41.55354, -72.01463
Daily/Weekly/Monthly **Rates: From 65 to 93 dollars**
Official website:
https://www.hiddenacrescamp.com
Spaces Available: 73
Max Length: 65

Amenities and services

Dump Station
Partial Handicap Access
Folding Tent Campers Allowed
Pet Restrictions on Size
Tent Camping Allowed
RV Park Model Rentals (1)
Cabin/Cottage Rentals (3)
WiFi Hotspots (6)
73 Sites with WiFi
Restroom and Showers
Restroom/Showers ($)
Laundry
Control Access Gate
ATM Machine
RV Supplies
Metered LP Gas
Firewood
Ice
Snack Bar
Groceries
Escort to Site

Restaurant
Fishing Supplies
Onsite Rentals (4)

Activities/Sports

- ✓ Swimming Pool
- ✓ River
- ✓ Fishing
- ✓ No Motors
- ✓ Body Of Water (Quinebaug River)
- ✓ Horseshoes
- ✓ Rec Hall
- ✓ Game Room
- ✓ Planned Activities
- ✓ Playground
- ✓ Outdoor Games
- ✓ Pavilion
- ✓ Nature Trails
- ✓ Frisbee Golf
- ✓ Pickle Ball

Salem Farms Campground

39 Alexander Rd
Salem, CT 06420
(860) 859-2320
Location: 41.49943, -72.31784
Daily/Weekly/Monthly **Rates: From 65 to 69 dollars**
Official website:
https://www.salemfarmscampground.com
Spaces Available: 40
Max Length: 60

Amenities and services:

Dump Station
Mobile Sewer Service
Emergency Phone
Folding Tent Campers Allowed
Pets Welcome
No Tents
RV Park Model Rentals (2)
WiFi Hotspots (3)
40 Sites with WiFi
Restroom and Showers
Restroom/Showers ($)
Laundry
Control Access Gate
ATM Machine
RV Supplies

Metered LP Gas
Firewood
Ice
Groceries
Escort to Site
Onsite RV Service
Cable
Staffed RV Wash
Onsite Rentals (2)
Dog Park
Pet Supplies

Restroom and Showers
Laundry
RV Supplies
Metered LP Gas
Firewood
Ice
Snack Bar
Onsite RV Service
Cable
Onsite Rentals (1)

Activities/Sports

✓ Swimming Pool
✓ Pond
✓ Fishing
✓ Horseshoes
✓ Rec Hall
✓ Game Room
✓ Planned Activities
✓ Playground
✓ Outdoor Games
✓ Pavilion
✓ Tennis
✓ Nature Trails
✓ Mini Golf

Activities/Sports

✓ Swimming Pool
✓ Stream
✓ Fishing
✓ Body Of Water (Branch Brook)
✓ Horseshoes
✓ Rec Hall
✓ Outdoor Games
✓ Pavilion
✓ Pickle Ball

Branch Brook Campground

435 Watertown Rd
Thomaston, CT 06787
(860) 283-8144
Location: 41.65469, -73.09328
Daily/Weekly/Monthly **Rates: 65 dollars**
Official website:
https://www.branchbrookcampgroundct.com
Spaces Available: 58
Max Length: 60

Amenities and services

Emergency Phone
Folding Tent Campers Allowed
Pets Welcome
Tent Camping Allowed
RV Park Model Rentals (1)
Dedicated Tenting Area
58 Sites with WiFi

MAINE

Freeport Village Station

Deport & Grove Streets
Freeport, ME 04032
207-552-7772
Official Website:
http://www.onefreeportvillagestation.com/
GPS: 43.8551, -70.1044
Number of Sites: 5
Pad Type: concrete
Elevation: 131 ft / 39 m

Airline Rips Campsite

Machias River Corridor
State Route 9
Wesley, ME 04686
207-941-4412
Official Website:
https://apps.web.maine.gov/cgi-
bin/online/doc/parksearch/index.pl
GPS: 44.9074, -67.8353
Number of Sites: 2
Open Seasonally: Yes
Elevation: 164 ft / 49 m
Tent Camping: Yes

Log Landing Campsite

Machias River Corridor
CCC Road
Wesley, ME 04686
207-941-4412
Official Website:
https://apps.web.maine.gov/cgi-
bin/online/doc/parksearch/index.pl
GPS: 44.9571, -67.8726
Number of Sites: 5
Open Seasonally: Yes
Elevation: 196 ft / 59 m
Tent Camping: Yes

Not Free Rv Camping

Lake Pemaquid Campground

100 Twin Cove Lane
Damariscotta, ME 04543
(207) 563-5202
Location: 44.03130, -69.46107
Daily/Weekly/Monthly **Rates: From 35 to 57 dollars**
Official website: https://lakepemaquid.com
Spaces Available: 233
Max Length: 70

Amenities and services:

Dump Station
Partial Handicap Access
Emergency Phone
Folding Tent Campers Allowed
Pets Welcome
Tent Camping Allowed
Cabin/Cottage Rentals (37)
Dedicated Tenting Area
233 Sites with WiFi
Restroom and Showers
Restroom/Showers ($)
Laundry
Control Access Gate
ATM Machine
RV Supplies
LP Bottles Only
Firewood
Ice
Groceries
Restaurant
Fishing Supplies
Onsite Rentals (37)
Enclosed Dog Run
Pet Supplies
Sells Fishing Licenses

Activities/Sports

- ✓ Heated Pool
- ✓ Hot Tub
- ✓ Lake
- ✓ Boating
- ✓ Fishing
- ✓ Dock
- ✓ Ramp
- ✓ Boat Rental
- ✓ Boat Marina
- ✓ Paddle Boats
- ✓ Body Of Water (Pemaquid Lake)
- ✓ Horseshoes
- ✓ Rec Hall
- ✓ Game Room
- ✓ Planned Activities
- ✓ Playground
- ✓ Outdoor Games
- ✓ Pavilion
- ✓ Sauna
- ✓ Tennis
- ✓ Mini Golf
- ✓ Kayaking/Canoeing

Old Orchard Beach Campground

27 Ocean Park Rd.
Old Orchard Beach, ME 04064
(207) 934-4477
Location: 43.50940, -70.42906
Daily/Weekly/Monthly Rates: From 65 to 150 dollars
Official website:
https://gocamping.com/?utm_source=Good Sam
Spaces Available: 252
Max Length: 80

Amenities and services

Dump Station
Partial Handicap Access
Folding Tent Campers Allowed
Pets Welcome
No Tents
Cabin/Cottage Rentals (9)
309 Sites with WiFi
Restroom and Showers
Laundry
Control Access Gate
RV Supplies
Firewood
Ice

Groceries
Cable
Guest Services
Onsite Rentals (9)
Dog Park
Pet Supplies

- ✓ Swimming Pool
- ✓ Hot Tub
- ✓ Swimming
- ✓ Wading Pool
- ✓ Horseshoes
- ✓ Rec Hall
- ✓ Game Room
- ✓ Playground
- ✓ Outdoor Games
- ✓ Pickle Ball

- ✓ Heated Pool
- ✓ Ocean
- ✓ Boating
- ✓ Swimming
- ✓ Fishing
- ✓ Dock
- ✓ Boat Rental
- ✓ Paddle Boats
- ✓ Body Of Water (Somes Sound)
- ✓ Horseshoes
- ✓ Planned Activities
- ✓ Playground
- ✓ Outdoor Games
- ✓ Nature Trails
- ✓ Kayaking/Canoeing

HTR Acadia

5 Spinnaker Way
Mount Desert, ME 04660
(207) 244-8094
Location: 44.33748, -68.32260
Daily/Weekly/Monthly **Rates: From 80 to 130 dollars**
Official website:
https://www.htrresorts.com/destinations/acadia
Spaces Available: 63
Max Length: 30

Amenities and services

Dump Station
Mobile Sewer Service
Emergency Phone
Age Restrictions May Apply
Pet Restriction on Quantity
Tent Camping Allowed
Teepee/Yurt Rentals (2)
Cabin/Cottage Rentals (4)
WiFi at Park Supports Streaming
63 Sites with WiFi
Restroom and Showers
Firewood
Ice
Escort to Site
Onsite Rentals (6)

Wassamki Springs Campground

56 Saco St.
Scarborough, ME 04074
(207) 839-4276
Location: 43.64687, -70.39875
Daily/Weekly/Monthly **Rates: From 55 to 87 dollars**
Official website:
https://wassamkisprings.com
Spaces Available: 165
Max Length: 60

Amenities and services

Dump Station
Mobile Sewer Service
Partial Handicap Access
Emergency Phone
Folding Tent Campers Allowed
Pets Welcome
Tent Camping Allowed
Overflow Area
Dedicated Tenting Area
WiFi Hotspots (12)
165 Sites with WiFi
Restroom and Showers
Laundry
Control Access Gate
ATM Machine
RV Supplies

Metered LP Gas
Firewood
Ice
Worship Services
Groceries
Cable
Self-Service RV Wash
Fishing Supplies
Enclosed Dog Run
Pet Supplies

Activities/Sports

- ✓ Boating
- ✓ Lake
- ✓ Swimming
- ✓ Fishing
- ✓ Electric Motors Only
- ✓ Boat Rental
- ✓ Paddle Boats
- ✓ Body Of Water (Wassamki Springs Lake)
- ✓ Horseshoes
- ✓ Rec Hall
- ✓ Game Room
- ✓ Planned Activities
- ✓ Playground
- ✓ Outdoor Games
- ✓ Driving Range
- ✓ Pavilion
- ✓ Frisbee Golf
- ✓ Pickle Ball
- ✓ Putting Green
- ✓ Rec Open to the Public

Mt Desert Narrows Camping Resort

1219 State Hwy 3
Bar Harbor, ME 04609
(888) 563-7040
Location: 44.42079, -68.33783
Daily/Weekly/Monthly **Rates: From 56 to 131 dollars**
Official website:
https://thousandtrails.com/maine/mt-desert-narrows-camping-resort
Spaces Available: 143
Max Length: 48

Amenities and services

Dump Station
Mobile Sewer Service
Partial Handicap Access
Emergency Phone
Folding Tent Campers Allowed
Pets Welcome
Tent Camping Allowed
RV Park Model Rentals (1)
Overflow Area
Dedicated Tenting Area
Privacy Barrier
WiFi at Park Supports Streaming
143 Sites with WiFi
Restroom and Showers
Laundry
RV Supplies
Metered LP Gas
Firewood
Ice
Groceries
Cable
Onsite Rentals (1)
Pet Supplies

Activities/Sports

- ✓ Heated Pool
- ✓ Ocean
- ✓ Boating
- ✓ Swimming
- ✓ Boat Rental
- ✓ Body Of Water (Frenchman's Bay)
- ✓ Horseshoes
- ✓ Rec Hall
- ✓ Game Room
- ✓ Playground
- ✓ Outdoor Games

MASSCHUSETTS

Cracker Barrel

Parking Lot
 Write a Review
215 Charlton Rd.
Sturbridge, MA 01566
508-347-8925
GPS: 42.1159, -72.0663
Number of Sites: 5
Pad Type: asphalt
Elevation: 557 ft / 169 m
Max Stay: 1
Max Length: 50 ft

Pearl Hill State Park

105 New Fitchburg Road, West Townsend, MA 01474
Official website:
https://www.mass.gov/locations/pearl-hill-state-park

Beartown State Forest

69 Blue Hill Road, Monterey, MA 01245
Official website:
https://www.mass.gov/locations/beartown-state-forest

Pine Lake RV Resort & Cottages

30 River Rd
Sturbridge, MA 01566
(508) 347-9570
Location: 42.08978, -72.08311
Daily/Weekly/Monthly Rates: **From 51 to 115 dollars**
Official website:
https://pinelakervresortandcottages.com
Spaces Available: 169
Max Length: 65

Amenities and services

Partial Handicap Access
Emergency Phone
Folding Tent Campers Allowed
Pets Welcome
No Tents
Max Length (65)
All-Weather Sites (169)
30 Amp
50 Amp
Seasonal Sites
Shaded (Some)
Big Rig Sites
Full Hookups (169)
Max Amps (50)
Pull-thrus (45)
Pull-thru Size (30 x 65)
Back-ins (30 x 45)
Room for Slideouts (Yes)
Site Length (65)
Fire Rings
Table at Site
Cabin/Cottage Rentals (55)
WiFi at Park Supports Streaming
On-Site WiFi Tech Support
169 Sites with WiFi
Restroom and Showers
Laundry
Control Access Gate
RV Supplies
Firewood
Ice
Groceries
Escort to Site
Cable
Fishing Supplies
Onsite Rentals (55)
Enclosed Dog Run
Dog Park
Pet Supplies

Activities/Sports

- ✓ Heated Pool
- ✓ Hot Tub
- ✓ Boating
- ✓ Lake
- ✓ Swimming
- ✓ Fishing
- ✓ Boat Rental
- ✓ No Motors
- ✓ Body Of Water (Pine Lake)
- ✓ Rec Hall
- ✓ Planned Activities
- ✓ Playground
- ✓ Outdoor Games
- ✓ Exercise Room
- ✓ Nature Trails
- ✓ Archery Range
- ✓ Kayaking/Canoeing

Martha's Vineyard Family Campground

569 Edgartown Rd
Vineyard Haven, MA 02568
(508) 693-3772
Location: 41.43530, -70.61029
Daily/Weekly/Monthly **Rates: From 108 to 130 dollars**
Official website: https://campmv.com
Spaces Available: 19
Max Length: 60

Amenities and services

Dump Station
Emergency Phone
Folding Tent Campers Allowed
Pet Restrictions on Size
Tent Camping Allowed

Cabin/Cottage Rentals (27)
Dedicated Tenting Area
WiFi at Park Supports Streaming
On-Site WiFi Tech Support
19 Sites with WiFi
Restroom and Showers
Laundry
ATM Machine
RV Supplies
Firewood / Ice
Groceries
Escort to Site
Fishing Guides
Onsite Rentals (27)
Ocean

Activities/Sports

- ✓ Body Of Water (Atlantic Ocean)
- ✓ Game Room
- ✓ Planned Activities
- ✓ Playground
- ✓ Outdoor Games
- ✓ Nature Trails
- ✓ Pedal Carts
- ✓ Bike Rentals
- ✓ Frisbee Golf

Circle CG Farm Campground

131 N Main St
Bellingham, MA 02019
(508) 966-1136
Location: 42.10128, -71.47256
Daily/Weekly/Monthly **Rates: From 55 to 75 dollars**
Official website: https://circlecgfarm.com
Spaces Available: 90
Max Length: 63

Amenities and services

Dump Station
Folding Tent Campers Allowed
Pets Welcome / Tent Camping Allowed
90 Sites with WiFi
Restroom and Showers
Laundry
Control Access Gate
RV Supplies

Metered LP Gas
Firewood
Ice
Groceries
Escort to Site
Onsite RV Service
Cable
Guest Services

Activities/Sports

- ✓ Swimming Pool
- ✓ Pond
- ✓ Fishing
- ✓ Horseshoes
- ✓ Rec Hall
- ✓ Game Room
- ✓ Planned Activities
- ✓ Outdoor Games
- ✓ Pavilion
- ✓ Nature Trails
- ✓ Mini Golf

Shady Knoll Campground

1709 Main St
Brewster, MA 02631
(508) 896-3002
Location: 41.75742, -70.08859
Daily/Weekly/Monthly **Rates: From 50 to 88 dollars**
Official website: https://shadyknoll.com
Spaces Available: 75
Max Length: 67

Amenities and services

Dump Station
Mobile Sewer Service
Emergency Phone
Folding Tent Campers Allowed
Pets Welcome
Tent Camping Allowed
75 Sites with WiFi
Restroom and Showers
Laundry
RV Supplies
Firewood / Ice
Onsite RV Service
Cable
Guest Services
Ocean

Activities/Sports

- ✓ Body Of Water (Atlantic Ocean)
- ✓ Rec Hall
- ✓ Game Room
- ✓ Playground
- ✓ Outdoor Games

Atlantic Oaks

3700 State Hwy
Eastham, MA 02642
(508) 255-1437
Location: 41.84536, -69.98421
Daily/Weekly/Monthly **Rates: From 70 to 104 dollars**
Official website: https://atlanticoaks.com
Spaces Available: 72
Max Length: 60

Amenities and services

Emergency Phone
Folding Tent Campers Allowed
Pets Welcome / Tent Camping Allowed
RV Park Model Rentals (2)
Dedicated Tenting Area
72 Sites with WiFi
Restroom and Showers
Laundry
Control Access Gate
RV Supplies
Metered LP Gas
Firewood
Ice
Groceries
Onsite RV Service
Cable
Guest Services
Fishing Supplies
Onsite Rentals (2)
Ocean
Body Of Water (Atlantic Ocean)
Horseshoes
Game Room
Playground
Outdoor Games
Nature Trails
Putting Green

NEW HAMPSHIRE

Free Rv Camping

Gale River Campground

White Mountain National Forest
Gale River Trail
Bethlehem, NH 03574
603-536-6100
Official Website:
https://www.fs.usda.gov/main/whitemountain/
GPS: 44.2432, -71.632
Number of Sites: 11
Pad Type: dirt
Open Seasonally: May - October
Elevation: 1,345 ft / 409 m
Max Stay: 14
Tent Camping: Yes

Haystack Road

White Mountain National Forest
Haystack Rd.
Bethlehem, NH 03574
603-536-6100
Official Website:
https://www.fs.usda.gov/whitemountain
GPS: 44.2502, -71.5788
Number of Sites: 11
Open Seasonally: Yes
Elevation: 1,607 ft / 489 m
Max Stay: 14
Tent Camping: Yes

Jefferson Notch Road

White Mountain National Forest
Jefferson Notch Rd.
Jefferson, NH 03583
603-466-2713
603-536-6100
Official Website:
https://www.fs.usda.gov/whitemountain
GPS: 44.3372, -71.3858

Not Free Rv Camping

Twin Tamarack Family Camping & RV Resort

41 Twin Tamarack Rd
New Hampton, NH 03256
(603) 279-4387
Location: 43.62182, -71.58923
Daily/Weekly/Monthly **Rates: From 45 to 65 dollars**
Official website:
http://www.twintamarackcampground.com
Spaces Available: 117
Max Length: 60

Amenities and services

Dump Station
Mobile Sewer Service
Emergency Phone
Folding Tent Campers Allowed
Pets Welcome
Tent Camping Allowed
RV Park Model Rentals (1)
Cabin/Cottage Rentals (8)
Privacy Barrier
Covered Area w/Picnic Table
WiFi at Park Supports Streaming
63 Sites with WiFi
Restroom and Showers
Laundry
Control Access Gate
RV Supplies
Firewood
Ice
Groceries
Onsite RV Service
Cable
Fishing Supplies
Near NASCAR® Track (20 mi to New Hampshire Motor Speedway)
Onsite Rentals (9)

Activities/Sports

✓ Swimming Pool
✓ Hot Tub
✓ Lake
✓ Boating

- ✓ Fishing
- ✓ Dock
- ✓ Ramp
- ✓ Boat Rental
- ✓ Paddle Boats
- ✓ Body Of Water (Pemigewasset Lake)
- ✓ Horseshoes
- ✓ Rec Hall
- ✓ Game Room
- ✓ Planned Activities
- ✓ Playground
- ✓ Outdoor Games
- ✓ Pavilion

- ✓ Swimming Pool
- ✓ Pond
- ✓ Wading Pool
- ✓ Fishing
- ✓ Horseshoes
- ✓ Rec Hall
- ✓ Game Room
- ✓ Planned Activities
- ✓ Playground
- ✓ Outdoor Games
- ✓ Pavilion
- ✓ Exercise Room

Tuxbury Pond RV Campground

167 Campground Road
South Hampton, NH 03827
(888) 563-7040
Location: 42.86754, -70.98739
Daily/Weekly/Monthly **Rates: From 78 to 101 dollars**
Official website:
https://thousandtrails.com/new-hampshire/tuxbury-pond-rv-resort
Spaces Available: 60
Max Length: 50

Amenities and services:
Dump Station
Pets Welcome
No Tents
Cabin/Cottage Rentals (7)
60 Sites with WiFi
Restroom and Showers
Restroom/Showers ($)
Laundry
Control Access Gate
RV Supplies
Firewood
Groceries
Cable
Self-Service RV Wash
Fishing Supplies
Onsite Rentals (7)
Enclosed Dog Run

Activities/Sports

Field & Stream RV Park

7 Dupaw-Gould Rd
Brookline, NH 03033
(603) 673-4677
Location: 42.74161, -71.68649
Daily/Weekly/Monthly Rates: 60 dollars
Official website: https://fsrvp.com
Spaces Available: 26
Max Length: 64

Amenities and services
Partial Handicap Access
Emergency Phone
Limited Facilities - Winter
Pet Restriction on Quantity
No Tents
WiFi at Park Supports Streaming
26 Sites with WiFi
Restroom and Showers
Laundry
Control Access Gate
Metered LP Gas
Firewood
Escort to Site
Cable
Enclosed Dog Run
Pond
Fishing
Planned Activities
Playground
Pavilion

Sandy Beach Campground

677 Clement Hill Rd

Contoocook, NH 03229
(888) 563-7040
Location: 43.20527, -71.75078
Daily/Weekly/Monthly **Rates: From 56 to 78 dollars**
Official website:
https://thousandtrails.com/new-hampshire/sandy-beach-rv-camping-resort
Spaces Available: 91
Max Length: 60

Amenities and services

Emergency Phone
Folding Tent Campers Allowed
Pets Welcome
Tent Camping Allowed
Cabin/Cottage Rentals (3)
Covered Area w/Picnic Table
84 Sites with WiFi
Restroom and Showers
Laundry
RV Supplies
LP Bottles Only
Firewood
Ice
Groceries
Escort to Site
Onsite RV Service
Cable
Fishing Supplies
Near NASCAR® Track (20 mi to New Hampshire Motor Speedway)
Onsite Rentals (3)

Activities/Sports

- ✓ Boating
- ✓ Pond
- ✓ Swimming
- ✓ Fishing
- ✓ Dock
- ✓ Electric Motors Only
- ✓ Paddle Boats
- ✓ Horseshoes
- ✓ Game Room
- ✓ Planned Activities
- ✓ Playground
- ✓ Outdoor Games
- ✓ Pavilion
- ✓ Tennis

Riverside Camping & RV Resort

94 Bridge Street
Lancaster, NH 03584
(603) 631-7433
Location: 44.49570, -71.58964
Daily/Weekly/Monthly **Rates: From 64 to 69 dollars**
Official website:
https://www.riversidecampingnh.com
Spaces Available: 40
Max Length: 85

Amenities and services

Folding Tent Campers Allowed
Pets Welcome
Tent Camping Allowed
RV Park Model Rentals (2)
Dedicated Tenting Area
WiFi at Park Supports Streaming
40 Sites with WiFi
Restroom and Showers
Laundry
LP Bottles Only
Firewood
Escort to Site
Onsite Rentals (2)

Activities/Sports

- ✓ Heated Pool
- ✓ River
- ✓ Swimming
- ✓ Fishing
- ✓ Body Of Water (Connecticut River)
- ✓ Planned Activities
- ✓ Outdoor Games
- ✓ Shuffleboard
- ✓ Nature Trails

NEW JERSEY

Pennsville, New Jersey - Wal Mart

Pennsville, New Jersey
GPS: 39.61243, -75.50301
Elevation: 16'

Brick Twp Walmart

1872 NJ-88
Brick Township, New Jersey
GPS: 40.07241, -74.12485
Elevation: 33'

Ocean City Campground and Beach Cabins

241 NJ 50
Ocean View, NJ 08230
(609) 390-3649
Location: 39.24260, -74.71278
Daily/Weekly/Monthly **Rates: From 70 to 119 dollars**
Official website:
https://www.oceancitycampground.com/?utm_source=GoodSam
Spaces Available: 64
Max Length: 45

Amenities and services

Dump Station
Partial Handicap Access
Pets Welcome
No Tents
Cabin/Cottage Rentals (9)
WiFi at Park Supports Streaming
64 Sites with WiFi
Restroom and Showers
Laundry
RV Supplies
Metered LP Gas
Firewood
Ice
Snack Bar
Groceries
Escort to Site
Cable
Onsite Rentals (9)
Dog Park
Dog Washing Station
Pet Supplies

Activities/Sports

✓ Splash Pad
✓ Swimming
✓ Body Of Water (Atlantic Ocean)
✓ Rec Hall
✓ Game Room
✓ Planned Activities
✓ Playground
✓ Outdoor Games
✓ Pavilion
✓ Nature Trails
✓ Mini Golf

King Nummy Trail Campground

205 Rte 47 S
Cape May Court House, NJ 08210
(609) 465-4242
Location: 39.07622, -74.89476
Daily/Weekly/Monthly **Rates: From 60 to 85 dollars**
Official website:
https://thousandtrails.com/new-jersey/king-nummy-trail-campground
Spaces Available: 39
Max Length: 40

Amenities and services

Dump Station
Mobile Sewer Service
Partial Handicap Access
Folding Tent Campers Allowed
Pets Welcome
Tent Camping Allowed
Cabin/Cottage Rentals (8)
Privacy Barrier
39 Sites with WiFi
Restroom and Showers
Restroom/Showers ($)
Laundry
Control Access Gate
RV Supplies
LP Bottles Only
Firewood
Ice
Groceries
Onsite RV Service
Cable
Guest Services
Self-Service RV Wash
Onsite Rentals (8)

Activities/Sports

✓ Swimming Pool
✓ Swimming

- ✓ Horseshoes
- ✓ Rec Hall
- ✓ Game Room
- ✓ Planned Activities
- ✓ Playground
- ✓ Outdoor Games
- ✓ Pavilion
- ✓ Shuffleboard
- ✓ Pickle Ball

Delaware River Family Campground

100 Rt 46
Columbia, NJ 07832
(908) 475-4517
Location: 40.88616, -75.06217
Daily/Weekly/Monthly **Rates: From 76 to 85 dollars**
Official website:
https://www.delawarerivercampground.com
Spaces Available: 48
Max Length: 50

Amenities and services

Dump Station
Mobile Sewer Service
Partial Handicap Access
Emergency Phone
Pets Welcome / Pet Supplies
Tent Camping Allowed
Tent Rentals (2)
Cabin/Cottage Rentals (16)
Dedicated Tenting Area
WiFi Hotspots (1)
Restroom and Showers
Laundry
Control Access Gate
ATM Machine
RV Supplies
Metered LP Gas
Firewood
Ice
Snack Bar
Groceries
Cable
Guest Services
Fishing Guides

Onsite Rentals (18)

Activities/Sports

- ✓ Heated Pool
- ✓ River
- ✓ Boating
- ✓ Wading Pool
- ✓ Fishing
- ✓ Ramp
- ✓ Boat Rental
- ✓ Body Of Water (Delaware River)
- ✓ Horseshoes
- ✓ Rec Hall
- ✓ Game Room
- ✓ Planned Activities
- ✓ Playground
- ✓ Outdoor Games
- ✓ Pavilion
- ✓ Mini Golf
- ✓ Kayaking/Canoeing

Holly Acres Campground

218 Frankfurt Ave
Egg Harbor City, NJ 08215
(609) 965-5055
Location: 39.52630, -74.59950
Daily/Weekly/Monthly **Rates: From 58 to 75 dollars**
Official website:
https://hollyacrescampground.com
Spaces Available: 60
Max Length: 60

Amenities and services

Dump Station
Emergency Phone
Folding Tent Campers Allowed
Pets Welcome
Tent Camping Allowed
RV Park Model Rentals (3)
60 Sites with WiFi
Restroom and Showers
Laundry
Control Access Gate
RV Supplies
Metered LP Gas
Firewood
Ice
Groceries

Escort to Site
Onsite RV Service
Cable
Fishing Supplies
Onsite Rentals (3)
Enclosed Dog Run
Dog Park

Activities/Sports

- ✓ Swimming Pool
- ✓ Pond
- ✓ Swimming
- ✓ Fishing
- ✓ Horseshoes
- ✓ Rec Hall
- ✓ Planned Activities
- ✓ Playground
- ✓ Outdoor Games
- ✓ Pavilion
- ✓ Mini Golf

Guest Services
Self-Service RV Wash
Fishing Supplies

Activities/Sports

- ✓ Swimming Pool
- ✓ Pond
- ✓ Wading Pool
- ✓ Fishing
- ✓ Horseshoes
- ✓ Rec Hall
- ✓ Game Room
- ✓ Planned Activities
- ✓ Playground
- ✓ Outdoor Games
- ✓ Nature Trails

Acorn Campground

419 Rt 47 S
Green Creek, NJ 08210
(609) 886-7119
Location: 39.04923, -74.90299
Daily/Weekly/Monthly **Rates: From 65 to 75 dollars**
Official website:
https://thousandtrails.com/new-jersey/acorn-campground
Spaces Available: 84
Max Length: 75

Amenities and services

Dump Station
Partial Handicap Access
Folding Tent Campers Allowed
Pet Restriction on Quantity
Tent Camping Allowed
WiFi Hotspots (1)
Restroom and Showers
Laundry
Control Access Gate
RV Supplies
LP Bottles Only
Firewood
Ice
Groceries
Cable

NEW YORK

Sugar Hill Fire Tower Designated Dispersed Camping

Sugar Hill State Forest
3360 Tower Hill Rd.
Watkins Glen, NY 14891
607-674-4017
607-776-2165
Official Website:
https://www.dec.ny.gov/lands/37446.html
GPS: 42.3905, -77.0033
Pad Type: grass
Open Seasonally: Late May - late October
Elevation: 2,001 ft / 609 m

Moose River Plains Camping Corridor

State Forest
Limekiln Lake Rd.
Inlet, NY 13360
518-863-4545
Official Website:
https://www.dec.ny.gov/lands/53596.html
GPS: 43.6892, -74.7505
Number of Sites: 116
Elevation: 1,870 ft / 569 m
Max Stay: 14
Tent Camping: Yes

Hamburg Gaming & Fairgrounds

Parking Lot
5820 South Park Ave.
Hamburg, NY 14075
716-646-6109
Official Website:
https://www.hamburggaming.com/
GPS: 42.7392, -78.8201

Camp Bell Campground

8700 SR 415
Campbell, NY 14821
(800) 587-3301
Location: 42.23565, -77.18454
Daily/Weekly/Monthly **Rates: From 36 to 50 dollars**
Official website:
https://campbellcampground.com
Spaces Available: 57
Max Length: 55

Amenities and services

Dump Station
Mobile Sewer Service
Folding Tent Campers Allowed
Pets Welcome
Tent Camping Allowed
RV Park Model Rentals (3)
Cabin/Cottage Rentals (4)
WiFi at Park Supports Streaming
57 Sites with WiFi
Restroom and Showers
Laundry
RV Supplies
Metered LP Gas
Firewood / Ice
Groceries
Cable
Guest Services
Fishing Guides
Near NASCAR® Track (21 mi to Watkins Glen International)
Onsite Rentals (7)
Enclosed Dog Run
Dog Park

Activities/Sports

- ✓ Heated Pool
- ✓ Swimming
- ✓ Horseshoes
- ✓ Rec Hall
- ✓ Game Room
- ✓ Planned Activities
- ✓ Playground

- ✓ Outdoor Games
- ✓ Pavilion
- ✓ Nature Trails
- ✓ Pedal Carts
- ✓ Bike Rentals
- ✓ Mini Golf
- ✓ Rec Open to the Public

The Villages at Turning Stone RV Park

5065 SR 365
Verona, NY 13478
(315) 361-7275
Location: 43.10667, -75.60643
Daily/Weekly/Monthly **Rates: From 60 to 70 dollars**
Official website:
https://www.turningstone.com/accommodations
Spaces Available: 175
Max Length: 60

Amenities and services

Dump Station
Folding Tent Campers Allowed
Pets Welcome
No Tents
175 Sites with WiFi
Restroom and Showers
Laundry
RV Supplies
Metered LP Gas
Firewood / Ice
Groceries
Cable
Guest Services
Fishing Supplies

Activities/Sports

- ✓ Heated Pool
- ✓ Hot Tub
- ✓ Pond
- ✓ Wading Pool
- ✓ Fishing
- ✓ Paddle Boats
- ✓ Horseshoes
- ✓ Game Room
- ✓ Planned Activities

- ✓ Playground
- ✓ Outdoor Games
- ✓ Golf
- ✓ Driving Range
- ✓ Pavilion
- ✓ Tennis
- ✓ Nature Trails
- ✓ Casino

Swan Bay Resort

43615 NY (State Route) 12
Alexandria Bay, NY 13607
(315) 482-7926
Location: 44.29896, -75.96354
Daily/Weekly/Monthly **Rates: Fr om 63 to 135dollars**
Official website: https://swanbayresort.com
Spaces Available: 165
Max Length: 80

Amenities and services

Dump Station
Pets Welcome / Dog Park
No Tents
Cabin/Cottage Rentals (15)
165 Sites with WiFi
Restroom and Showers
Laundry
Control Access Gate
RV Supplies
LP Bottles Only
Firewood / Ice
Groceries
Escort to Site
Onsite RV Service
Cocktail Lounge
Guest Services
Fishing Guides
Fishing Supplies
Golf Carts
Onsite Rentals (15)

Activities/Sports

- ✓ Heated Pool
- ✓ River
- ✓ Boating
- ✓ Fishing
- ✓ Dock

- ✓ Ramp
- ✓ Boat Rental
- ✓ Boat Marina
- ✓ Paddle Boats
- ✓ Body Of Water (St Lawrence River)
- ✓ Horseshoes
- ✓ Planned Activities
- ✓ Playground
- ✓ Outdoor Games
- ✓ Pavilion
- ✓ Bike Rentals
- ✓ Kayaking/Canoeing
- ✓ Watersports

Black Bear Campground

197 Wheeler Rd
Florida, NY 10921
(845) 651-7717
Location: 41.32242, -74.37340
Daily/Weekly/Monthly Rates: From 95 to 115 dollars
Official website:
https://blackbearcampground.com
Spaces Available: 74
Max Length: 75

Amenities and services

Emergency Phone
Limited Facilities - Winter
Pets Welcome
Pet Restriction on Quantity
No Tents
74 Sites with WiFi
Restroom and Showers
Laundry
RV Supplies
Firewood / Ice
Groceries
Guest Services
Fishing Supplies

Activities/Sports

- ✓ Heated Pool
- ✓ Pond
- ✓ Fishing
- ✓ Horseshoes
- ✓ Game Room
- ✓ Planned Activities
- ✓ Playground
- ✓ Outdoor Games

- ✓ Pavilion
- ✓ Shuffleboard
- ✓ Nature Trails
- ✓ Frisbee Golf
- ✓ Mini Golf

Ledgeview RV Park

321 SR-149
Lake George, NY 12845
(518) 798-6621
Location: 43.37792, -73.66963
Daily/Weekly/Monthly **Rates: From 64 to 74 dollars**
Official website: https://www.ledgeview.com
Spaces Available: 120
Max Length: 75

Amenities and services

Folding Tent Campers Allowed
No Pets
No Tents
RV Park Model Rentals (2)
120 Sites with WiFi
Restroom and Showers
Laundry
Control Access Gate
RV Supplies
Firewood / Ice
Groceries
Onsite RV Service
Cable
Onsite Rentals (2)

Activities/Sports

- ✓ Swimming Pool
- ✓ Horseshoes
- ✓ Game Room
- ✓ Playground
- ✓ Outdoor Games
- ✓ Pavilion
- ✓ Shuffleboard
- ✓ Pedal Carts
- ✓ Bike Rentals
- ✓ Mini Golf

PENNSYLVANIA

Free Rv Camping

Presque Isle Downs Casino

8199 Perry Highway
Erie, PA 16509
866-374-3386
Official Website:
https://www.presqueisledowns.com/
GPS: 42.0707, -80.0314

Mohegan Sun Pocono

1280 Pennsylvania 315
Wilkes-Barre, PA 18701
570-831-2100
Official Website: https://moheganpa.com/
GPS: 41.2715, -75.823

Cabela's

100 Cabela's Dr.
Hamburg, PA 19526
610-929-7000
Official Website:
https://stores.cabelas.com/us/wv/triadelphia/1-cabela-drive.html
GPS: 40.5583, -76.0061

Not Free Rv Camping

Pinch Pond Family Campground

3075 Pinch Rd
Manheim, PA 17545
(717) 665-7640
Location: 40.22955, -76.45227
Daily/Weekly/Monthly **Rates: From 48 to 52 dollars**
Official website: https://pinchpond.com
Spaces Available: 125
Max Length: 60

Amenities and services

Dump Station
Partial Handicap Access
Emergency Phone
Limited Facilities - Winter
Folding Tent Campers Allowed
Pets Welcome
Tent Camping Allowed
Cabin/Cottage Rentals (9)
Overflow Area
WiFi at Park $
WiFi at Overnite Sites $
63 Sites with WiFi
Restroom and Showers
Laundry
Control Access Gate
RV Supplies
Metered LP Gas
Firewood
Ice
Groceries
Escort to Site
Onsite RV Service
Cable
Guest Services
Self-Service RV Wash
Fishing Supplies
Onsite Rentals (9)

Activities/Sports

✓ Swimming Pool
✓ Pond
✓ Fishing

- ✓ Rec Hall
- ✓ Game Room
- ✓ Planned Activities
- ✓ Playground
- ✓ Outdoor Games
- ✓ Pavilion
- ✓ Nature Trails

Harrisburg East Campground & Storage

1134 Highspire Rd
Harrisburg, PA 17111
(717) 939-4331
Location: 40.23219, -76.79844
Daily/Weekly/Monthly **Rates: From 84 to 114 dollars**
Official website:
https://hbgeastcampground.com
Spaces Available: 42
Max Length: 60

Amenities and services

Dump Station
Emergency Phone
Folding Tent Campers Allowed
Pets Welcome
Tent Camping Allowed
Dedicated Tenting Area
On-Site WiFi Tech Support
42 Sites with WiFi
Restroom and Showers
Laundry
Metered LP Gas
Firewood
Ice
Escort to Site
Cable
Self-Service RV Wash

Activities/Sports

- ✓ Heated Pool
- ✓ Swimming
- ✓ Playground
- ✓ Outdoor Games

Drummer Boy Camping Resort

1 Rocky Grove Rd
Gettysburg, PA 17325
(888) 563-7040
Location: 39.82437, -77.19668
Daily/Weekly/Monthly **Rates: From 62 to 106 dollars**
Official website:
https://thousandtrails.com/pennsylvania/drummer-boy-camping-resort
Spaces Available: 139
Max Length: 70

Amenities and services

Dump Station
Partial Handicap Access
Emergency Phone
Folding Tent Campers Allowed
Pets Welcome
Tent Camping Allowed
Cabin/Cottage Rentals (51)
Dedicated Tenting Area
139 Sites with WiFi
Restroom and Showers
Laundry
ATM Machine
RV Supplies
Metered LP Gas
Firewood
Ice
Snack Bar
Groceries
Onsite RV Service
Cable
Fishing Supplies
Golf Carts
Onsite Rentals (51)

Activities/Sports

- ✓ Heated Pool
- ✓ Hot Tub
- ✓ Water Slide
- ✓ Water Umbrella
- ✓ Pond
- ✓ Wading Pool
- ✓ Fishing
- ✓ Rec Hall
- ✓ Game Room
- ✓ Planned Activities
- ✓ Playground

- ✓ Outdoor Games
- ✓ Pavilion
- ✓ Mini Golf

Round Top Campground

180 Knight Rd
Gettysburg, PA 17325
(877) 570-2267
Location: 39.77883, -77.23577
Daily/Weekly/Monthly **Rates: From 58 to 110 dollars**
Official website:
https://thousandtrails.com/pennsylvania/round-top-campground
Spaces Available: 101
Max Length: 63

Amenities and services

Dump Station
Mobile Sewer Service
Partial Handicap Access
Emergency Phone
Folding Tent Campers Allowed
Pet Restriction on Quantity
Tent Camping Allowed
Cabin/Cottage Rentals (27)
WiFi at Park Supports Streaming
On-Site WiFi Tech Support
WiFi Hotspots (2)
101 Sites with WiFi
Restroom and Showers
Laundry
ATM Machine
RV Supplies
Metered LP Gas
Firewood
Ice
Groceries
Cable
Guest Services
Onsite Rentals (27)
Pet Supplies

Activities/Sports

- ✓ Swimming Pool
- ✓ Wading Pool
- ✓ Horseshoes
- ✓ Rec Hall
- ✓ Game Room

- ✓ Planned Activities
- ✓ Playground
- ✓ Outdoor Games
- ✓ Pavilion
- ✓ Mini Golf

Thousand Trails Circle M

2111 Millersville Rd
Lancaster, PA 17603
(888) 563-7040
Location: 39.99789, -76.32282
Daily/Weekly/Monthly Rates: From 58 to 94 dollars
Official website:
https://thousandtrails.com/pennsylvania/circle-m-rv-camping-resort
Spaces Available: 203
Max Length: 50

Amenities and services

Dump Station
Mobile Sewer Service
Partial Handicap Access
Emergency Phone
Pcts Welcome / Pet Supplies

Tent Camping Allowed
Teepee/Yurt Rentals (4)
RV Park Model Rentals (28)
WiFi Hotspots (3)
Restroom and Showers
Laundry
Control Access Gate
RV Supplies
Metered LP Gas
Firewood
Ice
Snack Bar
Groceries
Escort to Site
Cable
Guest Services
Fishing Supplies
Onsite Rentals (32)

Activities/Sports

- ✓ Heated Pool
- ✓ Hot Tub
- ✓ River

- ✓ Wading Pool
- ✓ Fishing
- ✓ Body Of Water (Conestoga River)
- ✓ Horseshoes
- ✓ Game Room
- ✓ Planned Activities
- ✓ Playground
- ✓ Outdoor Games
- ✓ Pavilion
- ✓ Shuffleboard
- ✓ Pickle Ball
- ✓ Mini Golf
- ✓ Kayaking/Canoeing

RHODE ISLAND

Free Rv Camping

Twin River Casino

100 Twin River Rd.
Lincoln, RI 02865
401-723-3200
877-827-4837
Official Website:
https://casinos.ballys.com/lincoln/
GPS: 41.8909, -71.4528

Blackstone River Welcome Center

Rest Area
I-295 Beltway
Lincoln, RI 02865
Official Website:
http://www.dot.ri.gov/travel/
GPS: 41.9396, -71.4508

Not Free Rv Camping

Ginny-B Campground

7 Harrington Rd
Foster, RI 02825
(401) 397-9477
Location: 41.75356, -71.75441
Daily/Weekly/Monthly **Rates: From 42 to 43 dollars**
Official website: http://ginny-bcampground.com
Spaces Available: 75
Max Length: 60

<u>Amenities and services</u>
Dump Station
Mobile Sewer Service
Partial Handicap Access
Emergency Phone
Folding Tent Campers Allowed
Pets Welcome
Tent Camping Allowed
Dedicated Tenting Area
WiFi HotspotWiFi Hotspots (1)
Restroom and Showers
Laundry
RV Supplies
Firewood
Ice
Groceries
Escort to Site
Onsite RV Service
Fishing Supplies
Pond

<u>Activities/Sports</u>
- ✓ Swimming
- ✓ Fishing
- ✓ Horseshoes
- ✓ Rec Hall
- ✓ Planned Activities
- ✓ Playground
- ✓ Outdoor Games
- ✓ Pavilion
- ✓ Kayaking/Canoeing

Ashaway RV Resort

235 Ashaway Road
Ashaway, RI 02808
(401) 377-8100
Location: 41.41200, -71.75055
Daily/Weekly/Monthly **Rates: From 85 to 95 dollars**
Spaces Available: 260

Amenities and services

Partial Handicap Access
Emergency Phone
Pets Welcome
Pet Restrictions on Size
No Tents
Restroom and Showers
Laundry
Control Access Gate
ATM Machine
RV Supplies
Metered LP Gas
Firewood
Ice
Groceries
Onsite RV Service
Onsite Rentals (4)
Enclosed Dog Run

Activities/Sports

✓ Swimming Pool
✓ Hot Tub
✓ Splash Pad
✓ Horseshoes
✓ Rec Hall
✓ Game Room
✓ Planned Activities
✓ Playground
✓ Outdoor Games
✓ Pavilion
✓ Tennis
✓ Shuffleboard
✓ Exercise Room
✓ Nature Trails
✓ Pedal Carts
✓ Mini Golf
✓ Pickle Ball

Burlingame

1 Burlingame State Park

Charlestown, RI 02813
(401) 322-7337
Daily/Weekly/Monthly Rates: From 14 to 20 dollars
Spaces Available: 692
Max Length: 60

Amenities and services

Partial Handicap Access
Pets Welcome
Day Max Stay (14)
Tent Camping Allowed
Restroom and Showers
Control Access Gate
RV Supplies
LP Bottles Only

Activities/Sports

✓ Boating
✓ Pond
✓ Swimming
✓ Fishing
✓ Ramp
✓ Boat Rental
✓ Rec Hall
✓ Game Room
✓ Planned Activities
✓ Playground
✓ Kayaking/Canoeing

Charlestown Breachway Campground

Div of Parks & Rec, Charlestown Beach Rd
Charlestown, RI 02813
(401) 364-7000
Daily/Weekly/Monthly **Rates: From 14 to 20 dollars**
Spaces Available: 75
Max Length: 25

Amenities and services

Partial Handicap Access
No Pets
Day Max Stay (7)
No Tents
Restroom and Showers
Ocean

Activities/Sports

- ✓ Swimming
- ✓ Fishing
- ✓ Ramp
- ✓ Body Of Water (Block Island Sound)

George Washington Memorial Camping Area

2185 Putnam Pike
Chepachet, RI 02814
(401) 568-2085
Daily/Weekly/Monthly **Rates: From 14 to 35 dollars**
Spaces Available: 57

Amenities and services

Partial Handicap Access
No Pets
Tent Camping Allowed
Spaces Available (57)
Gravel Sites (57)
No Hookups (57)
Pit Toilets
Lake

Activities/Sports

- ✓ Swimming
- ✓ Fishing
- ✓ Ramp
- ✓ Body Of Water (Bowdish Reservoir)
- ✓ Horseshoes
- ✓ Playground

VERMONT

Free Rv Camping	Not Free Rv Camping

Bear's End Dispersed Camping

Green Mountain National Forest
NF-71
Shaftsbury, VT 05262
802-362-2307
802-747-6700
Official Website:
https://www.fs.usda.gov/main/gmfl/home
GPS: 42.9967, -72.976
Tent Camping: Yes

Montpelier Wastewater Treatment Plant

Dog River Road
Montpelier, VT 05601
802-223-9511
Official Website: https://www.montpelier-vt.org/Directory.aspx?did=10
GPS: 44.2547, -72.6003

Breadloaf Wilderness Dispersed Campsites

Green Mountain National Forest
TH11
Granville, VT 05747
802-767-4261
Official Website:
https://www.fs.usda.gov/recarea/gmfl/recarea/?recid=65041
GPS: 44.0002, -72.8776
Number of Sites: 5
Pad Type: grass
Open Seasonally: Yes
Elevation: 1,607 ft / 489 m
Max Stay: 14

Apple Island Resort

71 US Rte 2
South Hero, VT 05486
(802) 372-3800
Location: 44.63509, -73.26760
Daily/Weekly/Monthly **Rates: From 70 to 100 dollars**
Official website:
https://appleislandresort.com
Spaces Available: 220
Max Length: 70

Amenities and services

Dump Station
Folding Tent Campers Allowed
Pet Restriction on Quantity
Pet Restriction on Breed
Tent Camping Allowed
RV Park Model Rentals (6)
Cabin/Cottage Rentals (3)
Lodge Room Rentals (1)
Dedicated Tenting Area
WiFi at Park Supports Streaming
220 Sites with WiFi
Restroom and Showers
Laundry
ATM Machine
RV Supplies
Metered LP Gas
Firewood
Ice
Groceries
Escort to Site
Restaurant
Onsite RV Service
Guest Services
Fishing Supplies
Golf Carts
Onsite Rentals (10)

Activities/Sports

✓ Heated Pool
✓ Hot Tub
✓ Lake

- ✓ Boating
- ✓ Fishing
- ✓ Dock
- ✓ Ramp
- ✓ Boat Rental
- ✓ Boat Marina
- ✓ Paddle Boats
- ✓ Body Of Water (Lake Champlain)
- ✓ Horseshoes
- ✓ Rec Hall
- ✓ Planned Activities
- ✓ Playground
- ✓ Outdoor Games
- ✓ Golf
- ✓ Driving Range
- ✓ Pavilion
- ✓ Exercise Room
- ✓ Nature Trails
- ✓ Lawn Bowling
- ✓ Putting Green
- ✓ Kayaking/Canoeing
- ✓ Watersports

Laundry
RV Supplies
Metered LP Gas
Firewood
Ice
Groceries
Escort to Site
Onsite RV Service
Cable
Staffed RV Wash
Self-Service RV Wash
Onsite Rentals (2)

Activities/Sports

- ✓ Heated Pool
- ✓ Swimming
- ✓ Horseshoes
- ✓ Rec Hall
- ✓ Planned Activities
- ✓ Playground
- ✓ Outdoor Games
- ✓ Tennis
- ✓ Pedal Carts
- ✓ Mini Golf

Lone Pine Campsites

52 Sunset View Rd
Colchester, VT 05446
(802) 878-5447
Location: 44.55551, -73.18538
Daily/Weekly/Monthly **Rates: From 43 to 93 dollars**
Official website:
https://lonepinecampsites.com
Spaces Available: 150
Max Length: 66

Amenities and services

Dump Station
Mobile Sewer Service
Folding Tent Campers Allowed
Pets Welcome
Pet Restriction on Quantity
Tent Camping Allowed
RV Park Model Rentals (2)
WiFi at Park $
WiFi at Overnite Sites $
145 Sites with WiFi
Restroom and Showers
Restroom/Showers ($)

Horseshoe Acres

1978 Weston-Andover Rd
Andover, VT 05143
(802) 875-2960
Location: 43.28452, -72.71469
Daily/Weekly/Monthly **Rates: From 40 to 57 dollars**
Official website:
https://www.horseshoeacrescampground.com
Spaces Available: 50
Max Length: 58

Amenities and services

Dump Station
Mobile Sewer Service
Emergency Phone
lding Tent Campers Allowed
Pets Welcome
Tent Camping Allowed
RV Park Model Rentals (6)
Covered Area w/Picnic Table
50 Sites with WiFi

Restroom and Showers
Restroom/Showers ($)
Laundry
RV Supplies
LP Bottles Only
Firewood
Ice
Groceries
Escort to Site
Onsite RV Service
Onsite Rentals (6)

Activities/Sports

- ✓ Swimming Pool
- ✓ Pond
- ✓ Wading Pool
- ✓ Paddle Boats
- ✓ Horseshoes
- ✓ Rec Hall
- ✓ Game Room
- ✓ Planned Activities
- ✓ Playground
- ✓ Outdoor Games
- ✓ Pavilion
- ✓ Shuffleboard
- ✓ Nature Trails
- ✓ Bike Rentals
- ✓ Mini Golf

Sugar Ridge RV Village & Campground

24 Old Stagecoach Rd
Danville, VT 05828
(802) 684-2550
Location: 44.42216, -72.11483
Daily/Weekly/Monthly **Rates: From 48 to 55 dollars**
Official website:
https://www.sugarridgervpark.com
Spaces Available: 100
Max Length: 100

Amenities and services

Dump Station
Folding Tent Campers Allowed
Pets Welcome
Tent Camping Allowed
RV Park Model Rentals (6)

Dedicated Tenting Area
Cooking Counters
WiFi at Park /WiFi at Park $
WiFi at Overnite Sites $
100 Sites with WiFi
Restroom and Showers
Laundry
Control Access Gate
ATM Machine
RV Supplies
Metered LP Gas
Firewood
Ice
Groceries
Escort to Site
Onsite RV Service
Cable
Self-Service RV Wash
Fishing Supplies
Onsite Rentals (6)

Activities/Sports

- ✓ Heated Pool
- ✓ Pond
- ✓ Fishing
- ✓ Horseshoes
- ✓ Rec Hall
- ✓ Game Room
- ✓ Planned Activities
- ✓ Playground
- ✓ Outdoor Games
- ✓ Tennis
- ✓ Shuffleboard
- ✓ Nature Trails
- ✓ Bike Rentals
- ✓ Mini Golf
- ✓ Rec Open to the Public
- ✓ Kayaking/Canoeing

Rest N' Nest Campground

300 Latham Rd
East Thetford, VT 05043
(802) 785-2997
Location: 43.81570, -72.21069
Daily/Weekly/Monthly **Rates: From 43 to 50 dollars**
Official website: https://www.restnnest.com
Spaces Available: 54

Max Length: 92

Amenities and services:

Dump StationMobile Sewer Service
Folding Tent Campers Allowed
Pet Restrictions on Size
Tent Camping Allowed
RV Park Model Rentals (2)
Dedicated Tenting Area
54 Sites with WiFi
Restroom and Showers
Laundry
RV Supplies
Metered LP Gas
Firewood
Ice

Groceries
Escort to Site
Onsite RV Service
Self-Service RV Wash
Onsite Rentals (2)
Pet Supplies
Pond

Activities/Sports

✓ Swimming
✓ Horseshoes
✓ Rec Hall
✓ Game Room
✓ Planned Activities
✓ Playground
✓ Outdoor Games

DOWNLOAD HERE YOUR:

RV Logbook	Maintenance CheckList

Quick Guide to The 100+Best Free Campsites in the West

Made in the USA
Thornton, CO
11/27/24 14:11:48

410ad237-84dd-4743-a5f7-0c26aded1196R01